EU Anti-Dumping Measures Against Russian Exporters

T0316959

Schriften zum Europa- und Völkerrecht und zur Rechtsvergleichung

Herausgegeben von Manfred Zuleeg

Band 12

PETER LANG

Frankfurt am Main · Berlin · Bern · Bruxelles · New York · Oxford · Wien

Olesia Engelbutzeder

EU Anti-Dumping Measures
Against Russian Exporters

In View of Russian Accession
to the WTO and the EU Enlargement 2004

PETER LANG
Europäischer Verlag der Wissenschaften

Bibliographic Information published by Die Deutsche Bibliothek
Die Deutsche Bibliothek lists this publication in the Deutsche Nationalbibliografie; detailed bibliographic data is available in the internet at <http://dnb.ddb.de>.

Zugl.: Frankfurt (Main), Univ., Diss., 2004

D 30
ISSN 1436-2007
ISBN 3-631-53161-3
US-ISBN 0-8204-7379-0

© Peter Lang GmbH
Europäischer Verlag der Wissenschaften
Frankfurt am Main 2004
All rights reserved.

Printed in Germany 1 2 3 4 5   7

www.peterlang.de

For my parents and husband

Foreword

This research is a Dissertation, which was submitted to the Johann Wolfgang Goethe-University in Frankfurt am Main in Summer Semester 2004.

In the first line I would like to thank my Doctor father, Professor Dr. Dr. h.c. Manfred Zuleeg, Professor of the Frankfurt University and former Judge of the European Court of Justice. He was the supervisor of my Master's thesis in 2001/2002 academic year and encouraged me to continue my scientific research. I thank my Doctor father for fruitful work together and appreciate all his valuable suggestions and inspiration. I am very honoured that Prof. Dr. Dr. h.c. Manfred Zuleeg included my Dissertation in the series of publications under his supervision "Schriften zum Europa- und Völkerrecht und zur Rechtsvergleichung" at Peter Lang publishers.

I would like to thank Professor Dr. Boudewijn Sirks, who made excellent reference to my Dissertation. I also appreciate Professor Dr. Walter Kargl, who was the chairman at the official disputation of the Dissertation.

The consultations with scientists, practitioners in international trade law and officials of the EU and WTO contributed a lot to the present study. I appreciate their time and consideration for answering my enquiries, providing me with materials and inspiring me with new ideas. I thank Prof. Dr. Meinhard Hilf from the University of Hamburg for his kind consultation in Hamburg in spring 2003 and providing me with very useful publications, which were cited in this work.

On the separate note I would like to mention the staff of the Faculty of Law of the Johann Wolfgang Goethe-University for their great engagement and support. Mrs. Uta Bredemeier-Karbalaie from the Promotion office has greatly supervised the whole process of my promotion. Mrs. Heidrun Dudek and Mrs. Dr. Susanne Pelster from the Dean's office were in charge of the Master's course for foreign students and created very warm welcoming atmosphere.

This publication is dedicated to my parents, Ljudmila and Vladimir Zaglada and my husband Günter, who inspired, supported and believed in me.

Olesia Engelbutzeder

Frankfurt am Main, Summer 2004

CONTENTS

Introduction...17
PART ONE. RUSSIA AND THE EU
Bilateral trade relations with emphasis
on EU anti-dumping measures against Russia
A. Introduction 19
I. Background 19
II. Economical overview of the trade Relations
  between the EU-15 and Russia...21
B. Overview of trade relations between Russia and the EU.................27
I. Historical development of bilateral relations between
  Russia and the EU– a long way from opposition to partnership..............27
  1. Relations between the Soviet Union and the EU.......................27
  2. Conclusion of Partnership and Cooperation Agreement
     as a new chapter in EU-Russia Relations..............................28
II. Present state of the relations between Russia and the EU.
  Agreements and documents on trade issues between Russia and the EU....30
  1. Partnership and Cooperation Agreement as a cornerstone
     of bilateral relations 30
     a) Structure and key features of Partnership
        and Cooperation Agreement regarding trade 30
     b) Legal framework of Partnership and Cooperation
        Agreement in the Russian Federation 31
     c) Legal framework of Partnership and Cooperation
        Agreement in the European Union 31
     d) The institutional framework of Russia-EU relations 31
     e) Provisions of Partnership and Cooperation Agreement
        regarding anti-dumping investigations.........................33
        aa) Natural Comparative Advantages 34
     f) Conclusion 36
  2. The EU Common Strategy on Russia – Partnership
     with Russia in the light of the Amsterdam Treaty 37
     a) Legal framework of the EU Common Strategy
        on Russia in the EU law.......................................37
     b) Main goals of the EU Common Strategy on Russia 38
     c) Provisions regarding trade 38
     d) Critical observations.......................................38
  3. The Russian Federation Middle Term Strategy
     towards the European Union (2000 –2010).................. 40
     a) Main goals of the Russian Middle Term Strategy 40
     b) Provisions regarding trade 41
     c) Conclusion 42

4. Wider Europe Initiative 45
C. Future prospects 46
I. The Common European Economic Space 46
II. Russia's accession to the WTO and the EU 47
  1. Aims and objectives of the accession 47
  2. Legal framework of Russia's accession to the WTO...............48
  3. EU as a major negotiator in the Russia's WTO bid 50
  4. WTO Legal Issues—Is the EU energy demand WTO-Plus?... 52
  5. Reform of the trade legislation in view
     of the accession to the WTO..52
Conclusion of Part one 53
PART TWO. EU ANTI-DUMPING LAW AND PRACTICE
AGAINST RUSSIAN EXPORTERS
A. Legal framework of the EU anti-dumping law 55
I. The multinational WTO legal framework 55
II. The EC Framework 57
  1. Anti-dumping provisions in EC primary legislation 57
  2. Anti-dumping provisions in EC secondary legislation 57
     a) Scope of the Basic Anti-dumping Regulation.................57
  3. Increase of transparency in the EU Anti-dumping Acts 58
B. Substantive elements of the EU Anti-Dumping Investigation 59
I. Dumping...59
  1. Normal value determinations for imports
     from market economy countries 60
     a) Normal value based on domestic market price 60
     b) Grounds for disregarding domestic market prices 61
        aa) No or insufficient sales of like product 61
            (i) No sales 62
            (ii)Insufficient sales: the five per cent rule..............62
        bb) No sales in the ordinary course of trade 63
            (i) Sales below costs 63
            (ii)Associated parties and compensatory agreements ..64
        cc) Sales not permitting proper comparison 66
     c) The alternative normal value tests 66
        aa) Constructed value...66
            (i) Rules concerning the determination of costs 66
            ii) The elements of constructed value 67
        bb) Export price to third country 67
  2. Export price 69
     a) Notion of export price 69
     b) Notion of constructed export price..............................69
     c) Calculation of constructed export price 70

3. Comparison between normal value and export price...................71
4. Dumping margin 72
II. Injury 74
1. Notion of injury 74
2. Like product 74
3. Community industry 75
   a) Basic rule...75
   b) Exceptions...76
      aa) Exception 1: related parties and importers
          of dumped products 76
      bb) Exception 2: regional industry 78
4. Material injury 78
   a) Actual material injury 78
   b) Threat of material injury 79
   c) Material retardation of the establishment
      of a Community industry 81
III.Casual link between dumping and injury.......................................81
1. The causality tests 81
2. Cumulation...84
   a) Cumulation of imports from several exporters
      in a particular exporting country 84
   b) Cumulation of imports from several
      exporting countries..85
IV.Community interest 86
C. Anti-dumping procedure 86
I. Initiation of investigation 87
1. Lodging of a complain 87
2. Initiation of proceeding...88
II. Investigation 89
1. Anti-dumping questionnaire 89
2. Advantages of cooperation 89
3. Verification visits..91
4. Sampling 92
5. Rights of interested parties..93
   a) Access to the file and confidentiality 93
   b) Hearing..94
   c) Disclosure..95
6. Imposition of protective measured during investigation 95
   a) Provisional duties 95
   b) Registration of imports..97
7. Outcome of the investigation 97
III.Reviews 99

    1. Expiry review 100
    2. Interim review 101
    3. Combined expiry and interim review investigation 104
    4 New exporter review 104
    5. Anti-absorption review 105
    6. Anti-circumvention review... 106
IV.Refund procedure 108
V. Judicial review 109
    1. Direct actions 109
        a) Action for annulment 110
            aa) Acts reviewable under Art. 230 of the EC Treaty 110
            bb) Grounds for review under Art. 230 of the EC Treaty ..111
        b) Action for failure to act 111
        c) Action for damages 112
    2. Preliminary rulings...112
D. Anti-dumping measures 115
I. Anti-dumping duties...115
    1. Amount of duty 115
    2. Form of duty...117
II. Undertaking 117
    1. Notion and conditions for accepting an undertaking 117
    2. Advantages and drawbacks of undertakings for exporters 120
    3. Monitoring of undertakings 120
III.Imposition of different forms of duties on the example of
cases of Russian exporters 121
    1. Potassium chloride 122
    2. Ammonium nitrate 125
    3. Urea...126
Conclusion of Part two 128
**PART THREE. RUSSIA'S STATUS AS A MARKET ECONOMY
COUNTRY GRANTED BY THE EU IN 2002**
A. Historical Analysis 135
I. Background 135
II. Market and non-market economies in the context
of GATT/WTO anti-dumping rules 138
III.The concept of analogue country in the
EU Anti-dumping legislation 140
    1. Background 140
    2. Empirical selection process 142
    3. Conclusion 146
IV.Market and non-market economies in the EU anti-dumping law.
Historical overview 147

13

1. The period 1968-1994 – Russia as a State trading country.............147
2. The period 1994-1998 - Era of economic changes in Russia
   and sighing of Partnership and Cooperation Agreement..............148
3. The period from 1998 to 2002 - Conditional market
   economy treatment towards Russian exports..........................150
   a) Background 150
   b) Five market economy criteria....................................151
   c) Impact of market economy treatment on dumping margins 152
   d) The 2000 "conditional market economy" amendments
      to the Basic Regulation 153
   e) Results of application of a "hybrid" market economy status
      towards Russia..154
B. The 2002 amendment to the Basic Regulation –
   The granting of Market Economy Status to Russia.................156
I. Background 156
II. Legal framework of the Russian market economy status 157
III.2002 amendments to the Basic Anti-dumping Regulation 158
   1. Legal analysis..158
   2. Practice of the EU Commission..................................163
   3. Critical observations... 165
V. WTO consistency of the 2002 amendments............................166
VI.Ways of bringing the EU treatment of former non-market
   economies in line with international trade rules.... 167
   1. Signatories of Partnership and Cooperation Agreement 168
   2. WTO members..169
PART FOUR. PERSPECTIVES
A. The impact of EU Enlargement 2004 on anti-dumping
   measures against Russia 171
I. Background 171
II. Legal framework of the extension of the EU anti-dumping
    policy on new Member States 171
III. Partnership and Cooperation Agreement and the new
     EU Member States..172
IV. The previous experience of the extension of EU Anti-dumping
    measures upon accession of Austria, Finland and Sweden in 1995 174
V. Provisional evaluation of economical impact of the EU
   enlargement on EU Anti-dumping measures against Russia...............175
VI. Defending the interests of exporters in the enlarged EU....................177
VII. Conclusion 178
B. Accession to the WTO -The use of WTO Dispute
   Settlement Mechanism...178
I. Background...178

II.   Legal framework 179
III. The scope of dispute settlement..180
IV.   Challenging the legislation 180
V.   Overview of the WTO dispute settlement procedure 181
VI.   Panel and Appellate Body Recommendations..................................182
VII. Special standard of review...183
VIII. Non-appliance of exhaustion of local remedies rule........................184
IX.   Conclusion..185
Joint Conclusion 185
Afterword 189
Literature 195

TABLES
PART ONE. ANTI-DUMPING PROCEDURE

Diagram 1.   EU-Russia Trade 1996-2002 22
Table 1.   Trade between the EU Member States and Russia.......................23
Table 2.   The EU and Russia. Economic and Trade Indicators....................24
Diagram 2.   EU-15 exports by country of destination in 2002 25
Diagram 3.   EU–15 imports by country of origin in 2002..........................25
Diagram 4.   Russia's exports by country of destination in 2002..................26
Diagram 5.   Russia's imports by country of origin in 2002... 26
Diagram 6.   Institutional Framework of Russia – EU political dialog.. 33
Table 3.   Comparative analysis of the trade issues of the
             Russian Middle Term Strategy towards the EU (2000 - 2010)
             and the Common Strategy of the EU on Russia 43

PART TWO. EU ANTI-DUMPING LAW
AND PRACTICE AGAINST RUSSIAN EXPORTERS

Table 4.   WTO Anti-dumping Agreement provisions
             applicable to investigations......................................56
Table 5.   Normal value based on domestic market price: conditions 61
Table 6.   Sufficiency of sales. Application of 5% rule 62
Example 1.   Can the normal value for Model B be calculated
             on the basis of prices in Country A ?.............................64
Example 2.   Sales at prices below unit production cost 64
Table 7.   The elements of constructed value: Art.2 (3) 68
Example 3.   Calculation of constructed export price 71
Table 8.   Calculation of dumping margin - Art. 2 (11).......................73
Example 4.   Calculation of dumping margin (for Market economy countries).73
Table 9.   Determination of injury Art. 3. 80
Table 10.   Causal link between dumping and injury Art. 3 (6) and 3 (7)......83
Table 11.   EU anti-dumping proceedings initiated against Russia
             after collapse of the Soviet Union (1992-2003) 88

15

Table 12.   Provisional anti-dumping duties imposed
            on Russian exports (1992-2003).................. 96
Table 13.   New investigation against Russian exports concluded
            by imposition of definitive duties (1996-2003)........................98
Table 14.   New investigation against Russian exports terminated
            without the imposition of measures (1996-2003)............. 99
Table 15.   Expiry reviews (1996-2003)...101
Table 16.   Interim reviews (1996-2003)............... 103
Example 5. Refund proceedings........ 108
Table 17.   EU Anti-dumping proceeding timetable
            (for market economy countries) 112
Example 6. Determination of injury margin... 116
Example 7. Calculation of dumping margin in accordance with a lesser
            duty rule (for Market economy countries)......................... 116
Table 18.   Form of anti-dumping duties Case Potassium chloride
            originating in, inter alia, in Russia..................................124
Table 19.   Form of anti-dumping duties Case Ammonium nitrate
            originating in, inter alia, in Russia....................................125
Table 20.   Form of anti-dumping duties Case Urea originating in Russia...126
Table 21:   Number of EU anti-dumping measures against
            Russian exports (1996-2003).............................. 129
Table 22.   EU anti-dumping measures against Russian exports
            (on 1.03.2004)...130
Table 23.   Definitive anti-dumping measures in force against
            Russian exports (1996-2002)............................. 133

PART THREE. RUSSIA'S STATUS AS A MARKET ECONOMY COUNTRY GRANTED BY THE EU IN 2002

Table 24.   Comparison of dumping margins for market economy
            treatment and analogue price determinations 153
Table 25.   Status of Russia (correspondingly former Soviet Union)
            in the EU Anti-dumping Law 155

PART FOUR. PERSPECTIVES

Table 26.   Anti-dumping measures of the EU acceding
            countries against Russia (on 1.03.2004)............................176
Table 27.   Overview of procedural steps and time frames
            in WTO dispute settlement 181
Diagram 7. The WTO Dispute Settlement Procedure 187

Introduction

Anti-dumping is an instrument of trade policy whose use is permitted by the World Trade Organization Rules and is applied by many countries to protect national producers from unfair foreign competition. Dumping is, in general, a situation of international price discrimination, where the price of a product when sold to the importing country is less than the price of the same product when sold in the market of exporting country. It is generally accepted in the multilateral trading system that if dumping takes place, it might result in unfair trade as the domestic industry of the importing country might suffer harm as a result of the dumping. In this case, the authorities of the importing country may, if certain requirements are met, take action against dumping.

The subject of anti-dumping procedures has received growing attention in international trade policy and has become a source of tension between countries. The anti-dumping have been for years a key issue in the commercial and political relations of Russia with its biggest trading partner – the European Union. This issue is especially acute in view of the historical Enlargement of the EU and Russian forthcoming accession to the WTO. Following the EU Enlargement on 1st May 2004 the volume of Russian-EU bilateral trade will exceed 50%. In this regard one of the major Russian concern is EU anti-dumping policy against Russian exports, which is actively used by the EU institutions and bring significant losses to certain sectors of Russian economy.

The objective of this study, divided into four Parts, is to analyse the EU anti-dumping policy towards Russia. The Part one is dedicated to general legal analysis of trade relations between the EU and Russia with emphasis on EU anti-dumping law. The Part two provides detailed analysis of the EU anti-dumping rules and practice applicable to Russia, including the case study. In the Part three the author examines the essence of the historic amendments to the EU Anti-dumping legislation of 8 November 2002, which granted Russia a market economy status and expresses her view on the extent to which the anticipated practice of implementation of those amendments would be consistent with WTO Rules. Finally, the Part four gives the overview of the future prospects in view of the EU Enlargement and Russian membership in the WTO.

PART ONE. RUSSIA AND THE EU - Bilateral trade relations with emphasis on EU anti-dumping measures against Russia

A. Introduction

1. Background

"The partnership should be based on the same fundamental values and political principles, the same or similar strategic interests of the parties, high level of understanding and trust. In practice, the partnership is characterized by multiform, stable and intensive relations, by systematic coordination of actions..."

Yury Borko, Director of the Institute of Europe, Moscow[1]

The purpose of this Chapter is to analyse the legal framework of trade relations between the EU and Russia in view of the EU biggest enlargement ever and Russian accession to the WTO. The emphasis is made on the EU anti-dumping policy.

The relationship between Russia and the European Union is regarded as increasingly important both in Moscow and in Brussels. During the last decade, a set of bilateral and unilateral documents underlining the importance of these relations was adopted. The most important one are the Partnership and Cooperation Agreement (1994), the Common Strategy of the EU on Russia (1999) and the Medium-term Strategy for Development Relations between the Russian Federation and the European Union (1999). A network of permanent cooperation bodies was established according to the Partnership and Cooperation Agreement and started to work in 1999. The Russian Foreign Policy Doctrine mentioned relations with the EU among the top regional priorities. At the EU-Russia Summit of November 2003, in parallel to the WTO accession negotiations, the Concept paper on the Common European Economic Space, which aims at the elimination of trade barriers between the EU and Russia, was presented. Declarations about "strategic partnership" with the overall objective to prevent the emergence of new dividing lines in Europe are countless.

But in contrast to the official declarations, the level and intensiveness of EU-Russia cooperation are very modest and are characterized by separate actions in the absence of a strategic framework. The number of disputes is growing. One of them is EU anti-dumping policy towards Russian exports. Russian economy loses annually about $230-240 million[2] due to EU anti-dumping measures, this

---

[1] Cited from the Article of Kaveshnikov, Three stories about Strategic Partnership between Russia and the European Union, p.1

[2] Figures of the Russian Ministry for Russian Ministry of economic development and trade, www.economy.gov.ru

figure is expected to raise significantly due to the EU Enlargement. Producers of certain mineral fertilizers and metallurgy are the worst hit.

Both EU and Russia admit that the EU-Russian economical, and especially, trade relations are not always as straightforward as it could be. The EU have recently admitted that "there are positive elements to the relationship. But, overall, we [the EU] have to accept that the results of five years of increasingly intensive co-operation are not as positive as we have expected, and we have to do something about that".[3] In the recent Communication of the European Commission on relations with Russia the EU furthermore admitted that despite of ambitious political declarations agreed between Russia and the EU, as well as "common interests, growing economic interdependence and certain steps forward, there has been insufficient overall progress on substance".[4] In Russian[5] and international[6] papers there have been even rumours on "trade war" between the EU and Russia in connection with the EU Enlargement.

Up until now, the development of real cooperation with Russia was reduced to enforce Russia to play according the western rules and on the western conditions. The EU defends its interests very strictly and does not always take into account the Russian position; being the major trade partner, it shapes the agenda of the EU-Russia relations and often ignores Russia's initiatives; regarding Russia as unstable and unpredictable partner, the EU often chooses the less intensive forms of cooperation even if it is not profitable for the EU itself. The logic was rather simple: not being member of the WTO club, Russia has no right to veto. Not having sufficient political and economic resources to insist on its position yet, Russia can either count on benevolent and partnership attitude of the European countries, especially if some practical things should be done. The EU, as well as the West as a whole, is ready to develop cooperation, but depending on what progress Russia achieves in democratic reforms. EU and Russia should change the logic of cooperation. If there are common strategic purposes, it is

---

[3] See Speech by the Rt. Hon. Chris Patten at the European Parliament plenary Debate on Russia, Brussels, 26.02.04.
http://europa.eu.int/comm/external_relations/bews/patten/speech04_99.htm, called 01.03.04
[4] Communication from the Commission to the Council and the European Parliament on relations with Russia, COM (2004) 106, 09.02.04, www.eur.ru
[5] Numerous publications in Russian press, connected with the EU enlargement 2004, see e.g. www .rbc.ru, 24.02.04 "ЕС требует от России сдаться"- "The EU demand the capitulation of Russia", 25.02.03 www.rbc.ru "Евросоюз выставил ультиматум Путину"- "the EU made ultimatum to Putin" , www.kp.ru, 24.02.04 "Европа грозит России торговой войной"- "Europe threats Russia with trade war", www.gazeta.ru, 24.02.04, EU insists Russia expand partnership deal
6 See e.g. Daily Telegraph: "Russia faces EU sanctions over 'bullying' in Eastern Europe", Die Presse, Austria, 18.02.04:„Russland: Beziehungen zur EU immer angespannter", World Street Journal, 18.02.04: New Member States will deteriorate EU-Russian relations"

necessary to create common mechanisms for their realization. If the EU is interested in a democratic Russia, it is necessary to include it actively in the democratic space and community instead of dosing out cooperation.

The principal stumbling block in EU-Russia relations is the contradiction between Russia's claims for overall equality and the EU's desire to integrate Russia on a differentiated basis. Russian opposition to such an approach is perceived as an unwillingness to cooperate, which leads to an increase in practical disputes and to overall stagnation of the relations. The EU's approach demonstrates a lack of perspective: it isn't ready to make minor concessions today in the name of strategic gains in the near future.

The best result Russia can achieve, if it develops a stable and democratic political system, providing a legal and regulatory framework for economic growth and managing reasonable and predictable foreign policy, is to become a regional power. Some of these goals have been already achieved in the framework of the Russian ongoing accession to the WTO. The European Union is as interested in that process as Russia itself.

II. Economical overview of the trade Relations between the EU and Russia

Realistically speaking at present the key words characterising Russia's trade with the EU are energy and asymmetry (See Table 1, Diagram 1).

As we can see from the data analysed infra, the asymmetric nature of EU-Russia relations is evident and creates a considerable obstacle to the emergence of a strategic partnership. What a "strategic partnership" means in practice is never made explicit in detail, but the existence of a strategic partnership, which is different from any temporary cooperation, would seem to suggest the presence of shared values, common interests and mutual understanding. The Russian Middle Term Strategy towards EU furthermore emphasizes that partnership should be "on the basis of equality without dividing lines."[7] This strengthens the general idea that true partnership should always be between equals: partners of importance and prestige, which share common values. This is surely not the case in the EU-Russia relationship yet. The European Union is the major destination for Russian exports and the major part of Russia's total external trade is with the EU. After EU enlargement, Russia's exports to the EU will exceed 50% of its total exports so that the EU will become a "control share" over Russian external trade. On the opposite, Russia's share in EU external trade in 2002 was only 4.8% of imports and 3% of exports. The structure of bilateral trade continues to display a marked imbalance, with fuel and primary products representing the bulk of Russian exports (energy and fuels accounted for around 51% of Russian exports to the EU), as opposed to the predominance of finished industrial and consumer goods in imports from the EU.

---

[7] Дипломатический вестник (Diplomatic Bulletin), 1999, Nr. 11, p. 20-28, rec. 1.1

Russia is usually still characterized by the Western world, in brief, as a political heavyweight and an economic midget, in spite of increasing economical growths.[8] The EU, on the other hand, is both a political heavyweight and an economic giant. Still, this comparison does not come close to a full picture of the asymmetries between the Union and Russia.

The current EU population is approximately 380 million (and will rise to about 550 million after enlargement) compared to Russia's 145 million people. The Russian economy is between 5% and 12% of the size of the EU economy, depending on the method of calculation.[9] Even though the EU depends on Russia in certain sectors such as energy supply, the overall economic relationship is of asymmetric interdependence, with the EU playing a much more important role for the Russian economy than vice versa. Thus, in trade terms, Russia is hugely dependent on the EU market. As for the EU market, Russia has rather the same quantitative importance as Norway, and a clearly less important role than Switzerland. Thus, Russia badly needs the EU for trade. The same cannot be said of Russia's importance for the EU.

Unfortunately, very often Russia is considered by the EU as a small trading partner, which is very often a target of trade defence measures such as antidumping. In practice, there are some opinions, that EU protectionism has been helping to lock Russia into its place as a natural-resource supplier[10]. It remains to be seen how much difference the acceptance of Russia as a market economy and as a fully-fledged WTO member will make.

Diagram 1. EU-Russia Trade 1996-2002

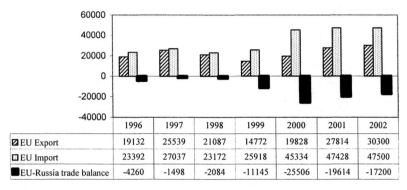

	1996	1997	1998	1999	2000	2001	2002
▨ EU Export	19132	25539	21087	14772	19828	27814	30300
▢ EU Import	23392	27037	23172	25918	45334	47428	47500
■ EU-Russia trade balance	-4260	-1498	-2084	-11145	-25506	-19614	-17200

(Source: Eurostat data)

---

[8] Sutela, P. Russia and Europe: Some Economic Aspects, p.17
[9] VAHL, M., "Just good friends?", Brussels, CEPS Working Document, n° 116, 03.2002, p. 4.
[10] Numerous publication in Russian and International Press, e.g. Hanson: Russia-EU economic relations. Dimensions and issues, p.8

Table 1. Trade between the EU Member States and Russia							
	Import				Export			
	1995		2002		1995		2002	
	In mio. USD	In %	In mio. USD	In %	In mio. USD	In %	In mio. USD	In %
Total	46709	100	46153	100	78217	100	106154	100
EU Member States	17944,5	38,6	18279,9	39,59	24218,2	33,6	37559,9	34,51
Austria	981,5	2,1	606,6	1,3	889,3	1,1	728,6	0,7
Belgium	866,5	1,9	763,4	1,7	1462,2	1,9	800,8	0,8
Great Britain	1099,5	2,4	1117,4	2,4	3065,6	3,9	3803,1	3,6
Germany	6483,1	13,9	6585,6	14,3	6207,6	7,9	8035,5	7,6
Greece	257,2	0,6	170,8	0,4	146,6	0,2	954,2	0,1
Denmark	483,3	1,0	512,8	1,1	455,0	0,6	414,9	0,4
Ireland	322,8	0,7	198,7	0,4	2634,8	3,4	259,9	0,2
Spain	241,0	0,5	576,3	1,2	209,8	0,4	1098,7	1,0
Italy	1850,6	4,0	2222,5	4,8	3376,3	4,3	7432,3	7,0
Luxemburg	32,8	0,1	11,4	0,02	14,7	0,0	55,7	0,01
Nederland	1646,0	3,5	1056,2	2,3	3191,5	4,1	7266,9	6,8
Portugal	19,2	0,0	33,8	0,07	16,6	0,0	136,3	0,1
Finland	2040,7	4,4	1514,6	3,3	386,5	3,1	2925,0	2,8
France	1073,7	2,3	1891,6	4,1	1518,7	1,9	2649,5	2,5
Sweden	546,6	1,2	1018,2	2,2	643,0	0,8	998,5	0,9
New EU Member States from 1 May 2004	4377,5	9,2	3366,3	7,23	9425	11,9	15340,8	14,4
Hungary	842,1	1,8	511,6	1,1	1627,0	2,1	2167,3	2,0
Cyprus	97,0	0,2	13,9	0,03	270,3	0,3	1562,0	1,5
Latvia	376,1	0,8	151,0	0,3	794,9	1,0	694,2	0,7
Lithuania	386,9	0,8	310,8	0,7	1080,9	1,4	1694,5	1,6
Malta	6,1	0,0	2,8	0,0	24,4	0,0	140,5	0,1
Poland	1321,4	2,8	1297,0	2,8	1688,1	2,2	3719,5	3,5
Slovakia	294,2	0,6	158,2	0,3	1735,7	2,2	2032,2	1,9
Slovenia	340,7	0,7	257,1	0,6	116,8	0,1	134,8	0,1
Czech Republic	438,2	0,9	559,8	1,2	1675,4	2,1	1509,1	1,4
Estonia	274,8	0,6	104,1	0,2	411,5	0,5	1686,7	1,6
Source: Data of the Russian State Customs Committee								

Table 2. The EU and Russia. Economic and Trade Indicators		
2002 data derived from Eurostat and Russian State Statistical Committee relatively	EU (15 Member States)	Russia
Population (million)	379.5	144.8
Area (1000 km^2)	3,191	17,075
Population density (inhabitants per km^2)	115	9
GDP (€ billion)	8,843	360
GDP per capita (€)	23,300	2,500
Exports (€ billion) (2002)	990.7	100
Imports (€ billion) (2002)	984.2	56
Balance (€ billion) (2002)	6.5	44
Russia's share in EU exports/ EU share in Russia's exports	3%	47.5%
Russia's share in EU imports/ EU share in Russia's imports	4.8%	54%
Russia's share in EU trade/ EU's share in Russia's trade	3.9%	49%
Exports as share of total world exports (2002)	20.0%	1.65%
Imports as share of total world imports (2002)	17.5%	0.67%
Source: The EU and Russia. Economic and Trade Indicators. Materials of the Delegation of the European Commission in Russia, 2003		

Diagram 2. EU-15 exports by country of destination in 2002[11]

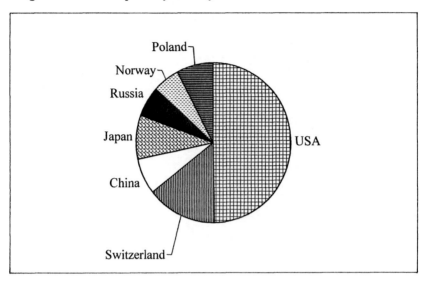

Diagram 3. EU-15 imports by country of origin in 2002

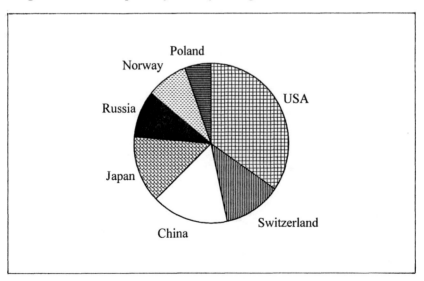

---

[11] Diagrams 2-5 source: Russia Trade Statistics, Materials of DG Trade, 2003

Diagram 4. Russia's exports by country of destination in 2002

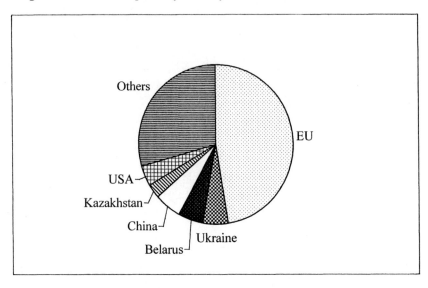

Diagram 5. Russia's imports by country of origin in 2002

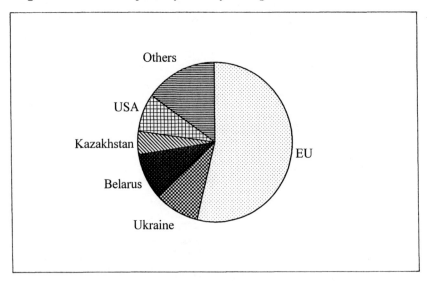

B. Overview of trade relations between the EU and Russia

I. Historical development of bilateral relations between Soviet Union and the EU – a long way from opposition to partnership

In this brief overview will be shown how two European giants, the EU and Russia, the relations of which were for such a long time governed by mistrust and fear, understood, that the cooperation and partnership relations are increasingly important for both sides.

The EU-Russian relations can be subdivided into two major periods of time, i.e. relations between the European Communities and Soviet Union in the period during 1952-1991 and relations between the European Union and Russia from 1991 till present time.

1. Relations between the Soviet Union and the EU

For many decades, trade and economic relations between Russia (and the former Soviet Union as a whole) and the European Communities were frozen by the conditions of the Cold war and were therefore quite limited. Until 1988 USSR and EU had relations of "useless ignorance"[12], i.e. during the Cold War era there were neither mutual recognition nor contractual relations between the European Community and the Council for Mutual Economic Assistance (CMEA, or also known as Comecon). From the outset, the Soviet leadership regarded the Community as an "economic basis of NATO" or the another version of the anti-Soviet bloc. Moreover, the Soviet leadership considered the European Communities to be weak formations, condemned to failure.

The defreezing of relations began together with disintegration of the Soviet and consequently CMEA system in 1985, when Mikhail Gorbachev became Secretary General of the Soviet Union. On 25 June 1988, when winds of perestroika began to blow in the Soviet Union, the framework agreement between CMEA and the Community in form of a Joint Declaration on mutual recognition was concluded[13]. This Declaration opened the way for the EU and its member states to establish diplomatic relations and regulate trade relations with CMEA countries on a bilateral basis. This was the first contractual link between the EU and Soviet Union, in form of "The Agreement on Trade and Commercial and Eco-

---

[12] De Smaiter "Russia and the European Union": history and perspectives of cooperation// Law of the European Union. Documents and commentaries, Moscow, 1999, p. 7

[13] Council Decision of 22 June 1988 on the conclusion of the Joint Declaration on the Establishment of official relations between the European Economic Community and the Council for Mutual Economic Assistance; OJ 1988, L. 157/34

nomic Cooperation" was concluded on 18 December 1989[14]. This was an essential part of the normalisation of bilateral relations. Under this Agreement, based on Articles 133 and 208 EC (ex 113 and 235), most favoured nation treatment was guaranteed and the EU was to abolish all specific quantitative restrictions on Soviet exports with the exception of some especially sensitive goods. Rules were specified for trade protection measures to be applied in certain cases. As in 1990 the Russian Federation accounted for 77 per cent of all Soviet exports and 68,5 per cent of all Soviet imports[15], this Agreement concerned, for the most part, trade between Russia and the EU. Though the Agreement established only the most general rules for these relations, leaving many problems, including anti-dumping, unsolved, it created favourable conditions for the development of bilateral trade. One of the most important problems that remained unsolved was the status of Soviet Union as state trading country, so that it did not qualify to benefit from a number of trade rules generally accepted among market economy countries, which mostly affected anti-dumping procedures.

2. Conclusion of Partnership and Cooperation Agreement as a new chapter in EU-Russia Relations

Also considered revolutionary, the Agreement on Trade and Commercial and Economic Cooperation between the Soviet Union and the European Communities soon became outdated due to the collapse of communist structures CMEA and its further dissolution in June 1991 but mostly because of the Soviet disintegration in the following December. A new structure, the Commonwealth of Independent States (CIS), was established in 1991[16]. The end of the Soviet Union meant a complete review of the EU's relations with what had once been a centralised superpower. The EU had to deal with a number of newly independent states of various states and structures and at different stages of development. Once the EEC/EC and its Member States formally recognized the new States in Eastern Europe and in the territory of the former Soviet Union,[17] an exchange of letters transformed The Agreement on Trade and Commercial and Economic Cooperation with USSR into a bundle of bilateral Trade and Cooperation

---

[14] Agreement between the European Economic Community and the European Atomic Energy Community and the Union of Soviet Socialist Republics on trade and commercial and economic cooperation , OJ, L.068, 15.03.1990, p.0002-0017

[15] Pinder/Shishkov "The EU&Russia. The promise of partnership", p.72

[16] The Presidents of Belarus, Russia and Ukraine, meeting in the outskirts of Minsk on 8 Dec. 1991, acknowledged the end of the Soviet Union and signed an agreement establishing a "Commonwealth of Independent States". On 21 Dec. 1991, eleven Presidents of the former Soviet Republics met in Alma Ata to sign the definite text of the Agreement establishing the CIS. The three Baltic States (Estonia, Latvia, and Lithuania) did not participate, nor did Georgia which joined later. The text of the CIS Charter can be found in Documents d'actualit'es internationales, No. 9, 1 May 1993, p. 171.

17 Bull. EC, 12-1991, point 1.4.13

Agreements with each newly independent state, including Russia[18]. Further, the Community decided to establish an entirely new type of agreement, in order to respond more adequately to the transformation of the former Soviet Union and to take into consideration the economic reforms launched by Russia.[19] It decided to offer these states a new kind of much further-reaching agreement intended to integrate them into a network of extensive economic, political and cultural relations. On the basis of the Council's negotiations directive of October 1992[20], after long and arduous negotiations, on 24 June 1994 Russian President Boris Yeltsin and the EU leaders signed at Corfu a multi-faceted Partnership and Cooperation Agreement establishing a partnership between European Communities and their Member States, of the one part, and the Russian Federation of the other part[21] which opened a new chapter in the EU-Russia relations. The aim of Partnership and Cooperation Agreement is to encourage political, commercial, economic and cultural cooperation between Russia and the EU. Apart from trade, the Partnership and Cooperation Agreement provides for more than thirty other areas of cooperation between EU and Russia.

The process of ratification of Partnership and Cooperation Agreement took more than three years: in October-November 1996 it was ratified by the State Duma and Federal Council[22], in October 1997 its ratification was completed by the EU member states. The Agreement came into force on 1 December 1997.

Up to that moment the parties' relations were regulated by the Interim Agreement on trade and trade-related matters[23], which was signed 17 June 1995 and came into force on 1 February 1996. The Agreement included many of the Partnership and Cooperation Agreement provisions, including provision regarding anti-dumping investigations, stating that "before definitive anti-dumping duties are imposed, the Parties shall do their utmost to bring about a constructive solution to the problem."

---

[18] The Russian Federation, recognized successor of the Soviet Union for international treaties, took over the EC-USSR Trade and Cooperation Agreement, see Documents d'Actualit´e Internationale, No. 7, 1 April, 1992.

[19] See the Communication of the Commission on the Relations between the Community and the Independent States, which suggested the replacement of the old TCA by another agreement taking into account the NIS political and economic transformation as well as the objectives of the new EU; Bull. EC 1/21992, point 1.4.2.

[20] European Parliament Fact Sheets. 6.3.4. The new independent States of the Former Soviet Union. www.euparl.eu.int/factsheets/6_3_4_en.html, called 27.10.2003

[21] OJ Nr. L327, 28.11.1997, pp. 0003-0068

[22] Federal Law of the Russian Federation of 25.11.1996 Nr. 135-FZ, published in Rossiiskaja Gazeta (Russian Newspaper) 26.11.1996. The PCA was published in Russian in Дипломатический Вестник (Diplomatic Bulletin) 1994, Nr. 15/16, S.29-59

[23] Interim Agreement on trade and trade-related matters between the European Community, the European Coal and Steel Community and the European Atomic Energy Community, of the one part, and the Russian Federation, on the other part, OJ L. 247, 13.10.1995, p.2

II. Present state of the relations between Russia and the EU. Agreements and documents on trade issues between Russia and the EU

1. Partnership and Cooperation Agreement as a cornerstone of bilateral relations.

a) Structure and key features of Partnership and Cooperation Agreement regarding trade

The Partnership and Cooperation Agreement is very ambitious in scope and consists of 112 articles, ten annexes, two protocols and a number of joint declarations, unilateral declarations and correspondence.

The key provisions of Partnership and Cooperation Agreement regarding trade are:

➢ Recognition in the Preamble that "Russia is no longer a state trading country" but "a country with an economy in transition". As projected under the Partnership and Cooperation Agreement, relations between Russia and the EU were to become similar to those that exist between the EU and market economies. Unfair trade restrictions that were in force during the Cold War era in relation to state trading countries were therefore no longer valid. According to some estimates, there were up to 600 such restrictions, including anti-dumping, costing Soviet Union several hundred million dollars a year[24]. As we can see this provision is not more up to date as the market economy status was granted to Russia by the EU in November 2002,[25] which will be discussed in details infra.

➢ Provisions regarding anti-dumping investigations and natural comparative advantages (see infra in details).

➢ Mutual granting of most favoured nation described in Article 1 paragraph 1 of the GATT (Art.10) and the removal of quantitative restrictions (Art.15), but not in trade in textiles, coal and steel products and nuclear materials.

➢ Statement, that Russia should bring commercial and other regulatory legislation closer in line with EU, i.e. the approximation of the legislation (Art.55).

➢ A commitment to create the necessary conditions for the establishment of a free trade area, and to examine, whether the circumstances allow for the beginning of negotiations for one (Art.1)

The negotiations on the regime of trade in goods were the most difficult part of negotiating of Partnership and Cooperation Agreement. The EU did not want to change the regime of trade in goods of the Trade Agreement of 1989 as it was concerned about the rapid growth of Russian raw materials export as a possible

---

[24] Pinder/Shishkov "The EU&Russia. The promise of partnership.",p.72

[25] See Council Regulation (EC) No. 1972/2002 of 5 November 2002 amending Regulation (EC) No. 2026/1997 on the protection against dumped imports from countries not members of the European Communities, OJ L305, 07.11.2002, p.1

consequence of trade liberalisation with Russia. However the regime of the Trade Agreement of 1989 became very negative for Russia in view of the growing dependence of Russian economy on export activities. Russia insisted on application of GATT/WTO Rules, which would favour the gradual adaptation of Russia to the GATT/WTO Rules in view of the decision of the Russia's application for accession to the WTO. As a result a compromises was found and the GATT/WTO rules are applied to the most part of elements of trade regime, while other elements are regulated by special agreements.

b) Legal framework of Partnership and Cooperation Agreement in the Russian Federation
The legal framework of international treaties in the Russia Federation is the Constitution of the Russian Federation of 12 December 1993[26] and the Federal Law on the International Treaties of the Russian Federation of 15 July 1995[27], which was adopted in accordance with Vienna Convention on the Law of Treaties of 1969[28].
In accordance with the Article 15 (4) of the Constitution of the Russian Federation of 12 December 1993 "international treaties and agreements of the Russian Federation shall be a component part of its legal system. If an international treaty or agreement of the Russian Federation fixes other rules than those envisaged by law, the rules of the international agreement shall be applied." As mentioned supra, the Partnership and Cooperation Agreement was ratified by Federal Law of the Russian Federation of 25.11.1996.

c) Legal framework of Partnership and Cooperation Agreement in the EU
The EC Treaty does not provide for a specific legal basis for such agreements as Partnership and Cooperation Agreement. Similarly to the Agreement on Trade and Commercial and Economic Cooperation with USSR of 1989 the Partnership and Cooperation Agreement is a mixed Agreement initially based on Articles 133 and 308 of the EC Treaty. It involves both EC exclusive competence (Common Commercial Policy) and shared competence between the Community and the Member States (economic cooperation).

d) The institutional framework of Russia-EU relations
The bilateral institutional framework is to large extend determined by the Partnership and Cooperation Agreement. The Diagram 7 will give a brief overview of the institutional hierarchy of the bilateral relations.

---

[26] Российская газета (Russian Newspaper) 25.12.1995.
[27] 15.07.1995, 101-FZ, Bulletin of the Russian Legislation, 1995, Nr. 29, p. 2757
[28] Soviet Union signed the Vienna Convention on the Law of Treaties of 1969 on 4 April 1986.

It should be noted that the structures created by the Partnership and Cooperation Agreement do function, but are intricate and excessively bureaucratic. This activity has, at least until recently, unfortunately been a disappointment to both the EU and Russia. In the words of one senior Commission official, it is a triumph of "process over substance"[29]. Moreover, these structures were formed in the mid nineties, when the dialog between Russia and the EU was not so active and diverse as now. As a result most of the problems had to be solved on the highest political level. Everyone would agree, that it is not the best way of a compromise finding. Therefore, it's a good time now to renew the present mechanisms of cooperation and accelerate its effectiveness. The Russia and EU have already passed the period when political declarations were of high importance and reached the stage of relations where the day-to-day problems are to be solved. Therefore it is necessary to modernise the political dialog between the EU and Russia by reducing the bureaucracy and accelerating the practical aspects of co-operation.

The EU and Russia are currently working together to finalize an efficient dispute settlement mechanism under the Partnership and Cooperation Agreement[30]. This is aimed to improve the predictability and transparency of trade relations and, will allow for the resolution of a number of long-standing trade disputes. The idea of a dispute settlement mechanism was agreed during the EU-Russian Summit of 29 May 2002 in Moscow, "aiming at a dynamic development of economic cooperation between Russia and the EU"[31]. It is expected, that the new system for resolving trade disputes will be a specially created arbitration tribunal, consisting of three arbiters. One of the arbiters will be appointed by the EU, a second by Russia, and the third by agreement of the parties. Where arbitration will recognize the claim of a party as justified, the parties will have to start talks to remove the violation. Failing removal of the violation, a mechanism of return measures or compensation for damage in another sector of the economy will be introduced. Mr. Maxim Medvedkov, Deputy Minister of Economic Development and Trade and Head of the Russian Group of WTO accession, emphasised, that this dispute resolution body fully duplicates the system of arbitration existing in the WTO, which gives Russia one more opportunity to adapt better to membership in the organization[32]. This mechanism would be very useful in view

---

[29] David Gowan "How the EU can help Russia", Center for European Reform, London, 2000, p.9

[30] The EU and Russia. Even closer partner in a wider Europe. Information material for the EU-Russia Summit of 31 May 2003 in St. Petersburg. www.eur.ru

[31] Joint Statement of the EU-Russian Summit 29 May 2002, www.eur.ru

[32] On Deputy Minister of Economic Development and Trade Maxim Medvedkov Press Conference on European Union's Designation of Russia as Market Economy, 30.05.2002, www.mid.ru

of the EU Enlargement, but, unfortunately it is at the moment solely on the stage of political declarations.

Diagram 6. Institutional Framework of Russia – EU political dialog according to the Partnership and Cooperation Agreement

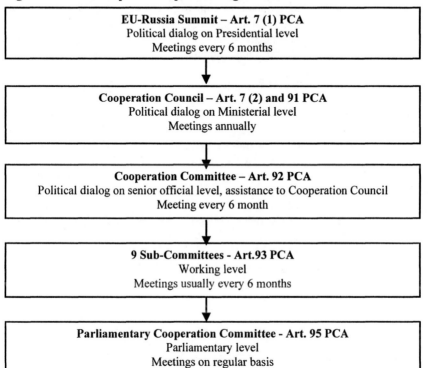

e) **Provisions of Partnership and Cooperation Agreement regarding anti-dumping investigations**

Article 18 of the Partnership and Cooperation agreement provides the rules and procedures of taking by the Parties of anti-dumping or countervailing measures by the direct reference to the respective GATT/WTO rules. The willingness of the EU to include the anti-dumping clause into the Agreement met very decisive resistance from Russian negotiators as anti-dumping had always been one of the largest and acute problems between EU and Russia[33].

---

[33] Timmermann, Die Beziehungen EU-Russland, p. 17

34

That is why the Agreement found a compromise and goes beyond the WTO rules by fixing in the Article 18 (2) that "in respect of anti-dumping or subsidy investigations, each Party agrees to examine submissions by the other Party and to inform the interested parties concerned of the essential facts and considerations on the basis of which a final decision is to be made. Before definitive anti-dumping and countervailing duties are imposed, the Parties shall do their utmost to bring about a constructive solution to the problem." Unfortunately, this very promising provision regarding the consultations of the Parties did not become the practice concerning EU anti-dumping measures against Russia.

aa) Natural Comparative Advantages
Another provision which was hardly negotiated and adopted at the request of Russian negotiators meant to be very beneficial for Russian exporters but remained just another political Declaration is Joint Declaration in relation to Article 18 of Partnership and Cooperation Agreement, in accordance to which the Parties agree that, without prejudice to their legislation and practice, when establishing normal value in anti-dumping and anti-subsidy cases due account shall be taken overall, in each case on its merits, when natural comparative advantages can be shown by the manufacturers involved to be held with regard to factors such as access to raw materials, production process, proximity of production to customers and special characteristics of the product. Due to the extreme flexibility and looseness of this formulation, it does not function to the advantage of Russian exporters as it meant to be.

For example, in anti-dumping case of 1998 "Potassium Chloride from Russia and Belarus[34]" the International Potash Company, exporter of potash from Russia and Belarus requested adjustments to the normal value calculated on the basis of Canada on the grounds that Russian and Belarusian mines enjoyed natural comparative advantages in terms of access to raw materials, production process, proximity of production to customers and special characteristics of the product, i.e. the size of the reserves, the general characteristics of the mines and their geographical location, and finally the characteristics of the ore. The various factors having been considered and on the basis of the information available, it was concluded that the natural comparative advantage of the depth of Russian and Belarusian mines is outstripped by the disadvantage of the quality of the ore which has, according to the conclusions of the European Commission, a bigger impact on costs. Taken as a whole, it came out that " it is more likely that Russian and Belarusian mines have an overall natural comparative disadvantage as compared to the Canadian mines." Therefore, an adjustment for natural comparative advantages for the Russian/Belarus mines as compared to the Canadian

---

[34] Potassium chloride originating in Belarus, Russia and Ukraine, Council Regulation (EC) No 449/98 of 23 February 1998, OJ L 058 , 27.02.1998 P. 0015 - 0026

mines was not warranted in this case and could therefore not be granted to the Russian exporter. Neither the natural comparative advantages were approved in the further investigation of 2000 regarding the same case.[35]

In the most recent case, Silicon from Russia,[36] all exporting producers made submissions arguing that the cost of electricity used at provisional stage should be amended. They emphasised that their main electricity supplier is a majority private-owned company and that its low price can be explained by the presence of the world's largest complex of hydro-electric power stations, based on a natural comparative advantage. However, the Commission services decided to rejected this claim and to confirm the provisional decision to use the electricity price charged by another electricity supplier in Russia by reasoning that "since it was found that electricity prices in Russia are regulated and that the price charged by this electricity supplier was very low, even when compared to other suppliers of electricity generated by hydro-electric power stations in the analogue country Norway and also in Canada." It should be noted that the low energy prices, which are natural comparative advantages of Russia have been a stumbling block in the EU-Russian trade relations, which slowed down the EU-Russian negotiations on the Russia's WTO bid.[37]

Until now there has not been any anti-dumping investigation where natural comparative advantages of Russian exporters were taken into account by the EU institutions.

Moreover, the EU went even further in its anti-dumping practice against Russia. In its latest amendments to the Anti-dumping law, which will be discussed later

---

[35]See Potassium chloride originating in Belarus, Russia and Ukraine, Council Regulation (EC) No 969/2000 of 8 May 2000, OJ L 112 , 11.05.2000 P. 0004 – 0026, in rec. 38 it was mentioned, that "International Potash Company made a number of comments regarding differences in quality and mining conditions between Belarus and Russia and the Community and Canada. Furthermore, most of the elements mentioned were already treated in the previous investigation, where it was concluded that any adjustment for natural comparative advantages would have been to the disadvantage of the Belarusian and Russian mines. As the essential circumstances have not materially changed since the previous investigation, and for the abovementioned reasons, there was no need for adjustments to normal value for physical differences or natural comparative advantages."

[36] Silicon originating Russia, Council Regulation (EC) No 2229/2003 of 22 December 2003, OJ L 339 , 24/12/2003 P. 0003 – 0013, rec. 27

[37] More detailed on this topic see in : David Tarr and Peter Thomson , The Merits of Dual Pricing of Russian Natural Gas,The World Bank, 2003. The analysis of the The World Bank reveals that, from Russia's perspective, there is no economic rationale to unify the price of natural gas it sells domestically and abroad. If Russia were to sell its natural gas to Europe at only full long run marginal cost plus transportation costs, Russia would lose between $5 billion and $7.5 billion per year. This would ruin Russian economy. The details are described in Part three of the present dissertation

in this research the EU armed itself with the perfect legal mechanism of disregarding the Russian natural comparative advantages.

f. Conclusion

The entry in force of Partnership and Cooperation Agreement was a milestone in the EU-Russia relations. It accelerated the dialog between the two European superpowers and is the legal basis for legislation in all fields of bilateral relations. The Partnership and Cooperation Agreement provided a stronger framework for trade and Cooperation and more developed institutions than the Trade and Cooperation Agreement of 1989. The idea of creating "the necessary conditions for the future establishment of a free trade area" was introduced, but without a date or a programme for moving towards it. The provisions of the Agreement regarding trade in goods are in the most part consistent with the WTO rules and were a big step towards Russian accession to the WTO and integration in the world trade system, where the market economy forces are governing. The Agreement declaratively put an end to the unilateral imposition of anti-dumping procedures without preliminary consultations. Unfortunately, the years practice has shown, that this very important provision regarding anti-dumping negotiations remained on the level of political declaration and was not implemented by the Parties, in the first place by the EU. Moreover, practice shows, that the institutional framework for EU-Russia relations requires renovation with emphasis on flexibility and reduce of bureaucracy in taking of day-to-day decisions, which are crucial for both Parties and reflect the latest developments in relations. It is strongly recommended to introduce the dispute settlement system for trade dispute resolutions and preliminary consultations, that has been a project for more than one year now. This system is badly needed in view of the EU Enlargement and Russian concerns regarding the extensions of the EU anti-dumping and other trade defence measures on 10 countries- traditional Russian trading partners. As Russian President Putin said on the Russia-EU Summit in Rome 6 November 2003 "What we need is detailed, flexible and effective dialogue at every level for the sake of attaining practical results and solving problems, which hinder successful cooperation. As far as specific instruments of work are concerned, we need a clear-cut and simple vertical for coordinating specific decisions, as well as clear-cut decision-making machinery; but, most importantly, such decisions must be translated into life.[38]"

As a conclusion the author would note, that the Partnership and Cooperation Agreement is not being used in the full power and it is very important to keep all trade practitioners on track of developments of bilateral relations in view of rapid changes in the world, in particular in world trade system. The author agrees with the words of President Putin, "that the European continent and the

---

[38] www.pravda.ru, called on 07.11.2003

entire world are experiencing major transformations at this stage and we can't be guided by obsolete working-interaction models today." Therefore it can be expected that upon the EU biggest Enlargement and Russia's accession to the WTO some provisions of the Partnership and Cooperation agreement will be modified paying respect to the changing of circumstances. One of the most important reason for modifying of the Agreement is the recently granted to Russia by the EU market economy status,[39] while the Agreement was oriented to Russia as a "country in a transition". In addition to political symbolism, the practical importance of a market economy status concerns mainly anti-dumping cases. In the case of a non-market economy, in which domestic prices cannot be regarded as reflecting true cost, the "normal value" used to measure dumping-export sales at below cost price-is defined in terms of costs and pricing of a comparable producer in a third country with market economy status. The newly won market economy status of Russia means that Russian companies accused of dumping can use their actual costs and prices, instead of the EU applying proxy costs and prices from a third country, when arguing the case. Market economy status will be examined in details infra.

2. The EU Common Strategy on Russia. Partnership with Russia in the light of the Amsterdam Treaty

a) Legal framework of the EU Common Strategy on Russia in the EU law

The reform of the Treaty on European Union introduced the Common Strategy as a new instrument of common foreign and security policy. Article 13 of the Treaty on European Union provides that:

"The European Council shall decide on common strategies to be implemented by the Union in areas where the member States have important interests in common. Common strategies shall set out their objectives, duration and the means to be made available by Union and the Member States. The Council shall recommend common strategies and shall implement them, in particular by adopting joint actions and common positions"

At the European Council Meeting in Cologne of June 1999, only one month after the Amsterdam Treaty entered into force, Russia became the first country to which the new instrument Common Strategy applied. This is no accident. The preferential treatment demonstrates the great importance the EU attaches to Russia's inclusion into the process of European cooperation. The reasoning behind this strategy is obvious: in one way or another, the developments in Russia are going to influence developments in the rest of Europe to a very high degree. Iso-

---

[39] See Council Regulation (EC) No. 1972/2002 of 5 November 2002 amending Regulation (EC) No. 2026/1997 on the protection against dumped imports from countries not members of the European Communities, OJ L305, 07.11.2002, p.1

lating Russia, even if it were anybody's intention to do so, is impossible because of Russia's size, its geographic location and potential.

The EU Common Strategy on Russia was adopted for an initial period of four years. However it was prolonged until 4 July 2004.

b) Main goals of the EU Common Strategy on Russia

Under the terms of the Common Strategy, the European Union intends to work together with Russia to meet the following principal objectives: to consolidate democracy; integrate Russia into a common European economic and social space; cooperate to strengthen stability and security in Europe and beyond; address common challenges on the European continent.

c) Provisions regarding trade

The economic part of the Common Strategy on Russia repeats, to the big disappointment of Russia, main points of the Partnership and Cooperation Agreement and adds nothing new.

According to the Common Strategy on Russia, the long-term goal is the "integration of Russia into a common European economic and social space" that will be preceded by establishing a common free trade zone. According to the Strategy "The Union is committed to the integration of Russia into the European and world economy. In this context, the Union will support Russia's efforts in meeting the requirements of WTO membership. It will also examine how to create the necessary conditions, in addition to WTO accession, for the future establishment of an EU-Russia Free Trade Area. The progressive approximation of legislation and standards between Russia and the European Union, in accordance with the Partnership and Cooperation Agreement, will facilitate the creation of a common economic area." EU undertook an obligation assist to the integration of Russia into a common European economic and social area, inter alia, "by encouraging Russia to remove obstacles to trade and investment, in particular through the improvement of border crossing procedures and facilities, and by examining, in accordance with EU rules and procedures, Russian concerns with respect to access to the EU market".

d) Critical observations

The common strategy was initially perceived by the scientific world as a remarkable and ingenious tool, in that it is both part of the EU's external relations and an internal institutional innovation.

The initial optimism with the Common Strategy was bound to fade, it was soon replaced by critical observations from both sides, most of them that the common strategies reiterated the words of the Partnership and Cooperation Agreements.[40] The most authoritative and unambiguously positive response from Moscow towards the Common Strategy on Russia can be found in the two Joint Statements of the EU-Russia Summits in Helsinki (October 1999) and in Moscow (May 2000). The Russian leadership has therefore agreed to appreciate the Common Strategy on Russia as one of the fundamental documents that long-term cooperation with the EU would be based upon. This political approach to the Common Strategy on Russia has been repeatedly confirmed by high-ranking Russian diplomats[41].

On the other side, most of the Russian researchers were of a critical opinion of EU Common Strategy on Russia[42]. The Strategy was evaluated as a document of an intermediate and technical nature only. From the point of view of its content, it is nothing but a simplified register of policy already carried out by the EU towards Russia.

The criticism of some experts arose from a deep dissatisfaction with the EU policy on Russia as a whole. Maxim Medvedkov's article under the unequivocal title "The Partnership and Cooperation Agreement has not confirmed expectations yet[43]" is, in fact, a large list of failures and unused possibilities of implementing the Partnership and Cooperation Agreement. The author's point of view deserves to be mentioned, above all, because of his position as a member of the Russian Delegation that negotiated the Partnership and Agreement in 1992-94 and a Head of Russian WTO negotiations group[44]. His principal thesis is that Russia and the EU are not inclined to fulfil the economic and institutional obligations taken within the Partnership and Cooperation Agreement framework, whereas the political arguments tend to prevail over the economic ones. In his opinion, both Russia and the Union are to blame for this weak result. Moreover, according to his forecast, the early death of the Partnership and Cooperation

---

[40] See e.g. Secretary General/High Representative: Common Strategies Report, Brussels, 21.12.2000, where the High Representative for Common Foreign and Security Policy, Javier Solana identified the gap between poor effectiveness and the big expectations raised by the common strategies. Joint report to the General Affairs Council by the Secretary General/High Representative and the Commission: The Effectiveness of Common Strategies of 23.01.2002 confirmed that "visible, but limited" progress has been made on implementation, and that Strategies have been used as tools of public diplomacy, rather than as internal policy instruments, are too broad in scope; and are little more than an inventory of existing policies and the value they add is limited. Available at: www.europa.eu.int

[41] Дипломатический вестник (Diplomatic Bulletin), Nr. 12/1999, 9

[42] See e.g. Leshukov, Igor "Russia and the European Union: A strategy of relations, Carnegie Center Moscow, p. 23-38

[43] Euro, Nr. 12, 1999: 30-32

[44] At the time of writing this article Mr. Medvedkov was the General Director of the Center for Trade Policy and Law, a private consulting agency, and has recently been appointed Deputy Minister of Economic Development and External Trade.

Agreement, resulting from the future accession of Russia to the WTO, seems to be possible. One cannot find even a single reference to the Common Strategy on Russia in Mr. Medvedkov's article. When asked about reasons, the author maintained he did this on purpose. To his mind, the Common Strategy on Russia is a political document, while the Partnership and Cooperation Agreement relates to the economic cooperation. The Agreement needs neither new areas for cooperation, nor new competencies of the EU institutions in external economic relations. In this sense the Common Strategy on Russia contains nothing new as far as the implementation of the Partnership and Cooperation Agreement is concerned.

3. The Russian Federation Middle Term Strategy towards the European Union (2000 – 2010)

Four months after the European Council adopted the Common Strategy on Russia, Vladimir Putin, who was then Prime Minister, delivered Russia's response at the EU-Russia Summit in Helsinki in October 1999. This was a "Medium-term Strategy for Development of Relations between the Russian Federation and the European Union (2000-2010)[45]. A British observer found it "a demanding and irritable response" which resented "what it felt to be a tone of condescension and hubris' in the Union's Common Strategy[46]".

a) Main goals of the Russian Middle Term Strategy

According to the Preamble, "the Strategy is primarily aimed at insuring national interests and enhancing the role and image of Russia in Europe and in the world".

Russia declared its intention to pursue its own way domestically as well as become a key area, a point of reference of its own internationally. Moreover, the Middle Term Strategy paper has stated with unprecedented clarity that Russia sees itself as a European and Asian power which has no intention to formally associate itself with or join the EU: "During the period under review, partnership between Russia and the European Union will be based on the treaty relations, i.e. without an officially stated objective of Russia's accession to or "association" with the EU. As a world power situated on two continents, Russia should retain its freedom to determine and implement its domestic and foreign policies, its status and advantages of an Euro-Asian state and the largest country of the Commonwealth of Independent States, independence of its position and activities at international organizations." Russia does not want to be a periphery but form a cosmos of its own, large and independent enough to be a central player.

---

[45] Дипломатический вестник (Diplomatic Bulletin), 1999, Nr. 11, p. 20-28
[46] Gowan, How the EU can help Russia, p.11

The Strategy determines numerous objectives of development of Russia's relations with the European Union for the current decade, including, in the first place development of mutual trade and investments and securing the Russian interests in an expanded European Union.

b) Provisions regarding trade

Cooperation in trade and investment is put in first place of the Russian Middle Term Strategy as a matter of highest economic priority. This approach results from the fact that the EU is the main trading partner of Russia, and there are no signs that the EU could be replaced by any country or regional association.

Chapter 3 of the Russian Strategy is dedicated to the development of mutual trade and investment. As an interested party of the EU export market, the Russia showed its big concern about the increasing of the EU market access by Russian exporters. It can be seen from the spirit of provisions regarding trade, that Russia is aimed to achieve the gradual abolition of the EU anti-dumping measures and other trade barriers against Russian exporters, which is at this stage particularly acute in view of the unprecedented enlargement of the EU.

It is not surprising that the first objective of Russia regarding trade issues was the objective "to continue the work on creating favourable conditions for access by Russian-made goods and services to the EU market and to eliminate elements of their discrimination, fully recognizing the market status of Russia's economy (Art. 3.1)[47]". Article 3.5. shows the clear intention of the Russian side to encourage, inter alia, "the positive review and phase-out of applicable antidumping procedures, the preservation of existing trade preferences and granting of additional ones, and the future abolishment of quotas on export to the EU of Russian steel products."

The Russian intention to access to the WTO reflected in the Art. 3.8. of the Strategy, which provides that Russian objective is "to seek a realistic and positive approach of the European Union to the terms of Russia's membership in the World Trade Organization. Before the "millennium round" of the multilateral trade negotiations within the framework of the WTO, to press for Russia's full participation in the round by using the European Union's position on the issue."

The position regarding the free trade area was stipulated in the Art. 3.9, which provides Russia's intention "together with the experts of the European Union to consider the availability of conditions for opening negotiations on the establishment of a free trade area under the provisions of the Partnership and Cooperation Agreement." Russia sees it appropriate "to be guided by the advisability of its gradual establishment after Russia's accession to the WTO on the basis of

---

[47] On the Russia-EU Summit 29 May 2002 Russia was granted a fully-fledged market economy status, which however can reduce, but not eliminate all anti-dumping duties against Russian exporters. Details see in Part three "Russia's status as a market economy country granted by the EU in 2002: a way forward or a status quo?"

Article XXIV of GATT-94 and of the agreed interpretation of this article." In Chapter 5 on the securing the Russian interests in an expanded European Union Russia emphasised that it is crucial "taking into account the ambivalent impact of the European Union's expansion on the terms of its cooperation with Russia and on the Russian interests, to strive for achieving the best advantages of such expansion while preventing, eliminating or setting off possible negative consequences[48]." Russia showed the importance of consultations with the EU, its individual members and candidates aimed at securing Russia's interests in view of the extension of the rules of the EU, inter alia, antidumping policies, to the countries of Central and Eastern Europe[49].

c) Conclusion

The conclusions relate primarily to two questions: Firstly, how does the EU Common Strategy compare with the Russian Mid-term Strategy?
In other words, what is the balance of common and divergent elements in these strategies? And secondly, how important are the Strategies in terms of influence, implementation and efficiency?
As far as the first point is concerned, one can see that the two Strategies are not incompatible in terms of strategic goals and principles, but are of contradictory character sometimes, especially as far as interpretation of goals and subordination of priorities is concerned. In principle, it is sufficient to conclude that these strategies have a substantial common ground for joint actions in a great number of areas. That the two EU and Russian documents scarcely connected is a reflection of the divergence between the EU and Russian agendas on the eve of Putin's presidency. The EU Common Strategy is little more than a restatement of current policy. It does not break much new ground and it makes the mistake of talking down to Russia[50]. On the one hand, the Russian Mid-Term Strategy is, to the large extend, a set of claims and discontentments focused on EU antidumping and restrictive measures applied to certain Russian export. On the other hand, the Common Strategy on Russia repeats the main guidelines of the Partnership and Cooperation Agreement and stays silent about the claims of the partner. But even if there is little common ground, the fact that the EU strategy

---

[48] Art. 5.1 of the Russian Middle Term Strategy
[49] Art. 5.2 of the Russian Middle Term Strategy
[50] The EU common Strategy regularly speaks about the EU's "assistance" and "contribution" to Russia. For its part, Moscow prefers another wording: Russia aims at utilizing "the economic potential and management experience of the EU with a view to promoting the development of the social market economy to be based on the principle of fair competition and the further building of the state of democracy and law". All in all, this is a difference of a donor and a recipient.

prompted a Russian reply was valuable itself. The EU and Russia may have been talking past each other, but at least they were doing it in the same room[51].

It is also essential that the Partnership and Cooperation Agreement has been confirmed as a basis for long-term cooperation between the EU and Russia.

However, this conclusion needs to be tested by the assessment of the divergent elements in both strategies. As mentioned above, both documents are typical examples of the art of diplomacy. They do not spell out the contradictions or disagreements between the EU and Russia in a direct way. Nevertheless, some sensitive issues are marked and most of them concern the EU trade barriers to Russian goods.

As regards the importance, implementation and efficiency of the both Strategies, there are two aspects to this question – political and practical.

From the political point of view, both the EU Common Strategy on Russia and Russian Middle Term Strategy towards EU are documents of paramount importance. By 1999, doubts and discussions within the EU had come to an end. The Union confirmed its political will to carry out the Partnership and Cooperation Agreement. The Common Strategy on Russia and Russia's prompt reply was a clear call for a fresh start in cooperation between the EU and Russia.

From the practical point of view, the implementation of the Strategies depends on a great many factors including the situation in Russia and in Europe and on the general climate of EU-Russia relations.

Table 3. Comparative analysis of the trade issues of the Russian Middle Term Strategy towards the EU (2000 - 2010) and the Common Strategy of the EU on Russia		
	Russian Middle Term Strategy towards the EU	**Common Strategy of the EU on Russia**
General provisions		
Period of validity	2000-2010	4.06.1999-1.06.2004
Main objectives	1. Consolidation of democracy, the rule of law and public institutions in Russia 2.Integration of Russia into a common European economic and social area 3.Cooperation to strengthen stability and security in Europe and beyond	1.Strategic character of Russia - EU partnership. 2. Improving the efficiency of the political dialogue. 3. Development of Mutual Trade and Investments. 4. Cooperation in the financial field. 5. Securing the Russian interests

---

[51] Gowan, How the EU can help Russia, p.13

	4.Common challenges on the European continent	in an expanded European Union. 6. Development of the pan-European cooperation infrastructure. 7. Cooperation in the field of science and technologies, protection of the intellectual property rights. 8. Transboundary co-operation. 9. Development of the legal basis for cooperation. Approximation of the economic legislation and technical standards. 10. Promotion of the role of business circles in cooperation development.
Certain Provisions regarding trade		
Russian Accession to the WTO	-seeking a realistic and positive approach of the EU to the terms of Russia's membership in the WTO. - pressing for Russia's full participation in the WTO "Millennium round" by using the EU's position on the issue. (Art. 3.8)	-supporting Russian efforts to meet the requirements for WTO accession, including legislative and institutional reform (Part II, Art. 2 (b), Abs.2).
Access of Russian goods to the EU market	-creating favourable conditions for access by Russian-made goods to the EU market -to eliminate elements of their discrimination (Art. 3.1)	-to examine Russian concerns with respect to access to the EU market (Part II, Art. 2 (b), Abs.3).
Anti-dumping	-positive review/phase-out of applicable antidumping procedures (Art. 3.5) - consultations with the EU and its candidates before the EU Enlargement aimed at securing Russia's interests regarding, inter alia, the EU anti-dumping policy (Art. 5.2)	No provisions

EU Enlarge- ment 2004	- to strive for achieving the best advantages of EU expansion for Russia - to prevent/eliminate possible negative consequences, e.g. in view of the expansion of the EU anti-dumping policy on the new member countries (Art. 5.1)	No provisions
Free trade area	-gradual establishment of free trade area after Russia's accession to the WTO. - to seek Russia's access to the entire European economic space -insisting that the respective obligations be set off by the advantages gained -not allowing that the arrangements are in conflict with the CIS legal mechanisms of economic integration.	- Examining how to create the necessary conditions, in addition to Russia's WTO accession, for the future establishment of an EU-Russia free trade area (Part II, Art. 2 (b), Abs.3).

4. Wider Europe Initiative

Another example of the EU political declarations, which do not propose any efficient solutions of outstanding trade issues between EU and third countries, including Russia is a Wider Europe initiative (with 'New Neighbours' and 'Proximity Policy' being used as alternative terms) within the framework of the biggest enlargement in the history of the EU.

The subject has been opened up by two documents from the European Commission[52], setting out a new framework for relations over the coming decade with Russia, the western newly independent states and the Southern Mediterranean - countries who do not currently have a perspective of membership but who will soon find themselves sharing a border with the Union. It suggests that, in return for concrete progress demonstrating shared values and effective implementation

---

[52] European Commission, Wider Europe – Neighbourhood: A New Framework for Relations with our Eastern and Southern Neighbours, COM(2003)104 final, 11.3.2003, europa.eu.int/comm/external_relations/ we/doc/com03_104_en.pdf ; and Paving the Way for a New Neighbourhood Instrument, COM(2003)393 final, 1 July 2003, europa.eu.int/comm/external_relations/ we/doc/com03_393_en.pdf, see also: European Parliament resolution on 'Wider Europe - Neighbourhood: A New Framework for Relations with our Eastern and Southern Neighbours (COM(2003) 104 - 2003/2018(INI)),www.europarl.eu.int/meetdocs/delegations/ esto/20031208/20031208.htm - 12k - 6. Dez. 2003

of political, economic and institutional reforms, all the neighbouring countries, including Russia, should be offered the prospect of a stake in the EU's internal market. The EU Commission Communication reaffirmed, that enlargement will serve to strengthen relations with Russia and other neighbour countries and stressed, that "the EU's neighbourhood should benefit from the prospects of closer economic integration with the EU." The Communication of 11 March 2003 also admitted, that the new neighbourhood policy will only constitute one pillar of the overall EU-Russia strategic partnership.

It is obvious that the content of the EU Neighbourhood policy so far is very thin and broad. It even does not try to touch upon any serious concern of the third countries connected with the enlargement, for example the extension of the EU anti-dumping policy on 10 new members. Moreover, although EU believes that it is possible to apply a single policy to relations with such a diverse ranch of neighbouring countries, one still cannot put Russia and Libya in the same basket.

The Wider Europe initiative risks being a flop, unless it is given more content and a credible institutional backup[53].

C. Future prospects

I. The Common European Economic Space

At the EU-Russia Summit of May 2001, in parallel to the WTO accession negotiations, the EU and Russia agreed to establish a joint High-Level Group to elaborate the concept of a Common European Economic Space, based on the wider goal of bringing the EU and Russia closer together. On 2 March 2002 the EU-Russia High-Level Group, co-chaired by representatives of Russia and the EU, was established.[54] The long-term objective of the initiative, which would cover essentially trade and economic issues, is the elimination of trade barriers between the EU and Russia.

The Concept paper on this initiative was presented to the EU-Russia Summit in November 2003 in Rome.[55] The Common European Economic Space was defined as "open and integrated market between the EU and Russia, based on the implementation of common or compatible rules and regulations". It shall ultimately cover substantially all sectors of economy. Paragraph 1.4. of the Concept provides that "The Common European Economic Space will be based on exist-

---

[53] Emerson, Institutionalising the Wider Europe, p.2

[54] 2002/240/EC: Decision of the Cooperation Council between the European Communities, and their Member States, of the one part, and the Russian Federation, of the other part, of 6 March 2002 to establish a joint High-Level Group to elaborate the concept of a common European economic space, OJ L 082 , 26/03/2002 P. 0009 - 0010

[55] See Documents of the 12th Russia-EU Summit in Rome, o6 November 2003, 13990/03 (Presse313), available at http://europa.eu.int/comm/external_relations/russia/intro/summit.htm

ing and future commitments of the Parties in the Partnership and Cooperation Agreement and WTO." However, "its scope shall be broader and deeper in comparison to the WTO and Partnership and Cooperation Agreement provisions."

Regarding the implementation of the Concept it was decided that the objectives will need to be transformed into specific goals and actions by way of action plans. The High Level Group will report progress to the EU-Russia Summit on a regular basis.

The Concept of the Common European Economic Space paper does little more than set forth the objectives of the dialogue and its scope with few details. All the work remains ahead. In view of increasing disagreements between the EU and Russia and numerous unsolved problems this idea is a very remote perspective. Moreover, the Concept is too vague to predict the practical implications of the Common European Economic Space on concrete trade issues, such as, e.g. anti-dumping.

II. Russia's accession to the WTO and the EU

1. Aims and objectives of the accession

Currently there are 146 member countries in the WTO and in the nearest future this number will increase.[56] This means that almost every nation aspiring to create a modern and effective economy and to participate in the world trade equally strives for WTO membership. Russia is not an exception. The membership in the WTO is increasingly seen as a necessary recognition by the international community of the reliability of one country's trade policy and a necessary step towards reaping the benefits of international trade. It is therefore not surprising that the number of countries requesting the accession to the WTO is increasing and spread to the various areas of the world.[57] Nor is it surprising that countries are ready to undergo lengthy negotiations in order to complete accessions process.

In June 1993, Russia applied for accession to GATT. In compliance with the procedures, a Working Party on accession was established on 16 June 1993. Russia's WTO accession negotiations started in 1995. Initially, they focused on a detailed study of the economic mechanisms, trade and political regime in Russia at multilateral level in terms of their conformity with the WTO rules and regula-

---

[56]Information on all WTO Members is available at:
http://www.wto.org/english/thewto_e/whatis_e/tif_e/org6_e.htm
[57] Accessions in progress: Algeria, Andorra, Azerbaijan, Bahamas, Belarus, Bhutan, Bosnia and Herzegovina, Cambodia, Cape Verde, Ethiopia, Kazakhstan, Lao People's Democratic Republic, Lebanese Republic, Nepal, Russian Federation, Samoa, Saudi Arabia, Serbia and Montenegro, Seychelles, Sudan, Tajikistan, Tonga, Ukraine, Uzbekistan, Vanuatu, Viet Nam, Yemen, available at: http://www.wto.org/english/thewto_e/acc_e/acc_e.htm

tions. Submitting initial tariff offers on goods and offers on government support for agriculture in 1998, and submitting the first draft of specific commitments on services with the list of exemptions from the Most Favoured Nation in 1999, allowed Russia to initiate a series of bilateral negotiations with all the interested members of Russia's WTO accession Working Party on the terms and conditions of Russia's membership in this international organization. At present, there are 67 member countries (EU counts as one) in the Working Party on Russia's WTO accession

The WTO membership offers a range of benefits. Enjoying these benefits is, pragmatically, the goal of joining the WTO. By acceding to the WTO Russia pursues the following goals:

➢ Improvement of existing conditions for access of Russian products to foreign markets and provision of non-discriminatory treatment for Russian exporters;
➢ Equal status with other WTO members in anti-dumping procedures and an end to all existing discriminatory measures against Russian exporters;
➢ Access to the WTO international dispute settlement mechanism;
➢ Creation of a more favourable climate for foreign investments as a result of legal system change in accordance with the WTO standards;
➢ Participation in negotiations of the international trade agreements taking into account national interests;
➢ Improvement of the image of Russia as a competent international trade participant.

The objective of the accession negotiations is to achieve the most favourable conditions for Russia joining the WTO, i.e. the best balance possible between the benefits of accession and the concessions in forms of tariffs reduction and domestic market opening. According to German Gref, The Minister of Economic Development and Trade, the balance of rights and obligations of Russia during its accession to the WTO should contribute to its economic growth and not vice versa.[58] Thus Russian WTO negotiators do not buy the ticket to the "moving WTO train" at any price.

2. Legal framework of Russia's accession to the WTO

Any state or customs territory having full autonomy in the conduct of its trade policies may become a member ("accede to") the WTO, but all WTO members must agree on the terms. This is done through the establishment of a working party of WTO members and through a process of negotiations. Article XII of the Marrakech Agreement Establishing the World Trade Organisation[59] states that

---

[58] Information regarding Russian accession to the WTO is available in Russian and English at: www.wto.ru

[59] The full text of Article XII of the WTO Agreement reads as follows:

"1. Any State or separate customs territory possessing full autonomy in the conduct of its external commercial relations and of other matters provided for in this Agreement and the Multilateral Trade Agreements may accede to this Agreement, on terms to be agreed between

accession to the WTO will be "on terms to be agreed" between the acceding government and the WTO. Accession to the WTO is essentially a process of negotiation — quite different from the process of accession to other international entities, which is largely an automatic process.

Article XII of the WTO Agreement does not stipulate any membership criteria, and this signals perhaps the most problematic legal aspect of the accession process. No guidance is given on the "terms to be agreed", these being left to negotiations between the WTO Members and the candidate. Furthermore, Article XII does not identify any concrete steps nor does it provide any advice when it comes to the procedures to be used for negotiating the terms of accession. Therefore, if an acceding country is a fairly large economy that presents a number of immediate opportunities to its trading partners, many WTO members will be directly involved in its accession negotiation and the process can then become lengthy and complex, as in case of Russia.[60] A single unresolved issue between an acceding country and one other WTO Member can slow down the entire process indefinitely. As will be seen infra it is obviously the case of negotiations between the EU and Russia.

Thus, although the WTO itself is based on the principle of legal clarity and predictability, its accession process follows an uneven road of laborious negotiations. The WTO accession process operates on case-by case basis, every case being driven by a set of distinct interests and priorities, and by very distinct realities.

It must be noted, that despite the broad mandate of Article XII of the WTO Agreement, the subsequent accession practice has shown an effort to preserve the uniformity of the WTO rule structure.[61] Since 1995, 20 countries have ac-

---

tilateral Trade Agreements may accede to this Agreement, on terms to be agreed between it and the WTO. Such accession shall apply to this Agreement and the Multilateral Trade Agreements annexed thereto.

2. Decisions on accession shall be taken by the Ministerial Conference. The Ministerial Conference shall approve the agreement on the terms of accession by a two-thirds majority of the Members of the WTO.

3. Accession to a Plurilateral Trade Agreement shall be governed by the provisions of this Agreement".The WTO texts of Agreements are available at www.wto.org

[60] E.g. counting from the initial application date to formal accession, it lasted 10 years for Bulgaria (September 1986 to December 1996)and Chinese Taipei (January 1992 to January 2002) and as long as 15 years for China (July 1986 to December 2001) to become a WTO Member.

[61] The WTO Secretariat, in consultation with WTO Members, has drawn up a set of procedures to be followed in the accession negotiations. See Technical Note on the Accession Process - Note by the Secretariat, 28.05.03, WT/ACC/10/Rev.1, available at: http://www.wto.org/english/thewto_e/acc_e/acc_e.htm. Although not legally binding, the procedures serve as a practical guide for WTO accessions and have helped to unify the accession processes.

ceded to the WTO, of which 13 are former centrally planned economies.[62] Each
of the 20 Protocols of accession has been made by its own provision "an integral
part of the WTO Agreement". Except in the case of China, the main text of each
protocol consists of no more that two pages of standardized provisions that address necessary procedural and technical matters of the accession.[63] The use of
such standardized text for the protocol of accession suggests that the acceding
Member is not subject to a different set of substantive rules from that applicable
to the original WTO Members.

3. EU as a major negotiator in the Russia's WTO bid

The EU recognises the fundamental role that membership of the WTO can play
in anchoring and solidifying Russia's economic reforms. Advantages stemming
from Russia's accession to the WTO will be reciprocal.[64]
However, there are several outstanding issues in EU-Russian talks that significantly slowed down the process of the accession process.[65] The European Commission made six energy demands on Russia: to raise internal prices for natural
gas, to end Gazprom's monopoly on gas exports,[66] to lift restrictions on gas transit, to allow foreign investors to build pipelines in Russia, introduce equal prices
for the transit of gas for domestic users and for exports, and to cancel gas export
tariffs.[67] Russia sees these demands as discriminatory and unacceptable.
The issue of lower energy prices in Russia has been the most contradictory and
highly disputed questions in Russia's decade-long effort to secure a place in the
WTO, especially when taking into account that on November 7, 2002 the EU
conferred market economy status on Russia. However, the very same day that

---

[62] The 20 countries are: Armenia, Former Yugoslav Republic of Macedonia, Ecuador,
Mongolia, Bulgaria, Panama, Kyrgyzstan, Latvia, Estonia, Jordan, Georgia, Croatia, Albania,
Oman, Lithuania, Moldova, China, Chinese Taipei, Nepal, Cambogia. Information on all
WTO accessions since 1995 is available at:
http://www.wto.org/english/thewto_e/acc_e/completeacc_e.htm#chn
[63] The Protocol of Accession of the People's Republic of China, WT/L/432 of 10.11.01,
available at http://www.wto.org/english/thewto_e/acc_e/completeacc_e.htm#chn consists of a
main text of 11 pages, nine annexes and 143 paragraphs incorporated by reference from the
Working Party Report. The main text of the Protocol has 17 sections of substantive provisions
(including 56 paragraphs and many additional subparagraphs). Most of the 143 paragraphs of
the Working Party Report incorporated into the Protocol contain commitments on rules. Thus,
covering a wide range of subjects, the China Protocol prescribes a set of special rules to be
applied between China and other WTO members.
[64] http://europa.eu.int/comm/trade/issues/bilateral/countries/russia/index_en.htm
[65] According to the estimates of the Russian Ministry of economic development and trade the
accession negotiation can be concluded not earlier, than end of 2004.,
see http://www.economy.gov.ru/
[66] OAO Gazprom has a monopoly, or is close to one, in the production, transmission and distribution of natural gas in Russia, information on www.gazprom.ru
[67] Barysh, Russia and the WTO, p. 33

Russia's Market economy status took effect, the Council of the European Union published an amendment to the EU regulation on antidumping.[68] Under the new guidelines, judgment in certain market situations, for example, where domestic market prices are artificially low or barter is common, will use a normal value defined on the basis of the company's actual production costs. If this fails, the costs will be adjusted or costs of similar companies

in the same country or information from other markets will be used. Thus, as long as the EU regards Russian energy, transportation and raw materials costs as being "artificially low," normal value can continue to be taken from another country (see detailed legal analysis infra Part three).

The EU indeed believes that energy prices in Russia are still subject to government controls and not subject to market mechanisms, which means that they do not reflect the true market price. Therefore, the EU claims that the gap between domestic Russian energy prices and world market prices bestows an unfair advantage on Russian producers. This leads to a double pricing system. EU and some other WTO member countries claim that dual energy pricing is an export subsidy for Russian exporters whose products embody energy.

Russian representatives argue that the difference between export and domestic prices for energy suppliers is Russian natural competitive advantages and that the EU demands exceed WTO requirements as agreed in the Uruguay round of multilateral trade negotiations. Moreover, Russian officials argue that dual energy pricing is an export subsidy only if the energy embodied in exported goods is priced lower than domestic energy—which, they argue, is not the case in the present situation. In the context of Russia's WTO accession, some members have sought a commitment by Russia to unify gas pricing. The request for unified energy pricing is perceived in Russia as imposing large economic costs in terms of lost profits on sales in Europe because of the decrease in export prices, or increased unemployment and resource misallocation costs at home caused by the imposition of higher prices, or a combination of both.[69]

Obviously, there is no evidence that Russian energy pricing structure causes real and serious damage to firms in the EU or other WTO member-states, which would be a precondition for it being defined as subsidies prohibited by the WTO. If Russia were to push up energy prices to world market levels too quickly, the result would be economic devastation on a scale that would easily outweigh the economic benefits of WTO accession. If Russia would accept the energy issue as part of the negotiation process, it would set an unfortunate

---

[68] See Council Regulation (EC) No. 1972/2002 of 5 November 2002 amending Regulation (EC) No. 2026/1997 on the protection against dumped imports from countries not members of the European Communities, OJ L305, 07.11.2002, p.1

[69] Russia maintains, moreover, that, as long as no specific industries are targeted for price discrimination, WTO rules do not prohibit it from charging different prices to domestic and foreign consumers (Inside U.S. Trade, April 26, 2002, p. 1).

precedent for assuming commitments in an area in which the WTO itself has not set any clear rules.

4. WTO Legal Issues—Is the EU energy demand WTO-Plus?
The Russian negotiators have noted that Article 2 of the WTO Agreement on Subsidies and Countervailing Measures[70] states that to be considered a subsidy, the subsidy has to be specific to an enterprise or group of enterprises. For example, Russia's earlier system of pricing energy at lower prices to the fertilizer industry would be a subsidy to the fertilizer industry. That system was eliminated. However, since the price in Russia for energy products does not vary with the user, Russian negotiators argue that dual energy pricing does not meet the criteria for a subsidy under WTO rules.

The following hypothetical example of specialists of the World Bank illustrates why the demand came to be labelled by the Russian negotiators as WTO-Plus, i.e. as a demand going beyond accession requirements: "If fertilizer producers elsewhere believe that dual energy pricing is a subsidy to Russian fertilizer exporters, they are permitted to initiate a countervailing duty investigation against Russian fertilizer exporters. Then, if Russia were a member of the WTO, it would have the right to appeal any such decision by another WTO member country to a WTO Dispute Settlement Panel. The Dispute Settlement Panel would resolve the matter according to WTO rules. Thus, if dual pricing were a subsidy under WTO rules, there would be no need to require its elimination as part of the accession negotiation since it would be possible to apply countervailing duties against Russian exports. On the other hand, if dual energy pricing is not a subsidy, then the Dispute Settlement Panel will rule in favour of Russia and the countervailing duty margins will be declared illegal."[71]

Anyway sooner or later Russia will be member of WTO and this problem will be solved by compromise. The author emphasised this issue to show how long the way of compromise can be. Every year that Russia is not member of WTO brings country significant losses, mainly because Russia cannot use the WTO dispute settlement mechanism in anti-dumping procedures. Moreover the Russian gas prises have direct connection with the EU anti-dumping legislation, as it will be shown infra.

5. Reform of the trade legislation in view of the accession to the WTO
On 21 June 2002 the Russian Government adopted the Regulation implementing the Action plan of bringing the Russian legislation in accordance with the WTO

---

[70] Available at : http://www.wto.org/english/docs_e/legal_e/24-scm_01_e.htm
[71] David Tarr and Peter Thomson, The Merits of Dual Pricing of Russian Natural Gas, The World Bank, 2003, p.3., available at www.wto.ru

law.[72] In accordance with this plan the following key legislation was adopted under Russia's WTO accession's bid:

➤ New Customs Code of 28.04.2003, which greatly simplified customs procedures.[73]
➤ A new law "On Special Safeguard, Anti-dumping and Countervailing Measures" [74] of 08.12.2003, which introduced clear and transparent procedures for anti-dumping procedures and provide increased certainty for Russian foreign trading partners.
➤ A new law "On State Regulation of Foreign Trade Activities"[75] of 08.12.2002 defined the exact scope of state competences in the area of foreign trade.

This legislation is the foundation for making all Russian foreign trade rules WTO compatible and the market more predictable and attractive for business partners. In general Russia have adopted or amended more than 50 legal acts in order to conform WTO standards, more amendments are in preparation.[76]

Conclusion of Part one

The diverse legal issues of trade cooperation have been analysed in the present Chapter. In the recent decade the certain progress in the EU-Russian bilateral trade relations was achieved. But going back to the Partnership and Cooperation Agreement between Russia and the EU as a cornerstone of bilateral relations the author would admit, that the structures of Russian interaction with the European Union were formed in the mid-1990s when the EU-Russian dialogue was not as diverse and active as today. As a result, many problems often have to be solved at the highest political level, which leads to unnecessary delays and misunderstandings. Moreover, everyone would agree that this is not the best way to

---

[72] See Распоряжение от 21 июня 2002 г. № 832-р (Regulation of the Government of the Russian Federation of 21.06.2002 № 832-р.)

[73] Таможенный кодекс Российской Федерации от 28.05.2003 N 61-ФЗ (Customs Code of the Russian Federation of 28.05.2003 N 61-ФЗ), "Российская газета", N 106, 03.06.2003, вступил в силу с 1.01.2004 года (published in Russian Newspaper, N 106, 03.06.2003, вступил в силу on 1.01.2004)

[74] Федеральный закон от 08.12.2003 № 165-ФЗ "О специальных защитных, антидемпинговых и компенсационных мерах при импорте товаров" (Federal Law of the Russian Federation "On Special Safeguard, Anti-dumping and Countervailing measures of 08.12.2003 № 165-ФЗ), "Российская газета", N 253, 17.12.2003 (published in Russian Newspaper, N 253, 17.12.2003)

[75] Федеральный закон от 08.12.2003 № 184-ФЗ "Об основах государственного регулирования внешнеторговой деятельности" (Federal Law of the Russian Federation of 08.12.2003 № 184-ФЗ), "Российская газета", N 254, 18.12.2003, вступает в силу по истечении шести месяцев со дня официального опубликования (published in Russian Newspaper, N 254, 18.12.2003, enters into force 6 months after official publication)

[76] Information of Russian Ministry of Economical Development and Trade

achieve compromises in the relations between states. Therefore, the existing mechanisms of cooperation should be renewed and made more effective.

The time has come to shift the many-sided dialogue between the Russia and the European Union to a totally pragmatic sphere, as should be the case between partners who are equal, who know each other well and trust each other. In view of the Russian accession to the WTO and EU enlargement, Russia and the EU have to leave behind the period when basic political declarations were important and have to reach a stage in bilateral relations when it is normal and natural to speak about one's benefits, to count one's money and in general tackle a multitude of day-to-day issues. This is especially relevant to EU anti-dumping investigations against Russian exports. Russia and EU sign promising political declarations and at the same time Russian industry suffers significant losses from the EU anti-dumping measures.

This should be the direction in "modernizing" the Partnership and Cooperation Agreement and other EU-Russian documents.

PART TWO. EU ANTI-DUMPING LAW AND PRACTICE AGAINST RUSSIAN EXPORTERS

A. Legal framework of the EU anti-dumping law and practice against Russian exporters

I. The multinational WTO legal framework

Since 1 January 1995 the rules of the multinational trading system relating to anti-dumping are found in the following World Trade Organisation ("WTO") provisions:

1. Article VI of the General Agreement on Tariffs and Trade 1994 ("GATT 1994"), which contains the basic provisions relating to anti-dumping action;
2. The Agreement on Implementation of Article VI of GATT 1994[77] (the "Anti-dumping Agreement), which contains detailed provisions relating to methodologies and procedural issues.

Although all Members of the WTO are also parties to the Anti-dumping Agreement, it is not mandatory for members to have in place a legal framework for anti-dumping action, or to take anti-dumping action when, or if, injurious dumping occurs. However, the Anti-dumping Agreement specifies that if a member chooses to take anti-dumping action, such action must be consistent with the rules set out therein and shall be preceded by the required investigation conducted on the basis of the provisions of the Anti-dumping Agreement.

In particular, Article 1 of the Anti-dumping Agreement provides that:

"An anti-dumping measure shall be applied only under the circumstances provided for in Article VI of GATT 1994 and pursuant to investigations initiated and conducted in accordance with the provisions of this Agreement".

Therefore, for WTO Members, the imposition of anti-dumping measures is subject to the following conditions:

➢ An investigation must have been initiated and conducted in accordance with the provisions of the Anti-dumping Agreement;
➢ As a result of that investigation it must have been determined that the imports concerned:
  o Are dumped;
  o That the domestic industry is suffering material injury, a threat of material injury, or that the establishment of a domestic industry is materially retarded; and
  o That the injury being suffered by the domestic industry is casually linked to the dumped imports.

WTO Members are precluded from taking action against injurious dumped im-

---

[77]See http://www.wto.org/english/docs_e/legal_e/final_e.htm for the texts of GATT 1994 and Anti-dumping Agreement.

ports other than the application of anti-dumping measures. Article 18.1 of the Anti-dumping Agreement provides: "No specific action against dumping of exports from another Member can be taken except in accordance with the provisions of GATT 1994, as interpreted by this Agreement".

The measures allowed by the Anti-dumping Agreement are provisional measures, definitive anti-dumping duties, and price undertakings.

The Anti-dumping Agreement contains detailed procedural rules which have to be observed in conducting investigations, as well as substantive rules regarding the methodologies to be applied in calculating the dumping margin, determining whether injury exists, and in establishing whether a causal link exists between the dumping and the injury.

Table gives an outline of the provisions of the Anti-dumping Agreement governing the procedural and the substantive aspects of investigations.

Table 4. WTO Anti-dumping Agreement provisions applicable to Investigations[78]	
Provision	**Issue**
Article 2	Definition and determination of dumping: Calculation of export price Calculation of normal value Adjustments to export price and normal value Calculation of dumping margin
Article 3	Determination of injury Causal link between the dumped imports and injury
Article 4	Definition of "domestic industry"
Article 5	Initiation of an investigation
Article 6	Investigation
Article 7	Provisional anti-dumping measures
Article 8	Price undertakings
Article 9	Definitive anti-dumping duties
Article 10	Retroactive imposition of anti-dumping duties
Article 11	Duration and reviews of anti-dumping duties
Article 12	Public notice and explanation of determinations
Article 13	Judicial review
Article 15	Special treatment for developing countries
Article 17	Special additional dispute settlement rules and procedures, i.e., an addition to those in the WTO Understanding on Rules and Procedures Governing the Settlement of Disputes, including standard of review rules.

---

[78] Czako/Human/Miranda , A Handbook on Anti-dumping investigations, p. 4

II. The EC Framework

1. Anti-dumping provisions in EC primary legislation

Article 3 (b) of the Treaty establishing the European Community[79] recognises that "a common commercial policy" is one of the objectives of the Community. The basic provision dealing with the common commercial policy is Article 133 EC, which provides the legal basis for the Community's trade protection instruments including anti-dumping.

This article does not define the term "common commercial policy", but simply offers a non-exhaustive enumeration of subjects covered by the common commercial policy, including "measures to protect trade such as those to be taken in the event of dumping"[80] emphasising that "common commercial policy shall be based on uniform principles".

2. Anti-dumping provisions in EC secondary legislation

The Community's anti-dumping and anti-subsidy legislation was first enacted in 1968 and has since been modified several times[81].

The current anti-dumping law, i.e. Council Regulation (EC) No 384/96 of 22 December 1995 on protection against dumped imports from countries not members of the European Community[82] ("Basic Regulation" or "Regulation 384/96"), which form the legal basis of anti-dumping investigations in the Community, entered into force in March 1996 and is based on WTO Anti-Dumping Agreement[83].

a) Scope of the Basic Anti-dumping Regulation

From a geographical point of view, even though not expressly mentioned in Regulation itself, the Basic Regulation applies to all countries that are not members of the European Union.

---

[79] See Consolidated versions of The Treaty on European Union and the Treaty establishing the European Community, OJ C 325, 24.12.02, also online
http://www.europa.eu.int/abc/treaties_en.htm

[80] Art. 133 (1) of the Treaty establishing the European Community

[81] Commission of the European Communities, 21st Anti-dumping report, 2002

[82] Council Regulation (EC) Nr. 484/96 of 22 December 1995 on protection against dumped imports from countries not members of the European Community (OJ L. 56, 6.3.1996, p.1), amended by Council Regulation (EC) Nr. 2331/96 of 2 December 1996 (OJ L. 317, 6.12.1996, p.1), amended by Council Regulation (EC) Nr. 905/98 of 27 April 1998 (OJ. L128, 30.04.1998, p.18), amended by Council Regulation (EC) Nr. 2238/2000 of 9 October 2000 (OJ L. 257, 11.10.2000, p.2), amended by Council Regulation (EC) Nr. 1972/2002 of 5 November 2002 (OJ L. 305, 7.11.2002, p.1), amended by Council Regulation (EC) Nr. 461/2004 of 8 March 2004 (OJ L.77, 13.3.2004, p.12)

[83] The issues of WTO conformity of some provisions of Basic Regulation will be discussed in Part three

It applies to WTO members and non-members alike, although Community authorities are theoretically empowered under Art. 22 (c) of the Regulation to adopt "special measures" with respect to imports from non-WTO members[84].

The Community adopted specific provisions in relation to countries without a market economy or whose economy is in transition[85].

The Regulation also stipulates that its provisions do not preclude the application of any special rules laid down in agreements concluded between the Community and third countries.

From a physical point of view, the Regulation applies to products in general[86], but not to services.

3. Increase of transparency in the EU Anti-dumping Acts

On 8 March 2004 the EU amended the Basic Anti-dumping Regulation to introduce greater transparency, efficiency and predictability in the use of anti-dumping.[87] Under the new rules, which enter into force on 20th March 2004, definitive anti-dumping measures will be considered adopted unless a simple majority of EU Members States opposes the move. The EU will also introduce mandatory deadlines to complete review investigations, which will lead to faster investigations and will also introduce clearer rules on enforcement of trade defence measures. On the eve of the EU's enlargement, these changes are aimed to make the use of trade defence instruments more efficient, workable and transparent for EU operators as well as third countries subject to trade defence cases in the EU. [88]

The latest changes in the anti-dumping Regulation in detail:

➤ Streamlined decision-making: a clearer and more transparent system for EU operators. Definitive anti-dumping measures will be considered adopted unless a simple majority of Member States rejects the measures within one month after the Commission has made a proposal. The new rules do not upset the balance of powers between the Commission and the Council: the simple

---

[84] This has only happened in one case under Regulation 459/68: Steel nuts (Taiwan), OJ 1977 L 286/7. These measures were repealed by Regulation 1948/92, OJ 1992 L 197/1 (Data from Van Bael/Bellis, EC Anti-dumping Laws, p. 41)

[85] Regulation 384/96, Art. 2(7)

[86] However, with regard to agricultural products, particularly products where common market organisations protect Community production through the use of levies, the provisions of the anti-dumping regulation may be applied by way of complement to and in derogation from any provisions, which preclude the application of anti-dumping duties (Regulation 384/96, Art. 22).

[87] Council Regulation (EC) No. 461/2004 of 8.03.2004 amending Regulation (EC) No. 384/96 on protection against dumped imports from countries not members of the European Community and Regulation (EC) No. 2026/97 on protection against subsidised imports from countries not members of the European Community, OJ 13.03.2004, L 77/12

[88] http://europa.eu.int/comm/trade/issues/index_en.htm, called 10.03.2004

majority principle will continue to operate. But it will require affirmative action by Member States to overturn a Commission proposal.

Before: a simple majority of EU Member States was necessary to impose definitive measures. This means that abstentions were counted as being votes against.

➢ Faster Investigations: transparency and predictability for EU operators and third country exporters

From now on: investigations aimed at reviewing existing anti-dumping or anti-subsidy measures and changes in form or in the level of such measures (review investigations) will be subject to strict mandatory deadlines. This should put an end to concerns about uncertainty regarding measures that remain in force while - sometimes lengthy – reviews are ongoing. This responds to calls from economic operators (in particular importers and exporters from third countries) for greater predictability. However, the provisions regarding deadlines of most revives are only applicable two years after the entry into force of amending Regulation, i.e. on 20th March 2006.[89]

Before: review investigations were subject to an indicative period of completion of 12-month. Experience gained in the past shows that reviews have lasted longer than the normal timeframe. The introduction of mandatory deadlines will thus speed up the conduct of reviews.

➢ Clearer rules for companies on enforcement of anti-dumping and measures. The changes also introduce rules aimed at clarifying the application of anti-dumping measures on exporters from third countries and importers in the EU.

➢ Clearer rules are also introduced to in respect to price undertaking, fight against circumvention of anti-dumping measures as well as against the absorption of the duties.

B. Substantive elements of the EU Anti-Dumping Investigation

There are four substantive elements of the EU Anti-dumping investigation:

1. The existence of dumping
2. The existence of injury
3. Causality between dumping and injury
4. Community interest

I. Dumping

Establishing whether dumping has occurred is the first essential step in any proceeding under the Basic Regulation. In accordance with the Art. 1 (1) of the Basic Regulation, "a product is to be considered as being dumped if its export price to the Community is less than a comparable price for the like product, in the or-

---

[89] Art. 3 (b) of Regulation (EC) No. 461/2004 of 8.03.2004 amending Regulation (EC) No. 384/96, OJ 13.03.2004, L 77/12

dinary course of trade, as established for the exporting country." Dumping is different from the ordinary cheap sales, which are made due to low costs or higher productivity. Decisive factor is not a correlation between export price and market price in importing country, but the correlation between the export price and normal value.

The rules concerning dumping determinations are set out in Art. 2 of the Basic Regulation. Under these rules a dumping determination involves four basic steps:

1. the determination of "normal value" – Art. 2.A
2. the determination of "export price" – Art. 2.B
3. the comparison of "normal value" and "export price" – Art. 2.C
4. the calculation of the "dumping margin" – Art. 2.D

1. Normal value determinations for imports from market economy countries

Determining "normal value" is the first step in any dumping determination. Complex rules govern the determination of normal value, particularly the selection of the test by which the normal value will be assessed[90].

An initial distinction must be made between imports from market economy countries and those from non-market economy countries as different rules govern these two types of imports. Russia is considered as a market economy country from 8 November 2002[91].

a) Normal value based on domestic market price

The normal value is, as general rule, "normally to be based on the prices paid or payable, in the ordinary course of trade, by independent customers in the exporting country"[92]. In other words, the primary basis for determining normal value is the domestic price paid or payable for the like product in the exporting country.

However even from the formulation "normally" in Art. 2(1) Abs.1 of Regulation 384/96 one can come to the conclusion, that normal value cannot be determined in this way in all cases. The reason is that in some cases the goods in question are not sold in exporting countries or sold in insufficient quantities or the price building does not reflect market forces.

The Table gives an overview over conditions for determining of normal value based on domestic market prices. The exceptions to the general rule of determining normal value are listed in Art. 2, paragraph 1 to 7 of the Basic Regulation.

---

[90] Regulation 384/96, Art. 2(1) to 2(7)
[91] OJ L 305 of 7.11.2002, p.1, detailed see Part three
[92] Regulation 384/96, Art. 2(1) Abs. 1

Table 5. Normal value based on domestic market price: conditions	
Condition	**Legal framework**
Sales of the like product in the domestic market of the exporting country	Art. 2 A (1) Abs.1 read together with Art. 2 A (1) Abs. 4
Representative sales (5% test)	Art. 2 A (1) Abs. 2
Sales in the domestic market are made in the ordinary course of trade	Art. 2 A (1) Abs.1 read together with Art. 2 A (1) Abs. 4
Sales in the domestic market permit a proper comparison	Art. 2 A (1) Abs.3

b) Grounds for disregarding domestic market prices
The Regulation 384/96 identifies a number of circumstances in which the domestic market price may be disregarded for normal value purposes and alternative tests may be used instead. A summary of the applicable rules is set out below:
1. The domestic market price may be disregarded in the following circumstances:
   a. when there are "no or insufficient sales of the like product" on the domestic market of the exporting country[93]; or
   b. when there are no sales or insufficient sales of the like product "in the ordinary course of trade" on the domestic market of the exporting country[94]; or
   c. when such sales, because of particular market situation, do not permit a proper comparison[95].
2. The alternative normal value tests that may be used when the domestic market price may be disregarded are:
   a. the constructed value; or
   b. the export prices, in the ordinary course of trade, to an appropriate third country, provided that these prices are representative[96].

aa) No or insufficient sales of like product
The first ground for not using the domestic market price as the basis to calculate normal value is the absence of sales or insufficient sales of the like product[97] on the domestic market in the exporting country.

---

[93] Regulation 384/96, Art. 2 (1), 2 (2)
[94] Regulation 384/96, Art. 2 (1), 2 (4)
[95] Regulation 384/96, Art. 2(3)
[96] Regulation 384/96, Art. 2(3)

(i) No sales

In accordance with Art. 2(1) subparagraph 2 of the Basic Regulation "where the exporter in the exporting country does not produce or does not sell the like product, the normal value may be established on the basis of prices of other sellers or producers." This situation can occur, for instance, in case when the product in question is only sold in export markets or because the models sold on the domestic market are different from those sold in the EU.

If, however, the difference between the products sold for export and on the domestic market are relatively minor, the Commission will tend to treat them as like product, but will allow an adjustment to be made to take the differences in physical characteristics into account[98].

(ii) Insufficient sales: the five per cent rule

From the quantitative point of view Art. 2(2) of the Regulation 384/96 requires that sales volumes constitute 5% or more of the sales volume of the product under consideration to the Community. It must be noted, however, that this Article allows the authorities to depart from the five per cent rule and calculate the normal value on the basis of domestic market prices even if the domestic sales volume represent less than five per cent of the sales volume to the Community. Thus, in accordance with Art. 2(2) sentence 2 of the Regulation 384/96 "a lower volume of sales may be used when, for example, the prices charged are considered representative for the market concerned."

Table 6. Sufficiency of sales. Application of 5% rule[99]				
Model	Export volume to the EU	Sales volume in the domestic market	Percentage of Export sales	Representative Sales YES/NO
Total	2,000,000	372,000	18,6%	YES
Model A	1,000,000	40,000	4%	NO
Model B	500,000	40,000	8%	YES
Model C	0	200,000	-	irrelevant

---

[97] Art. 1(4) of the Regulation 384/96 defines the "like product" as "a product which is identical, that to say, alike in all respects, to the product under consideration, or in the absence of such a product, another product which although not alike in all respects, has characteristics closely resembling those of the product under consideration". It should be noted that the term "like product" is not only relevant for the dumping determination, but also for the injury determination.

[98] Van Bael/Bellis, EC Anti-dumping Laws, p. 69

[99] Müller, Der AD-rechtliche Rahmen, p. 31

bb) No sales in the ordinary course of trade
The second ground for not using the domestic market price as the basis to calculate normal value is the absence of sales of the like product "in the ordinary course of trade" in the domestic market in the exporting country. The purpose of the requirement that there must be domestic sales in the ordinary course of trade is to make sure that the prices used in the normal value determination reflect normal trading conditions[100]. The concept of "the ordinary course of trade" helps to circumvent anti-dumping measures through artificially low prices in export country.
The Regulation 384/96 specifies three sets of circumstances under which sales may be considered as not having been made in the ordinary course of trade:
1. sales below cost of production[101];
2. sales between associated parties[102]; and
3. sales between parties having a compensatory agreement[103].
This list has only exemplary character and is not exhaustive.

(i) Sales below costs
Art. 2(4) of the Regulation 384/96 reproduce the provisions of Art. 2.2.1 of the WTO Anti-dumping Agreement laying down the principle that sales of the like product in the domestic market, or export sales to a third country, at prices below per unit (fixed and variable) costs of production plus selling, general and administrative costs may be considered as not having been made in the ordinary course of trade by reason of price. The introduction of cost arguments in the normal value calculation was subject of criticism in the professional literature. The reason of these critics was that a sale below costs is solely question of competition, which should not be affected by trade policy measures[104]. Not least because of all that critics the Basic Regulation 384/96 concretized and specified more precisely the requirements set for sales below costs[105]. Thus domestic prices may be disregarded in determining normal value by reason of price but only if it is determined that such sales:
1. "are made within an extended period (normally one year but shall in no case less than six months) in substantial quantities (when the weighted average selling price is below the weighted average unit cost, or the volume of sales

---

[100] The concept of "ordinary course of trade" is also relevant in connection with the calculation of constructed value in that Regulation 384/96, Art. 2 (6) provides that for purposes of calculating the cost of production, "the amounts for selling, for general and administrative costs and for profits shall be based on actual data pertaining to production and sales, in the ordinary course of trade..."
[101] Regulation 384/96, Art. 2(4)
[102] Regulation 384/96, Art. 2(1)
[103] Regulation 384/96, Art. 2(1)
[104] Bail/Schädel/Hutter, Antidumping VO, Rn. 23
[105] Friedrichs, EGV/Antidumpingrecht, p. 17

below unit cost is not less than 20 % of sales being used to determine normal value)", and

2. "are at prices which do not provide for the recovery of all costs within a reasonable period of time."

Example 1.[106] Can the normal value for Model B be calculated on the basis of prices in Country A?		
	Quantity	Price per unit
Export sales in EU	500.000	$100
Sales in country A	40.000	$120
Production costs		$130
Conclusion: although sales of Model B are representative, but not in ordinary course of trade, because they are unprofitable		

Example 2. [107] Sales at prices below unit production cost
What is normal value of Model A from Country B?
Export sales in the EU: 100.000 units at $100 per unit
Sales in the domestic market of country B:

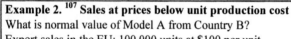

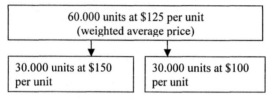

60.000 units at $125 per unit
(weighted average price)

30.000 units at $150 per unit

30.000 units at $100 per unit

Cost of production: $120 per unit
Answer: Normal value is **$150** (half of the domestic sales are at price below unit production costs and therefore are disregarded in determining normal value)

(ii) Associated parties and compensatory agreements

Art. 2(1) subparagraph 3 of the Regulation 384/96 provides that prices between parties "which appear to be associated " may not be considered as being made in the ordinary course of trade. These prices may not be used to determine normal value unless it is determined that they are unaffected by the relationship. The term "associated" is defined neither in the WTO Anti-dumping Agreement nor in the Regulation 384/96, awaiting further clarification in the case law. Article 2 (1) subparagraph 3 of the Basic Regulation gives the EU authorities a wide dis-

---

[106] Müller, Der AD-rechtliche Rahmen, p. 33
[107] Müller, Der Ad-rechtliche Rahmen, p. 33

cretion, allowing them to disregard transactions between parties, which "appear" to be associated[108].

The questionnaire for producers and exporters usually contains the following statement:

"For the purpose of completing this questionnaire, a purchaser should be considered to be related if it holds directly or indirectly mare than 1% of your capital or otherwise controls your company of if your company holds more than 5% of its share capital or you otherwise control it"[109].

Thus, a stock participation of more than one per cent could be a sufficient basis for a finding that there is an association between parties, although it would not appear to be conclusive evidence of such an association.

Where parties are considered to form a "single economic unit", e.g. where one party acts as a related sales company, then sales by the sales company will usually be assimilated to the sales of the exporter[110].

The amendments to the Basic Regulation of 2002 introduced the additional provision (subparagraph 4) to the Art. 2(1), which puts some light to the definition of "associated parties". The Art. 2(1) subparagraph 4 provides, that "in order to determine whether two parties are associated account may be taken of the definition of related parties set out in Article 143[111] of Commission Regulation (EEC) 2454/93 of 2 July 1993 laying down provisions for the implementation of Council Regulation (EEC) No 2913/92 establishing the Community Customs Code".[112] However the permissive language of the provision ("account may be taken") and shortage of relevant EU practice since November 2002 does not al-

---

[108] See e.g. Van Bael/Bellis, EC Anti-dumping Laws, p. 73, Netteshim in: Grabitz/ von Bogdandy/ Nettesheim, p. 205

[109] Anti-dumping Handbook for Russian Exporters, p. 134

[110] Van Bael/Bellis, EC Anti-dumping Laws, p. 74

[111] Art. 143 of Commission Regulation (EEC) 2454/93 of 2 July 1993 reads as follows: 'For the purposes of Title II, Chapter 3 of the Code and of this Title, persons shall be deemed to be related only if : (a) they are officers or directors of one another's businesses; (b) they are legally recognized partners in business; (c) they are employer and employee; (d) any person directly or indirectly owns, controls or holds 5 % or more of the outstanding voting stock or shares of both of them; (e) one of them directly or indirectly controls the other; (f) both of them are directly or indirectly controlled by a third person; (g) together they directly or indirectly control a third person; or (h) they are members of the same family. Persons shall be deemed to be members of the same family only if they stand in any of the following relationships to one another:- husband and wife; - parent and child; - brother and sister (whether by whole or half blood); - grandparent and grandchild; - uncle or aunt and nephew or niece; - parent-in-law and son-in-law or daughter-in-law; - brother-in-law and sister-in-law.
2. For the purposes of this title, persons who are associated in business with one another in that one is the sole agent, sole distributor or sole concessionaire, however described, of the other shall be deemed to be related only if they fall within the criteria of paragraph 1.

[112] OJ L 253, 11.10.1993, p.1. Regulation as last amended by Commission Regulation (EC) No 444/2002 (OJ L 68, 12.3.2002, p.11)

low to make any conclusion whether the 2002 amendments would bring any clarity to the definition of "associated parties".

Parties that appear to have a compensatory arrangement with each other are treated like associated parties under the Regulation 384/96[113]. The term "compensatory arrangement" is not defined in the Regulation. According to legal doctrine it mean arrangement between companies, where low sales prices are compensated by other deals[114], such as buy-back arrangements, swap deals and conversion arrangements[115].

cc) Sales not permitting proper comparison

The third ground for not using the domestic market price as the basis to calculate normal value is in accordance with Art. 2 (3) of Regulation 384/96 the case "where because of the particular market situation such sales do not permit a proper comparison". Before the amendments to the Basic Regulation of November 2002 the doctrine used to interpret the "particular market situation" as e.g. sales during seasonal clearances or advertising campaigns[116]. The latest amendments to the Regulation 384/96 gave a following definition to the term "particular market situation": "A particular market situation for the product concerned within the meaning of the preceding sentence may be deemed to exist, inter alia, when prices are artificially low, when there is significant barter trade, or when there are non-commercial processing arrangements."[117]

c) The alternative normal value tests

Whenever there are grounds for disregarding the domestic price paid for the like product in the exporting country, Art. 2 (3) of the Regulation 384/96 leaves the EU authorities the entire discretion to base normal value either on the export price of the like product when exported to a third country or on constructed value. In practice, the EU tends to use the constructed value in such a case[118].

aa) Constructed value
(i) Rules concerning the determination of costs

Article 2 (5) of the Basic Regulation lays down the following rules concerning the determination of costs.

   1. Use of the party's records

---

[113] Regulation 384/96, Art. 2(1)
[114] Bail/Schädel/Hutter, Antidumping VO, Rn. 23
[115] Van Bael/Bellis, EC Anti-dumping Laws, p. 75
[116] Bail/Schädel/Hutter, Antidumping VO, Rn. 12
[117] The possible impact of this amendments on anti-dumping measures against Russia see in details in Part three
[118] Van Bael/Bellis, EC Anti-dumping Laws, p. 64

2. Cost allocations

3. Start-up operations

Regarding the first rule it should be noted, that the Article 2 (5) of the Basic Regulation provides that costs will normally be calculated on the basis of records kept by the party under investigation, provided that such records are in accordance with the generally accepted accounting principles of the country concerned and that it is shown that the records reasonably reflect the costs associated with the production and sale of the product under consideration.

The amendments to the Basic Regulation in November 2002 added the clause to the Article 2 (5) of the Regulation 384/96, providing that if costs associated with the production and sale of the product under investigation are not reasonably reflected in the records of the party concerned, they will be adjusted or established on the basis of the costs of other producers or exporters in the same country or, where such information is not available or cannot be used, on any other reasonable basis, including information from other representative markets.

Thus, while the Regulation sets out the principle that the company's accounting records should be used, it nevertheless leaves a wide margin of discretion to the Commission to revise the costs reported in the accounting records. This discretion might be definitely used very widely in future as the term "information from other representative markets" is not defined.

(ii)The elements of constructed value

Constructed value is determined on the basis of cost of production in the country of origin plus a reasonable amount for selling, general and administrative costs (SGA) and for profit[119].

Table 7 (See next page) gives an outline of the elements of constructed value in accordance with the provisions of the Basic Regulation.

bb) Export price to third country

The second alternative normal value test that may be used when there are no or insufficient sales of the like product in the ordinary course of trade on the domestic market, or where such sales do not permit a proper comparison are "the export prices, in the ordinary course of trade, to an appropriate third country".[120]

Regulation 384/96 itself only states that the third country should be "appropriate" and that the export prices should be "representative". It is clear from the definitions, that the EU authorities have wide discretion at this alternative test. The Commission has the power to decide which third country is "appropriate".

Until the latest amendments to the Basic Regulation the EU authorities practically never relied on export prices to a third country to determine normal value

---

[119] Regulation 384/96, Art. 2 (3)

[120] Regulation 384/96, Art. 2(3)

when domestic market prices cannot be used. The rationale traditionally put forward by the EU institutions to justify their refusal to use export prices to a third country is that such sales might be made at dumping prices.[121] In such a case, they normally computed normal value on the basis of constructed value.[122] However, the legal doctrine has reasons to believe that this method of normal value calculation will be more frequently used after granting a market economy status to Russia as the Russian law gas prices have always been a stumbling block in Russia-EU trade.[123]

Table 7. The elements of constructed value. Art. 2(3)	
1. Cost of production in the country of origin	➤ Cost of materials ➤ Cost of direct labor (basic pay, employee benefits, other employee-related expenses) Manufacturing overheads (indirect labor, including contract labor, supervision, sub-contractor fees, depreciation, rent, power, maintenance and repairs, accounting adjustments to inventory)
2. Selling, general and administrative costs (SGA)	**SGA cost and profit based on : (Art. 2 (6)):** ➤ Basic rule: actual data pertaining to production and sales, in the ordinary course of trade, of the like product, by the exporter or producer under investigation.
3. Profit	➤ Alternative methods: a) the weighted average of the actual amounts determined for other exporters or producers subject to investigation in respect of production and sales of the like product in the domestic market of the country of origin; (b) the actual amounts applicable to production and sales, in the ordinary course of trade, of the same general category of products for the exporter or producer in question in the domestic market of the country of origin; (c) any other reasonable method.

---

[121] Bierwagen, in: Europäische Zeitschrift für Wirtschaftsrecht (EuZW) 1995, S. 232
[122] Van Bael/Bellis, EC Anti-dumping Laws, p. 92
[123] See in details in Part three

2. Export price

a) Notion of export price

The second step in a dumping determination involves an inquiry into the export price. Article 2B of the Regulation 384/96 provides for two alternative export price tests:

➢ Basic principle: actual export price, i.e. "the price actually paid or payable for the product when sold from the exporting country to the Community";[124] or

➢ The constructed export price.[125]

In accordance with Art. 2B of the Basic Regulation, costs occurred after the export are irrelevant, i.e. they are deducted from price actually paid[126]. The EU Commission defines the export price not as the selling price of the product in the EU, but the price at the moment of export from the country of origin. As a rule export price do not exist and the formation of the weighted average figure is necessary. The calculation methods of the Commission are quite vague. All export prices that are higher than calculated before normal value, are counted only on the basis of this normal value. Export prices below normal value are counted in their actual value. This calculation method inevitably produces an export price, which lies below normal value.[127] In case when export price for the product cannot be determined directly, the EU Commission calculates the value by deducting the costs payable between the export and entry of product in the EU (see Example 3 p. 71).

It should be noted that, regardless of the rules set out in Art. 2 of the Basic Regulation, the EU institutions are authorized under Art. 18 (1) to make determinations "on the basis of facts available" in cases where interested parties refuse access to, or otherwise do not provide, necessary information within a reasonable period, or significantly impede the investigation. In a number of cases, the institutions have relied on this provision to determine the export price on the basis other than those referred to in Art. 2 (8) and 2 (9).[128]

b) Notion of constructed export price

Article 2(9) provides that the export price may be determined on the basis of the constructed export price in the following two cases:

1. Where there is no export price;

---

[124] Regulation 384/96, Art. 2(8)
[125] Regulation 384/96, Art. 2(9)
[126] Nettesheim, in: Grabitz/von Bogdandy/Nettesheim, S.214
[127] Egeln/Klann, Antidumpingpolitik der EG, S.25
[128] Van Bael/Bellis, EC Anti-dumping Laws, p. 92

2. Where it appears that the export price is unreliable because of an association or a compensatory arrangement between the exporter and the importer or a third party.

The language of Art. 2 (9) is permissive. The EU institutions "may", but are not required to, resort to a constructed export price where one of the circumstances referred to in Art. 2 (9) occurs. Needless to say, the EU institutions will have no choice but to resort to the constructed export price where there is no actual export price or where they have actually determined that the actual export price is unreliable. In contrast, where the unreliability of the actual export price is merely assumed from the existence of an association or compensatory arrangement between the parties and it is determined that the actual export price is nevertheless reliable, Art. 2 (9) allows the actual export price to be used. In practice however the provision regarding association or compensatory arrangements is frequently used by the EU Commission in anti-dumping proceedings. When the importer of the product under consideration is a subsidiary of the exporter, the EU institutions generally disregard the actual export price and use the constructed export price instead.[129] This is the case even where the exporter's subsidiary in the EU acts like an agent and does not keep any stock on its own.[130]

c) Calculation of constructed export price

There are two methods on the basis of which a constructed export price may be determined:[131]

1. The primary method is "the price at which the imported product are first resold to an independent buyer";
2. The alternative method is "any reasonable basis", which may be used only in the following two cases:
   a) where the products are not resold to an independent buyer, or
   b) where they are not resold in the condition imported.

However, to the knowledge of author, by the end of 2003 the EU institutions had not expressly used this alternative method in any decided case.

Regarding the basic rule of export price calculation, i.e. the price at which the imported product are first resold to an independent buyer, the export price will be "worked back" from the price at which the product is first sold to an unrelated party. This method implies that "adjustment for all costs, including duties and taxes, incurred between importation and resale, and for profits accruing, shall be made so as to establish a reliable export price, at the Community frontier level." Art. 2 (9) provides that the items for which adjustments shall be made include "those normally borne by an importer but paid by any party, either

---

[129] Van Bael/Bellis, EC Anti-dumping Laws, p. 107
[130] See e.g. Video cassette recorders (Japan, Korea), OJ 1988 L240/5
[131] Regulation 384/96, Art. 2 (9)

inside or outside the Community, which appears to be associated or to have a compensatory arrangement with the importer or exporter".

As provided for in Art. 2(9), the allowances deducted from the price of first resale to the independent buyer include, in particular, the following:

> - usual transport, insurance, handling, loading and ancillary costs;
> - customs duties, any anti-dumping duties, and other taxes payable in the importing country by reason of the importation or sale of the goods;
> - and a reasonable margin for selling, general and administrative costs and profit.

In other words, the assumption on which this method is based is that the arm's-length price which an independent importer would be prepared to pay would be such that it would allow the importer to resell the product as a price which covers all its direct and indirect costs and yields a reasonable profit.[132]

In practice, the exporter operating through an affiliated distribution network in the EU may find himself at a disadvantage compared with the exporter who sells his product through unrelated importers and distributors.[133] The use of a constructed export price tends to lead to higher dumping margins than the use of actual export price.[134] The large scope of discretion which the EU Commission enjoys in investigations involving constructed export prices makes it extremely difficult for exporters to set the resale price of their products so as to avoid a potential dumping finding.

Example 3.[135] Calculation of constructed export price

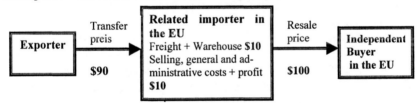

Conclusion: Export price=$ 80

3. Comparison between normal value and export price

Art. 2 (10) provides that "a fair comparison shall be made between the export price and the normal value." The basic principle is that "this comparison shall be made at the same level of trade and in respect of sales made at as nearly as pos-

---

[132] Van Bael/Bellis, EC Anti-dumping Laws, p. 108
[133] Anti-dumping Handbook for Russian Exporters, p. 20
[134] Van Bael/Bellis, EC Anti-dumping Laws, p. 112
[135] Müller, Der AD-rechtliche Rahmen

sible the same time and with due account taken of other differences which affect price comparability."

In case when the normal value and export price are not on comparable basis due allowances, in the form of adjustments shall be made in each case, on its merits, for differences in factors, which are claimed, and demonstrated, to affect prices and price comparability.

Art. 2 (10) allows those specific adjustments which are listed in paragraphs (a) to (i), i.e. physical characteristics; import charges and indirect taxes; discounts, rebates and quantities; level of trade; transport, insurance, handling, loading and ancillary costs; packing; credit; after-sales costs; commissions; currency conversions. Art. 2(10) lays down the principle that "any duplication when making adjustments shall be avoided in particular in relation to discounts, rebates, quantities and level of trade".

It should be noted that adjustments must be claimed by the interested party on whom rests the duty to "demonstrate" that they concern factors, which effect price comparability. It is important to bear in mind that Art. 2.4 of the WTO Anti-dumping Agreement requires the authorities to indicate to the parties in question what information is necessary to ensure a fair comparison and not to impose an unreasonable burden of proof on them.

4. Dumping margin

The fourth and last step in dumping determination involves the calculation of the dumping margin, i.e. "the amount by which the normal value exceeds the export price".[136]

As a rule, the institutions calculate the dumping margin in specific amounts, which are then generally translated into percentage terms on the basis of the CIF export price of the product under consideration. The formula used to calculate this percentage is the following:[137]

Formula: Determination of dumping margin

$$\frac{(\text{Normal value} - \text{Export price})}{\text{CIF export price (duty unpaid) EU frontier}} = \text{Dumping margin (\%)}$$

As provided in Art. 2 (12) of the Regulation 384/96, "where dumping margins vary, a weighted average dumping margin may be established".

In accordance with the Art. 9(3) of the Basic Regulation, only dumping margins higher than 2% can lead to anti-dumping measures.

---

[136] Regulation 384/96, Art. 2(12)
[137] Van Bael/Bellis, EC Anti-dumping Laws, p. 137

Finally, reference should be also be made to the EU practice of refusing to compute individual dumping margins for exporters in non-market economy countries.

The following Table gives a brief overview of rules concerning determination of dumping margins provided by Art. 2 (11) of the Basic Regulation.

Table 8. Calculation of dumping margin - Art. 2 (11)	
Method 1 (Basic rule)	Normal value* – Export price*
Method 2 (rarely used)	Normal value pro transaction – Export price pro transaction
Method 3 (exception)	Normal value* – individual Export price
* weighted average **only if there is a pattern of export prices which differs significantly among different purchasers, regions or time periods and Methods 1 and 2 are therefore not applicable	

The rules and methods of calculation of anti-dumping margin are obviously set up to determine normal value especially high and export price especially law. The EU Commission prefers to use weighted average and constructed values instead of actual values, which arise in course of trade. Therefore, the room of discretion of the EU Commission is very wide and the possibility to verify the results is almost impossible.

Example 4.[138] Calculation of dumping margin (for Market economy countries)

Representative and profitable sales of product in the domestic market of company A.
    1. Average price for unit= $100, $3 of which are transport costs. There are no more selling costs.
      Normal value = 100-3=$97
    2. Export price on the EU frontier = $95, $10 of which are transport costs.
      Constructed export price = 95-10=$85
    3. **Dumping = 97-85=$12**
    4. **Dumping margin** as a percentage on the basis of the CIF export price (duty unpaid) EU frontier = **12/95×100=12,6%**

---

[138]Anti-dumping Handbook for Russian Exporters, S.21

II. Injury

1. Notion of injury

Proving "injury" to domestic injury is a second material element of dumping and an essential prerequisite for adopting anti-dumping measures under the Basic Regulation. In accordance with Art. 1 (1) of the Regulation 384/96, "an anti-dumping duty may be applied to any dumped product whose release for free circulation in the Community causes injury." The rules governing injury determinations are laid down in Art. 3 of the Basic Regulation.

An injury determination involves three basic steps:

1. It must be determined whether the product under investigation and the product of domestic producers are "like products".
2. It must be determined whether domestic producers of the like product constitute a "Community industry" within the sense of Art. 4 of the Regulation 384/96.
3. It must be determined whether the Community industry is experiencing "injury" within the sense of Art. 3 of the Regulation. The concept of injury in the Regulation includes "material injury", "threat of material injury" and "material retardation of the establishment of industry".

It should be noted that finding of "no injury" in EU anti-dumping proceedings are uncommon, and usually occur in review proceedings.[139] It can be explained by the fact that the Commission has good information on injury at the complaint stage, and week claims may be rejected then.

2. Like product

Identifying the "like product" is a first step in any injury investigation in anti-dumping proceedings. The effect of the dumped imports must be analysed in relation to domestic producers of the like product[140].

Art. 1 (4) of Regulation 384/96 defines the like product as:

"a product which is identical, that is to say, alike in all respects, to the product under consideration, or in the absence of such a product, another product which although not alike in all respects, has characteristics closely resembling those of the product under consideration."

---

[139] McGovern, EC Anti-dumping law and practice, p.31:2

[140] Article 3 (8) of the Regulation 384/96 provides that "the effect of the dumped imports shall be assessed in relation to the production of the Community industry of the like product when available data permit the separate identification of that production on the basis of such criteria as the production process, producers' sales and profits. If such separate identification of that production is not possible, the effects of the dumped imports shall be assessed by examination of the production of the narrowest group or range of products, which includes the like product, for which the necessary information can be provided.

The definition, which is taken from Art. 2.6 of the WTO Anti-dumping Agreement, focuses on the physical characteristics of the product: the exported and domestic products must be identical or, at least, bear a close resemblance to the other. If two products are distinct, they will not be regarded as "like products" even if they are in competition with one another. For example, in Mechanical wrist-watches from the USSR[141], the complainant raised the argument that dumped imports of the product concerned could have an influence on the marketability of other wrist-watches, that is, analogue and digital quartz watches. The Commission rejected the argument on the grounds that since quartz watches use a completely different movement technology in comparison with mechanical watches, they could not be considered as "like product" to the mechanical watches imported from the USSR.

3. Community industry
a) Basic rule
This section considers the question of which firms should be examined in considering whether injury is being suffered – these comprise the Community industry. Art. 4 (1) states that a Community industry consists of Community producers as a whole of the like products or to those of them whose collective output of the products constitutes a major proportion of the total Community production of those products. The "major proportion" is defined in Art. 5 (4) and contains a double criterion: producers accounting for 50 percent of the production of those supporting or opposing the anti-dumping complaint criterion, provided these account for 25 percent or more of the production. This wording is identical to that of Art. 5.4 of the WTO Anti-dumping Agreement. This means, in practice, that domestic producers accounting for at least 25 percent of total EU production may be regarded as the "Community industry" unless domestic producers accounting for a larger share of EU production express opposition to the complaint.

In the EU anti-dumping practice there are numerous examples that prove the fact that the EU producers of some products apply for and get protection against imports from third countries. For example, as on 30th September 2003 there were anti-dumping measures in force against imports of urea from 12 different countries, including Russia, against steel ropes and cables- against 10 countries, including Russia.[142] Such practice of EU institutions encourages the successive and successful applications of anti-dumping measures in favour of the same Community industry against a number of third countries. It seems that the decisive point in such anti-dumping practice are not unfair prices of exporters, but protection of some sensible Community industries which by various reasons got

---

[141] See mechanical wrist-watches originating in the USSR, Council Regulation (EEC) No 2686/90 of 17.09.1990, OJ L 256, 20.09.1990 p. 0010

[142] Anti-Dumping Statistics covering the Year 2003, p. 37

into crisis. This practice supports the opinion in the legal doctrine, that anti-dumping measures developed into the substitute of protection of market from unwanted competitors for troubled Community industries.[143] The further circumstantial evidence for this point is long term of validity of anti-dumping measures that are constantly extended.[144] For example, the market of potassium chloride has been protected by anti-dumping measures against exporters from Russia and Belarus from October 1992 till present time.[145]

b) Exceptions
There are also two exceptions to the Basic rule.

aa) Exception 1: related parties and importers of dumped products
Firstly, producers who are related to the exporters or who are themselves importers of the allegedly dumped imports may be excluded from the Community industry.[146]
Producers will be considered to be related to exporters or importers only if:
(a) one of them directly or indirectly controls the other (i.e. is legally or operationally in a position to exercise restraint or direction over the latter); or
(b) both of them are directly or indirectly controlled by a third person; or
(c) together they directly or indirectly control a third person
provided that there are grounds for believing or suspecting that the effect of the relationship is such as to cause the producer concerned to behave differently from non-related producers.
Exclusion is discretionary[147] and, according to the Commission, the exclusion of Community producers that are related to the exporters in the exporting countries concerned must be decided on case-by-case basis, on reasonable and equitable grounds, and by taking into consideration all the legal and economic aspects involved.[148]
The cases where EU producers import the dumped product, or dumped components, in order, for example, to fulfil their delivery contracts[149], are not rare in practice. Court of Justice gave the Commission the discretion to decide whether

---

[143] Wessely, Antidumping- und kartellrecht in der EG, p. 71

[144] E.g. in 2002 13 expiry review investigations were initiated. In 12 cases, the investigations were concluded with confirmation of the duty. See in: 21st Anti-dumping report, 2002, p. 9

[145] Weekly updated anti-dumping and anti-subsidy measures list of the EU, http://europa.eu.int/comm/trade/issues/respectrules/anti_dumping/stats.htm, called 04.02.04

[146] Art. 4(1)(a)

[147] E.g., Judgment of the Court of 14 March 1990, Case C-156/87, (Gestetner v Council and Commission), ECR 1990, I-781 (para 43); Judgment of the Court (Fifth Chamber) of 10 March 1992, Case C-179/87, (Sharp v Council), ECR 1992, I-1635

[148] Van Bael/Bellis, EC Anti-dumping Laws, p. 140

[149] See e.g. Drams originating in the Republic of Korea, Council Regulation (EEC) Nr. 2686/92, OJ L 272 , 17.09.1992 p. 0013

such importers are to be excluded from the Community industry.[150] According to the Court of Justice's case law, the following factors were found to be decisive in justifying the inclusion of Community producers in the scope of the Community industry:

> The total of imports made by the Community producer in question was always relatively low and only a few models, all of them at the lower end of the range, were imported to fill gaps existing in their range of products;[151]

> The imports of dumped products were temporary. For example, in one instance, the Court of Justice regarded the fact that the Community producer had committed itself to replace imported components with ones manufactured in the Community, as relevant to its inclusion in the Community industry.[152]

According to the opinion of Advocate General Van Gerven in Noelle v. Hauptzollamt Bremen-Freihafen[153], it is not sufficient for the Community institutions to state that the above-mentioned criteria are fulfilled. Positive evidence that the importation of dumped products by Community producers was justified, as a defensive measure must be provided.

If the firm goes beyond the mere protection of its market position and is making a business of importing the dumped articles it is likely to be excluded from considerations.

The Commission has summarized its practice as follows: importing Community producers will be excluded "only when they are either shielded from the effect of the dumped imports, draw undue benefits from them or import such quantities in relation to their own production that they can not be considered any longer as being committed to production in the Community". [154]

---

[150] See e.g. Judgment of the Court of First Instance of 28 September 1995, Case T-164/94 (Ferchimex v Council), ECR 1995, II-02681. Recital 98 provides that "as is apparent from the wording of Article 4(5) of the basic regulation, and in particular the use of the word "may", the Community institutions have a wide discretion when deciding whether or not to exclude from the "Community industry" producers who are themselves importers of the dumped product."

[151] Judgment of the Court of 5 October 1988, Joined cases 260/85 and 106/86, (Tokyo Electric Company Ltd (TEC) v Council), ECR 1988, 05855

[152] Judgment of the Court of 14 March 1990, Case C-156/87, (Gestetner v Council and Commission), ECR 1990, I-00781(para. 59)

[153] Judgment of the Court of 22 October 1991, Case C-16/90, ("Eugen Nölle" v Hauptzollamt Bremen-Freihafen), ECR 1991, I-05163

[154] Large electrolytic aluminium capacitors originating in Japan, Council Regulation (EEC) No 3482/92 of 30.11.1992, OJ L 353 , 03.12.1992 p. 0001 - 0006

bb) Exception 2: regional industry

Injury determinations should in principle be made on a EU-wide basis. Article 4(1)(b) of Regulation 384/96 however provides that "in exceptional circumstances the territory of the Community may, for the production in question, be divided into two or more competitive markets and the producers within each market may be regarded as a separate industry if:

(a) the producers within such a market sell all or almost all of their production of the product in question in that market; and

(b) the demand in that market is not to any substantial degree supplied by producers of the product in question located elsewhere in the Community.

Article 4(1)(b) further provides that, in such circumstances, injury may be found to exist even where a major portion of the total Community industry is not injured, provided

(a) there is a concentration of dumped imports into such an isolated market and

(b) the dumped imports are causing injury to the producers of all or almost all of the production within such a market.

There have been very few occasions on which the EU has accepted that those conditions have been met.[155] However, the fact that there are only few cases in which the Commission established the existence of a separate market does not mean that injury determinations in other cases are always made on real Community-wide basis. On the contrary, there have been a number of cases where the focus of the investigation has been on producers in one member state without the need to apply Art. 4 (1)(b). In those cases, the producers in the member state concerned accounted for a "major proportion" of the Community industry in accordance with the Art. 5 (4).

4. Material injury

A crucial step in any injury investigation I the assessment of whether the domestic industry is experiencing "material injury".

Art. 3 (1) of the Basic Regulation provides three tests for determining "material injury":

1. actual material injury;
2. threat of material injury; or
3. material retardation of the establishment of a Community industry.

a) Actual material injury

Art. 3 of the Basic Regulation does not contain any definition of "material injury". Instead, it lists a number of criteria that should be considered in order to

---

[155] E.g. Ammonium nitrate origination in Russia and Lithuania (94/293/EC: Commission Decision of 13.04.94, OJ L 129 , 21.05.1994 p. 0024 – 0037. Recital 7 provided that "Community industry allegedly being injured refers to that represented by UK producers."

determine whether the material injury is present. A determination of injury must be based on positive evidence and involve an objective examination of:

1. the volume of the dumped imports;
2. the effect of the dumped imports on prices in the Community market for like products; and
3. the consequent impact of the dumped imports on the Community industry.[156]

Art. 3(3) and 3(5) expressly provide that no one or several of the factors that must be considered to assess injury can necessarily give decisive guidance. The Court of Justice reaffirmed the wording of these paragraphs in several cases, conducted under previous versions of the Basic Regulation, stating that the law does not require a "comprehensive analysis of the market as a whole", and that the list is merely indicative so that the Community is free to take the view that the most relevant factors contained therein are in themselves a sufficient basis for forming a judgment".[157]

Thus there is no mathematical formula for determining the existence of injury. The decision whether the standard of material injury has been satisfied is essentially a matter of judgment about which few general principles can be stated.[158] It involves the assessment of complex economic matters of which the Community institutions enjoy a wide discretion; the fact that some criteria do not show injury will not discredit affirmative finding.[159]

b) Threat of material injury

The term "injury" is defined in Art. 3 (1) of Regulation 384/96 to include "threat of material injury.

Art. 3 (9) provides that:

"A determination of a threat of material injury shall be based on facts and not merely on allegation, conjecture or remote possibility. The change in circum-

---

[156] Regulation 384/96, Art. 3(2)

[157] Judgment of the Court of 5 October 1988 (Canon v Council), Joined cases 277/85 and 300/85, ECR, 1988, 05731, rec. 44 and 56; See also Judgment of the Court of 11 July 1990 (Enital v Commission and Council), Joined cases C-304/86 and C-185/87, ECR 1990 I-02939, para. 4 provides that "the examination of injury must involve a whole series of factors no one or several of which can give decisive guidance." The Court upheld the Council's decision to assess injury on the basis of several factors instead of only on the basis of the decreasing market share held by imports.

[158] McGovern, EC Anti-dumping law and practice, p.31:2

[159] See Judgement of the Court of First Instance of 30 March 2000, Case T-51/96, (Miwon v. Council of the European Union), ECR II-1841, para. 94, See also e.g. Judgment of the Court of First Instance of 29 January 1998 (Sinochem v Council), Case T-97/95, ECR 1998, II-85, para. 108; Judgment of the Court of 10 March 1992, Case C-176/87(Konishiroku v Council), ECR 1992, I-1493, para. 31

stances, which would create a situation in which the dumping would cause injury, must be clearly foreseen and imminent.

Further Art. 3 (9) provides an indicative list of factors that should be taken into consideration in making a determination regarding the existence of a threat of material injury.[160]

According to the EU Commission practice, the decisive factor in the finding of the threat of injury has been the production and export capacities in exporting country, which may possibly lead to the significant increase of export.[161] Findings of threat on injury are rare, in practice no case has been based on finding of threat of injury alone.[162] In the cases where a threat of injury was found to exist, it was in combination with an actual injury finding.[163] However, an analogues finding is made during the course of "expiry" reviews (whether expiry of duty would be followed by renewed dumping and injury).

Table 9. Determination of injury (Art. 3)[164]	
The volume of the dumped imports Art. 3 (3)	**Significant increase in dumped imports** ➤ in absolute terms or relative to production in the EU or relative to consumption in the EU
The effect of the dumped imports in the Community market for like products Art. 3 (3)	**Price comparison between dumped imports and like product in the EU** ➤ significant price undercutting or ➤ significant depression of prices or ➤ significant prevention of price increases, which would otherwise have occurred

---

[160] These factors are: (a) a significant rate of increase of dumped imports into the Community market indicating the likelihood of substantially increased imports; (b) sufficient freely disposable capacity of the exporter or an imminent and substantial increase in such capacity indicating the likelihood of substantially increased dumped exports to the Community, account being taken of the availability of other export markets to absorb any additional exports;

(c) whether imports are entering at prices that would, to a significant degree, depress prices or prevent price increases which otherwise would have occurred, and would probably increase demand for further imports; and (d) inventories of the product being investigated.

No one of the factors listed above by itself can necessarily give decisive guidance but the totality of the factors considered must lead to the conclusion that further dumped exports are imminent and that, unless protective action is taken, material injury will occur.

[161] Reszel, Feststellung der Schädigung, S. 178 Fn.297

[162] McGovern, EC Anti-dumping law and practice, p.31:3

[163] Wenig, in: Dauses, a.a.O, KII, Rn.82

[164] The list is not exhaustive, no one or more of these factors can necessarily give decisive guidance, Regulation 384/96, Art. 3 (3) and 3(5)

The impact of the dumped imports on the Community industry Art. 3 (5)	Evaluation of all relevant economic factors and indices having a bearing on the state of the industry, including: ➤ the fact that an industry is still in the process of recovering from the effects of past dumping or subsidization, the magnitude of the actual margin of dumping, ➤ actual and potential decline in sales, profits, output, market share, productivity, return on investments, utilization of capacity; ➤ factors affecting Community prices; actual and potential negative effects on cash flow, inventories, employment, wages, growth, ability to raise capital or investments.

c) Material retardation of the establishment of a Community industry

Apart from the actual material injury and threat of injury, the material retardation of the establishment of a Community industry can be basis for a determination of injury.[165] It is unclear which considerations would be relevant to a finding of material retardation, as the Basic Regulation does not contain any specific provisions on this issue. Thus, this determination is left to the discretion of the EU Commission.[166] There seems to be only one investigation, which resulted in a finding of a material retardation.[167]

III. Casual link between dumping and injury

1. The causality tests

The injury of the Community industry is relevant only in case they were caused by dumped imports. In other words, there must be a causal link between dumping and injury. The Art. 3(6) of the Regulation 384/96 provides that "it must be demonstrated, from all the relevant evidence that the dumped imports are causing injury within the meaning of this Regulation." Specifically, this shall entail a demonstration that the volume and/or price levels are responsible for an impact on the Community industry, and that this impact exists to a degree which enables it to be classified as material."

The Basic Regulation does not require dumping imports to be sole or even principal cause of injury. In practice, it is enough that dumping attribute the small

---

[165] Regulation 384/96, Art. 3(1)

[166] Egeln/Klann, Antidumpingpolitik der EG, S. 26

[167] Electronic microcircuits known as DRAMs originating in Japan, Commission Regulation (EEC) No 165/90 of 23 January 1990, OJ L20, 1990, p.5

share to the injury.[168] The Court of Justice held that as the law does not require dumping to be principal cause of injury, it is therefore possible to attribute to an importer responsibility for injury caused by dumping even if the losses due to the dumping are merely part of more extensive injury attributable to other factors.[169]

It should be separately noted that the wording of the causality test laid down in Art. 3 (6) of Regulation 384/96 is not identical to that of Art. 3.5. of the WTO Anti-dumping Agreement.[170] In contrast to the WTO Anti-dumping Agreement, Art. 3(6) of the Basic Regulation does not specifically require injury to be caused "through the effects of dumping". According to the legal doctrine, it may be seen as an attempt to water down still further the concept of causality.[171]

For example, in the Silicon originating from Russia[172] exporting producers argued that even if the finding of material injury is confirmed, this injury was not caused by the Russian imports of silicon. A number of other factors were alleged to be the true cause of the injury, suffered by the Community industry. Other third countries with a much larger share of imports compared with Russia[173], Community industry's self-inflicted injury, the export performance of the Community industry, imports of silicon by the community industry itself, and the differences in the markets for chemical and metallurgical silicon were all cited as explanations for any injury suffered by the Community industry. One Russian producer also alleged that there was a 16 % difference between prices of the Community industry and Russian prices during the period of investigation, and that such a large difference showed that there is no price competition between the silicon from the two sources on the Community market. However the EU Commission confirmed, that "these other factors do not break the causal link between the dumped imports and the injury suffered by the Community industry."

---

[168] Reuter, Außenwirtschafts- und Exportkontrollrechts Deutschland/ Europäische Union, Rn.374

[169] Judgment of the Court of 5 October 1988 (Canon v Council), Joined cases 277/85 and 300/85, ECR, 1988, 05731, para. 62; E.g. E.g. Ammonium nitrate origination in Russia and Lithuania (94/293/EC: Commission Decision of 13.04.94, OJ L 129 , 21.05.1994 p. 0024 – 0037.

[170] Art. 3.5. of the WTO Anti-dumping Agreement provides that: "It must be demonstrated that the dumped imports are, through the effects of dumping, as set forth in paragraphs 2 and 4 of this Article, causing injury within the meaning of this Agreement. The demonstration of a causal relationship between the dumped imports and the injury to domestic industry shall be based on an examination of all relevant evidence before the authorities".

[171] Van Bael/Bellis, EC Anti-dumping Laws, p. 187

[172] Silicon originating in Russia, provisional duties- Commission Regulation (EC) No 1235/2003 of 10 July 2003, OJ L 173 , 11/07/2003 P. 0014 – 0034, recs. 74-102 ; definitive duties-Council Regulation (EC) No 2229/2003 of 22 December, OJ L 339 , 24.12.2003 P. 0003 – 0013, recs. 49-68

[173] Over the period under consideration imports from Norway and Brazil were several times the level of Russian imports, South Africa and China also contributed to the injury suffered

Even though Regulation 384/96 does not require dumping to be principle cause of injury, Art. 3 (7) provides that known factors other than the dumped imports, which at the same time are injuring the Community industry must also be examined to ensure that injury caused by these other factors are not attributed to dumped imports. Art. 3 (7), implementing Art. 3.5 of the WTO Anti-dumping Agreement, provides that other injury factors which may be considered in this respect include, inter alia, the volume and prices of imports not sold at dumping prices, contraction in demand or changes in the patterns of consumption, restrictive trade practices of, and competition between, third country and Community producers, developments in technology and the export performance and productivity of the Community industry.

The question of the contribution of other imports involves the assessment of complex economic matters regarding which the Community institutions have a wide discretion.[174] The fact that an industry's difficulties are in part attributable to causes other than dumping is not a reason for depriving it of protection against injury caused by dumping imports.[175]

Since Art. 3 (7) states that the factors must be "known", the Community is under no obligation to initiate a search for them. They are usually proposed by the exporter or an importer.[176] In one case the Court of Justice annulled an anti-dumping measure because the Community had failed to consider the "other factors" put forward by one of the importers.

Generally, examples of injury being attributed to other causes to the exclusion of the dumped imports are rare. In some instances the EU has reduced the injury margin when it has concluded that dumping was not the exclusive cause of injury[177].

Table 10. Causal link between dumping and injury Art. 3 (6) and 3 (7)
Regulation384/96 does not demand dumping to be the sole or principle cause of injury

Causality test I Art. 3 (6)	Demonstration that: a) the volume of the dumped imports and/or price levels are responsible for an impact on the Community industry; and b) this impact exists to a degree which enables it to be classified as material (i.e. effect of price development + sales of the Community industry on the general economical situation of the Community industry)

---

[174] Judgment of the Court of First Instance of 28 September 1995, Case T-164/94 (Ferchimex v Council), ECR 1995, II-02681, para. 131

[175] Judgment of the Court of 5 October 1988, Case 250/85, (Brother v Council), ECR, 1988 Page 05683, para. 42; Judgment of the Court of First Instance of 29 January 1998 (Sinochem v Council), Case T-97/95, ECR 1998, II-85, para. 100

[176] McGovern, EC Anti-dumping law and practice, p.32:4

[177] McGovern, EC Anti-dumping law and practice, p.32:5

Causality test II Art. 3 (7)	Only when Causality test I is positive Causality test II has Double-check character Purpose: to make sure that that injury caused by factors other than the dumped imports, which at the same time are injuring the Community, industry is not attributed to the dumped imports. Possible other factors (not exhaustive): ➤ the volume and prices of imports not sold at dumping prices, ➤ contraction in demand or changes in the patterns of consumption, ➤ restrictive trade practices of, and competition between, third country and Community producers, ➤ developments in technology ➤ the export performance and productivity of the Community industry.

2. Cumulation

The issue of cumulation of imports arises in two contexts:

1. Where there are several exporters in the exporting country under investigation; and
2. Where there are several exporting countries.

In these two contexts, the question may arise as to whether the dumped imports must be cumulated or considered on individual basis. The Community's normal practice is to cumulate, one rationale being that to treat any exporter in isolation would be to discriminate against the rest.[178] However it can have a consequence that anti-dumping measures would be applied against all exporters involved, whereas their imports on individual basis would not cause any significant injury.[179]

a) Cumulation of imports from several exporters in a particular exporting country

In 1987 the Court of Justice approved in general terms the practice of cumulation of several exporters in a particular exporting country. It ruled that the injury to the Community industry should be assessed on a global basis, without it being necessary nor possible to individualize the part of the injury caused by each of the exporters involved.[180]

---

[178] In iron or steel coils originating in Argentina, Brazil, Canada and Venezuela (Commission Decision No 2182/83/ECSC of 27 July 1983, OJ L 210 , 02/08/1983 p. 0005 - 0006), rec. D provides that: "should the Commission treat any one country in isolation it would be acting in a discriminatory manner against the rest."

[179] Friedrichs, EGV/Antidumpingrecht, S.29

[180] Judgment of the Court of 7 May 1987, Case 255/84, (Nachi Fujikoshi Corp. v Council), ECR 1987, 01861, rec. 46. See also Judgment of the Court of 5 October 1988, Joined cases 294/86 and 77/87, (Technointorg v Commission and Council), ECR 1988, Page 06077, rec.

Since then it is the standard practice of the EU to cumulate the factors of injury caused by several exporters from one exporting country.[181]

b) Cumulation of imports from several exporting countries

Cumulation of the effects of imports from more than one country is now dealt with explicitly by the Art. 3 (4) of Basic Regulation, which is in line with the WTO Anti-dumping Agreement.

Art. 3 (4) provides for two conditions of cumulation. According to the first condition of Art. 3 (4), the effects of imports from more than one country should be cumulatively assessed provided that (1) the dumping margin established in respect of each exporting country is two per cent or more and (2) imports from each exporting country represent a market share of one per cent or more, unless imports from such exporting countries accounting for less than one per cent of the market collectively account for three per cent or more of Community consumption.[182] The second condition is that a cumulative assessment of the effects of the imports is appropriate in light of the conditions of competition between imported products and the conditions of competition between the imported products and the like Community product.

In case Unwrought magnesium originating in Russia and Ukraine[183] the Commission mentioned the following factors to be examined:

absolute and relative level of imports from the exporting countries concerned during the investigation period; comparability of the products imported in terms of physical characteristics and interchangeability of end use; and similarity of market behaviour.

A review of the EU anti-dumping practice shows that the cumulation of dumped imports from different exporting countries has been the rule. Cases where dumped imports from a particular exporting country have been examined in isolation have been rare.[184]

The consequence of cumulating exports is that all volume and price effects will be considered together rather than on a country-by-country basis, which is not always in favour of each individual exporter. In this case the outcome of investigation will depend on the fact which other exporters were involved.

---

40 and 41; Judgment of the Court of First Instance 20 October 1999, Case T-171/97 (Swedish Match Philippines Inc. v. Council), ECR 1999, II-3241, rec.. 64

[181] E.g. in Silicon originating in Russia anti-dumping measures were imposed against 3 different exporting producers, Council Regulation (EC) No 2229/2003 of 22 December, OJ L 339 , 24.12.2003 P. 0003 – 0013

[182] Regulation 384/96, Art. 5(7)

[183] Commission Regulation (EC) No 2997/95 of 20 December, OJ L 312 , 23.12.1995 p. 0037 – 0049, rec. 43

[184] McGovern, EC Anti-dumping law and practice, p.32:6

IV. Community interest

The WTO Anti-dumping Agreement has no specific requirement that the investigating authorities should consider the public interest before imposing anti-dumping measures. However, some Members including EU have chosen to include public interest provisions in their anti-dumping legal framework.

Once the dumping has been determined, it has to be established that the application of measures would not be contrary to the overall interest of the Community. The "Community interest" is a pure political criterion, which also takes into consideration all possible political consequences of anti-dumping measures in question.185 Art. 21(1) of the Basic Regulation provides that "a determination as to whether the Community interest calls for intervention shall be based on an appreciation of all the various interests taken as a whole, including the interests of the domestic industry and users and consumers." It further provides that "measures, as determined on the basis of the dumping and injury found, may not be applied where the authorities, on the basis of all the information submitted, can clearly conclude that it is not in the Community interest to apply such measures."

This public interest is determined only on the stage of imposition of anti-dumping measures. It is impossible to check the Community interest on the earlier stages of initiation of an investigation and anti-dumping investigation itself, because other factors necessary for determination of the Community interest are determined at these stages.[186]

The anti-dumping practice of the EU institutions showed that the Community interest requirement has only played a minor role thus far.[187]

Legal doctrine stated that "in many cases, once dumping and injury are found and measures are likely to give relief to the complainant industry, there is a presumption that such measures would be in the Community interests".[188] In the great majority of cases the Community interest criterion has impact neither on application of anti-dumping measures nor on the level of duty. It is clear from the wording of Art. 7(1) and 9(4) of the Basic Regulation that "Community interest" comes into play only to determine whether "intervention is called for but that, once a decision to intervene has been made, the level of the duty must be fixed exclusively on the basis of dumping and injury findings.

C. Anti-dumping procedure

The procedure became the very important part of the EU anti-dumping law. Almost in all cases, in which the Court annulled the Council Regulation imposing

---

[185] Egeln/Klann, Antidumpingpolitik der EG, p.27
[186] Wenig, in: Dauses, rec.127
[187] Wenig, in: Dauses, rec.128
[188] Van Bael/Bellis, EC Anti-dumping Laws, p. 209

anti-dumping duties, the procedural aspects played the decisive part.[189] The Court has generally shown itself rather unwilling to intervene in the detailed investigation conducted by the Commission, unless there has been an infringement of an essential procedural requirement.[190] One of the major factors is that through application of procedural requirements Court tries to compensate the fact, that the vague notions of material law, such as e.g. "injury" or "Community interest" are very often beyond the scope of its judicial review and it is in general very difficult to deal with them.[191]

The anti-dumping procedure is divided into initiation of investigation, investigation itself, imposition of measures or termination with no measures and review investigations.

I. Initiation of investigation

1. Lodging of a complain

In accordance with the Art. 5(1) an anti-dumping investigation "shall be initiated upon a written complaint by any natural or legal person, or any association not having legal personality, acting on behalf of the Community industry."[192]

Typically, complaints are brought by associations, which can be either the existing trade associations grouping the European manufacturers of the product sector concerned or ad hoc associations especially formed for the purposes of lodging of a complaint.[193]

Regulation 384/96 imposes on the Commission the obligation to take active steps to examine the degree of support for the complaint among the Community producers of the like product.[194] A complaint will be considered to have been made by or on the behalf of the Community industry if:

---

[189] Rolf, Die Rechtsstellung Betroffener bei der Anwendung außenhandelspolitischer Schutzinstrumente in den USA und der Gemeinschaft, p.23

[190] Van Bael/Bellis, EC Anti-dumping Laws, p. 327

[191] Friedrichs, EGV/Antidumpingrecht, p.32

[192]The Commission issued a "Guide on How to Draft an Anti-dumping Complaint", which provides detailed explanations and insights into the contents of anti-dumping complaints, available at
http://europa.eu.int/comm/trade/issues/respectrules/anti_dumping/complaint/index_en.htm.

[193] E.g. in Silicon originating in Russia the anti-dumping proceeding was initiated following a complaint lodged by Euroalliages (Liaison Committee of the Ferro-Alloy Industry) on behalf of producers representing 100 % of the Community production of silicon (OJ L 173 , 11/07/2003 P. 0014 – 0034); in Potassium Chloride originating in Russia- by a complaint from the European Potash Producers' Association (EPPA), acting on behalf of producers accounting for the Community's entire potash output (OJ L 110 , 28/04/1992 p. 0005); in Urea originating, inter alia, in Russia- by a complaint lodged by the European Fertiliser Manufacturers Association (EFMA) on behalf of a major proportion of Community producers (OJ L 075 , 24/03/2000 p. 0003 - 0017.

[194] Regulation 384/96, Art. 5(4)

1. it is supported by those Community producers whose collective output constitutes more than 50 % of the total production of the like product produced by
   that portion of the Community industry expressing either support for or opposition to the complaint; and
2. the Community producers found to be expressly supporting the complaint represent at least 25 % of total production of the like product produced by the
   Community industry.

The complain must be in writing and include evidence of dumping, injury and a
causal link between the allegedly dumped imports and the alleged injury.[195]
Where it appears, after consultation, that insufficient evidence has been presented, the complainant will be informed accordingly.[196] Such information is not
made public but a letter received by the complainant to that effect may be the
subject of an appeal to the Court of First Instance (Art. 230 (4) EC).

2. Initiation of proceeding

Where, after consultation, it is apparent that there is sufficient evidence to justify
initiating a proceeding, the Commission shall do so within 45 days of the lodging of the complaint and shall publish a notice in the Official Journal of the
European Communities.[197] In addition to publishing the notice of initiation, the
Commission must also directly inform the exporters, importers and representative associations of importers or exporters known to it to be concerned, as well
as representatives of the exporting country and the complainants, of the initiation of the proceedings and provide the full text of the written complaint. [198] Art.
3 (11) of the Basic Regulation also provides, that the Commission may choose
to provide the full text of the complaint only to the authorities of the exporting
country or to the relevant trade association where the number of exporters involved is particularly high.

Table 11. EU anti-dumping proceedings initiated against Russia after collapse of the Soviet Union (1992-2003)			
Year	Proceedings against Russia	Total initiations by the EU	Share in EU total annual proceedings
1992	3	39	7,7%
1993	1	21	4,8%
1994	3	43	7%
1995	1	33	3%
1996	1	25	4%

---

[195] Regulation 384/96, Art. 5(2) (a)-(d) contains a detailed list of the data to be provided.
[196] Regulation 384/96, Art. 5(9)
[197] Regulation 384/96, Art. 5(9)
[198] Regulation 384/96, Art. 5 (11)

1997	2	45	4,4%
1998	-	29	-
1999	1	86	0,9%
2000	2	31	6,5%
2001	2	33	6%
2002	3	23	13%
2003	-	6	-
Total	**19**	**414**	**5%**

Source: European Commission, the Community's Anti-dumping and anti-subsidy and safeguard activities, annual reports from the Commission to the European Parliament

II. Investigation
1. Anti-dumping questionnaire
The anti-dumping proceeding begins when the Commission sends the anti-dumping questionnaires to the parties that are given at least 30 days to reply.[199] For exporters, the time limit is counted from the date the questionnaire is received. Receipt is deemed to occur one week from the day it was sent to the exporter or transmitted to the appropriate diplomatic representative of the exporting country. Although the Regulation 384/96 provides for a period of at least 30 days, longer periods are very seldom granted.[200]

2. Advantages of cooperation
The cooperation of exporters in the anti-dumping investigation is on voluntarily basis, i.e. they neither have any legal obligation to answer the anti-dumping questionnaire, nor are obliged to tolerate the verification visits of the Commission staff.[201] The Commission has no power to compel the disclosure of certain information, but in the absence of voluntarily submission, the Commission may make its preliminary or final findings "on the basis of facts available".[202] For this reason, most parties find it to be in their interest to co-operate actively since otherwise the Commission is likely to base its findings on the least favourable information available. In the majority of cases "the facts available" has meant the allegations set out in the complaint or official import statistics. According to the Commission, such an approach is justified since the use of a more favourable method would constitute "a bonus for non-cooperation and would create an opportunity for circumvention of duty".[203] For the exporter this approach means

---

[199] Regulation 384/96, Art. 6 (2)
[200] Anti-dumping Handbook for Russian Exporters, p. 134
[201] Wenig, in: Dauses, KII Rec.169
[202] Regulation 384/96, Art. 18(1)
[203] Van Bael/Bellis, EC Anti-dumping Laws, p. 263

the much higher anti-dumping duty than in the case of cooperation.[204] Art. 18 (6) of the Basic Regulation clearly provides that "if an interested party does not co-operate, or cooperates only partially, so that relevant information is thereby withheld, the result may be less favourable to that party than if it had cooper-ated."

A particular problem exists where none of the exporters of the country con-cerned cooperate. In such case, the Commission will then normally base its find-ings on the allegations set out in the complaint.[205] Findings may also be based on the facts available where a party only partially replies to the Commission's re-quest for information.[206]

Therefore the unwillingness to cooperate is the major mistake the exporters can make during an anti-dumping investigation. Art. 18 (1) sets out some examples of non-cooperation: party refuses access to, or otherwise does not provide, nec-essary information within the time limits provided in this Regulation; signifi-cantly impedes the investigation; supplies false or misleading information.

Furthermore, as a rule the non-cooperation has a consequence that undertakings, provided in Art. 8 of Regulation 384/96, which are sometimes the sole opportu-nity for export of product in question to the EU, are not accepted by the Com-mission. Thus, e.g. in Ammonium nitrate originating in Russia, an undertaking from a Russian producer was not accepted "due to the total lack of cooperation from all Russian producers/exporters."[207]

It is also of a highest importance for exporters to keep the deadlines. Thus, e.g., in expiry review Ammonium nitrate originating in Russia, where two of export-ers failed to submit their reply to the Commission's questionnaire within a rea-sonable period of time, they were therefore considered as non-cooperating with the investigation and the market economy status applications[208] were not proc-essed.[209] In seamless pipes and tubes of iron or non-alloy steel originating in, in-ter alia, in Russia, where Russian exporters failed to submit reply to question-naires within time limits, the Commission clearly states that "it would be dis-criminatory to other interested parties cooperating with the investigation if in-formation were taken into account which was submitted days, weeks and some-times months after the deadline for submitting it has passed."[210]

---

[204] Wenig, in: Dauses, KII Rec.174

[205] Van Bael/Bellis, EC Anti-dumping Laws, p. 263

[206] Anti-dumping Handbook for Russian Exporters, p. 33

[207] Council Regulation (EC) No 663/98 of 23 March 1998, OJ L 093 , 26/03/1998 p. 0001 – 0007, rec. 35

[208] Before the Amendments to the Basic Regulation of 08.11.2002 the market economy status was granted to Russian companies on case-by-case basis, detailed see in Part three

[209] Council Regulation (EC) No 658/2002 of 15 April (OJ L 102 , 18/04/2002 P. 0001 – 0011), rec. 20

[210] Council Regulation (EC) No 2320/97 of 17 November 1997, Official Journal L 322 , 25/11/1997 P. 0001 – 0024, rec. 29

Therefore, in order to be considered as cooperative exporters must provide information, which is accurate, complete, in the form and within deadlines requested. The latter forces exporters, many of which never dealt with EU anti-dumping law before, work under enormous time pressure and seek help of expensive advisers. It is no wonder that given the considerable amount of time and manpower to be spent in preparing questionnaire responses, many Russian exporters preferred not to cooperate, because they were unaware of consequences. The Russian Ministry of Trade and Economic Development has done a great amount of work to clarify Russian exporters consequences of non-cooperation with EU anti-dumping investigation and in the last years the level of cooperation has grown drastically.[211]

3. Verification visits

The Commission has the right, where it considers it appropriate, carry out visits to examine the records of parties concerned (including in third countries) and to verify information provided on dumping and injury, provided that the companies concerned and the government in question have been officially notified and raise no objection. [212] In the event that an interested party or a third country was to refuse to submit to the investigation, the Commission might make its preliminary or final findings "on the basis of the facts available". Hence, it is usually to the advantage of the interested parties to cooperate. This principle is valid for exporters as well for complainants.

The purpose of a verification visit is to ensure that questionnaire responses are complete and accurate. The investigators will verify whether the figures contained in the questionnaire response correspond to figures in the company's accounting record. The basic principle which a company must keep in mind is that it should be able to explain to the Commission the process by which each figure has been derived from the accounting records.[213]

As a rule Russian cooperating companies affected by EU anti-dumping investigation appoint several people from managing staff responsible for EU anti-dumping questionnaire and verification visits. This responsible team consists as a rule of head accountant, sales manager and production manager. Therefore the company favours the efficiency of the verification visit and tries to prevent possible negative impact of such visit on the daily activity of the company. It also

---

[211] E.g. in the latest case Silicon metal originating in Russia the cooperating Russian exporting producers represented 100 % of the Russian production of silicon (OL 173 , 11/07/2003 P. 0014 – 0034, rec. 18), in grain oriented electrical sheets originating in Russia "the level of cooperation in the present proceeding was high. Both known Russian exporting producers cooperated and replied to the Commission questionnaire." (OJ L 025 , 30/01/2003 P. 0007 – 0020)

[212] Regulation 384/96, Art. 16 (1)-(2)

[213] Van Bael/Bellis, EC Anti-dumping Laws, p. 268

helps the EU officials to receive timely all information needed and minimize the risk that EU will carry out investigation based on other information. Thus the right actions of companies help them to receive the better outcome of the anti-dumping investigation. It is interesting to note that even in the Soviet era, when Soviet export organizations did not officially recognize the EU, they nevertheless found it in their interests to co-operate.[214]

4. Sampling

Some anti-dumping investigations involve such a large number of complainants, producers/exporters or product types, that it is hardly possible to complete the investigation within a reasonable time frame. As a solution to this problem, the Art. 17 (1) of the Basic Regulation provides that "in cases where the number of complainants, exporters or importers, types of product or transactions is large, the investigation may be limited to a reasonable number of parties, products or transactions by using samples". This sample techniques means the selection of a number of representative companies which are thoroughly investigated and whose results in turn form the basis of the determinations for those companies not forming part of the sample.

The selection of the companies to be included in the sample rests with the Commission, although preferably after consultations with the concerned parties. Where possible, the parties should agree with the sample selected. Concerned parties wishing to participate in the selection process must make themselves known and provide sufficient information within three weeks of initiation.[215] This strict time limit, which puts exporters under extreme time pressure, is not found in the WTO Anti-dumping agreement.

For exporters included in the sample, in individual company-specific dumping margin will be calculated. Other cooperating exporters, not included in the sample, will receive the weighted average dumping margin established for the companies included in the sample.

As an exception to the above general rule, the Regulation 384/96 provides that individual dumping margins will nevertheless be calculated for companies which were not included in the sample, on condition that: the company has submitted the necessary information within the time limits provided; or the number of exporters or producers is not so large that individual examinations would be unduly burdensome and prevent completion of the investigation within the time-limit.[216]

---

[214] See e.g. Photographic enlargers originating, inter alia, in the USSR (Commission Regulation (EEC) No 53/83 of 7 January 1983, OJ L 009 , 12.01.83 P. 0005), Upright pianos (84/638/EEC: Commission Decision of 17 December 1984 ,OJ L 332 , 20/12/1984 p. 0079)
[215] Regulation 384/96, Art. 17(2)
[216] Regulation 384/96, Art. 17(3)

The Regulation 384/96 provides for cases of non-cooperation on the part of the exporters or producers forming part of a sample. If such non-cooperation "is likely to materially affect" the result of the investigation, the Commission can either select a new sample or, if there is not enough time for such selection or the non-cooperation persists to a material degree, proceed on the basis of the fact available,[217] which is the worst for exporters.

The advantage of the sampling for an exporter is that if it is not selected as sample, it will be relieved of the burden of the replying to the questionnaire. The disadvantage that the outcome of an investigation depends on the parties selected as a sample, their data and willingness to cooperate with the Commission.

5. Rights of interested parties

Art. 6 (7) of the Regulation 484/96 considers as interested parties " complainants, importers and exporters, their representative associations, users and consumer organizations."

All interested parties have following rights in the anti-dumping investigation:

a) Access to the file and confidentiality

Interested parties, as well as the representatives of the exporting country concerned, may, upon written request, inspect all information made available to the Commission by any party to an investigation, to the extent that it is relevant to the defence of their interests and is used by the Commission in the investigation.[218]

Confidential documents and internal documents prepared by the EU authorities or the member states are non-accessible in virtue of Art. 6(7) and 19(5) of the Basic Regulation. Art. 19 (1) defines confidential information as "any information which is by nature confidential, (for example, because its disclosure would be of significant competitive advantage to a competitor or would have a significantly adverse effect upon a person supplying the information or upon a person from whom he has acquired the information) or which is provided on a confidential basis by parties to an investigation."

Interested parties providing confidential information are required to furnish non-confidential summaries thereof unless they are able to demonstrate that the information cannot be summarized in non-confidential form. In such exceptional cases, the party requesting confidentiality must provide a statement of reasons.[219]

Although the Regulation 384/96 provides that non-confidential summaries should be in sufficient detail to permit a reasonable understanding of the sub-

---

[217] Regulation 384/96, Art. 17 (4) referring to Art. 18
[218] Regulation 384/96, Art. 6 (7)
[219] Regulation 384/96, Art. 19 (2)

stance of the information submitted in confidence, non-confidential information made available to interested parties is as a rule extremely limited.[220]

The Regulation expressly provides that the information received by the authorities may only be used "for the purpose for which it was requested".[221] This provision guarantees the interested parties that the price information submitted in the context of an anti-dumping proceeding will not be passed, for example, on to Directorate General for Competition.[222]

The confidentiality requirement of the Regulation, however, do not prevent the Community authorities from disclosing general information, in particular the reasons on which decisions are based; and the evidence relied upon in "so far as is necessary to explain those reasons in court proceedings".[223] Nevertheless, Art. 19 (4) of the Basic Regulation provides that when the EU authorities make such disclosure, they must respect the legitimate interest of the parties involved "that their business secrets should not be divulged".

b) Hearing

The interested parties have a right to be heard by virtue of the Art. 6 of the Basic Regulation.

In the historical decision on the rights of interested parties in Al-Jubali Fertilizers[224] the Court ruled that: "with regard to the right to a fair hearing, any action taken by the Community institutions must be all the more scrupulous in view of the fact that, as they stand at present, the rules in question do not provide all the procedural guarantees for the protection of the individual which may exist in certain national legal systems."

Regulation 384/96 provides for two kinds of hearing: an oral hearing, i.e. a meeting between a given party and members of the Commission staff,[225] which is more common in practice; and a so-called confrontation meeting, i.e. a hearing attended by the parties directly concerned and presided over by a Commission official.[226]

---

[220] Van Bael/Bellis, EC Anti-dumping Laws, p. 273

[221] Regulation 384/96, Art. 19 (6). See e.g. the Order of the Court of 30 March 1982 in Celanese Co. Inc. v. Council and Commission Order of the Court of 30 March 1982 (case 236/81), ECR 1982, Page 01183, concerning the documents placed before the Court relating to the business secrets of undertakings and confidential treatment, see also: Judgment of the Court of 5 October 1988 (Canon v Council), Joined cases 277/85 and 300/85, ECR, 1988, 05731, rec. 70-71;

[222] Van Bael/Bellis, EC Anti-dumping Laws, p. 273

[223] Regulation 384/96, Art. 19 (4)

[224] Judgment of the Court of 27 June 1991, Case C-49/88, (Al-Jubail Fertilizer Co. v Council), ECR 1991 I-03187, rec. 16

[225] Regulation 384/96, Art. 6(5)

[226] Regulation 384/96, Art. 6(6)

The Commission may hear parties at any time in the course of the proceeding. However, parties who want to be heard, must within the period laid down in the notice of initiation, "make a written request for a hearing showing that they are an interested party likely to be affected by the result of the proceeding and that there are particular reasons why they should be heard."

c) Disclosure

In accordance with the Art. 20 of the Basic Regulation, the complainants, importers and exporters and their representative associations, and representatives of the exporting country, have a right to request disclosure of the details underlying the essential facts and considerations on the basis of which provisional and final measures have been imposed.

In the landmark Judgment Al-Jubali Fertilizers[227] the Court held that the right to disclosure constitutes a fundamental right.

Art. 20 of the Basic Regulation sets out detailed rules applicable to the disclosure procedure.

6. Imposition of protective measured during investigation

a) Provisional duties

Provisional measures may be imposed at any stage of the investigation, provided the proceeding has been formally initiated. They shall be applied in critical circumstances where delay would cause damage which would be difficult to repair, making immediate action necessary, and where a preliminary determination provides clear evidence that increased imports have caused, or are threatening to cause, serious injury.[228] Provisional duties must be imposed by Regulation.[229]

In spite of the use of the terms "preliminary examination" and "provisional duties" in the Basic Regulation, the Commission's fact-finding leading to the imposition of a provisional duty tends to be more final than preliminary in nature and is used not only in critical circumstances. As a rule, provisional antidumping duties are imposed only after verification visits.[230]

Upon a preliminary finding that dumping has caused injury to a Community industry, it has become the Commission's practice to impose a provisional antidumping duty.[231]

---

[227] Judgment of the Court of 27 June 1991, Case C-49/88, (Al-Jubail Fertilizer Co. v Council), ECR 1991 I-03187
[228] Regulation 384/96, Art. 7(1)
[229] Regulation 384/96, Art. 14(1)
[230] 21st Anti-dumping report, 2002, p. 21
[231] Van Bael/Bellis, EC Anti-dumping Laws, p. 279

When a provisional duty is imposed, the release of the products concerned for free circulation in the Community must be conditional upon the provision of guarantee for the amount of the provisional duty.[232]

The form of such guarantee is governed by the national law of the member state concerned and as a rule it is a bank guarantee. Where a provisional duty has been applied and the facts as finally established show that there is dumping and injury, the Council shall decide, irrespective of whether a definitive anti-dumping duty is to be imposed, what proportion of the provisional duty is to be definitively collected.[233]

Art. 7 (7) provides for a normal term of validity of provisional measures of 6 months, which may be extended for an additional three-months period.[234] The Commission may also decide to impose the provisional duty for a nine-month period. However, a three month extension or immediate imposition of provisional duties for a nine-month period is only possible provided exporters representing a significant percentage of trade involved so request or do not object it.[235]

No later than one month before the period of validity of the provisional duty expires, the Commission must submit to the Council its proposal for definitive duties.[236] Once the period of validity of the provisional duty expires, the guarantee must be released to the extent that the Council has not decided to collect it definitively.[237]

Table 12. Provisional anti-dumping duties imposed on Russian exports (1992-2003)		
Year	Product	Commission Regulation Nr.
1992	Potassium chloride	1031/92, 23.04.92, L110, 28.04.92, p.5
1994	Ferro-silico-marganese	3119/94, 19.12.94 L330, 21.12.94
1995	Grain oriented electrical sheets	L252, 20.10.95, p.2
	Magnesium unwrought	L 312, 23.12.95, p.37
1997	Zinc (unwrought unalloyed)	593/97, 25.03.97, L. 89, 4.04.97
	Seamless steel pipes and tubes	981/97, 29.05.97, L. 141, 31.05.97
1998	Hardboard	1742/98, 05.08.98, L218, 06.08.98, p.16

---

[232] Regulation 384/96, Art. 7(3)

[233] Regulation 384/96, Art. 10(2)

[234] See e.g. Council Regulation (EC) No 866/95 of 10 April 1995 extending the provisional anti-dumping duty on imports of ferro-silico-manganese originating in Russia, Ukraine, Brazil and South Africa (OJ L 089 , 21/04/1995 p. 1)

[235] Regulation 384/96, Art. 7(1)

[236] Regulation 384/96, Art. 9(4)

[237] Regulation 384/96, Art. 10(2)

2000	Solutions of urea and ammonium nitrate	617/00,16.03.2000, L75, 24.03.00, p.3
2001	Steel ropes and cables	230/01, 02.02.2001, L34, 03.02.01, p.4
2002	Tube and pipe fittings	358/02, 26.02.2002, L 56, 27.02.02, p.4
2003	Silicon metal	1235/03, 10.07.03, L 173, 11.07.03, p.14
Source: European Commission, the Community's Anti-dumping and anti-subsidy and safeguard activities, annual reports from the Commission to the European Parliament		

b) Registration of imports

Another form of provisional measures is registration of imports, where the Commission has a right to instruct customs authorities to register imports of the product concerned.

In accordance with the Basic Regulation registration may be imposed in the following cases:

> ➢ breach or withdrawal of undertakings;[238]
> ➢ retroactive imposition of definitive duties:[239]
> ➢ newcomer reviews;[240]
> ➢ anti-circumvention investigations.[241]

The decision to impose registration is to be taken by the Commission, after consultation of the Advisory Committee, either on its own initiative or following the request by the Community industry, which contains sufficient evidence to justify such action.[242] Imports may not be made subject to registration for a period longer than nine months.

7. Outcome of the investigation

An anti-dumping investigation is, whenever possible, to be concluded within one year. In any event, such investigations must in all cases be concluded within 15 months of initiation.[243] Although not expressly stated, the proceeding will be terminated where no definitive duties have been imposed or undertaking ac-

---

[238] Regulation 384/96, Art 10(5)

[239] Regulation 384/96, Art 10(4)

[240] Regulation 384/96, Art 11(4)

[241] Regulation 384/96, Art 13 (3), See e.g. Certain seamless pipes and tubes of iron or non-alloy steel originating in Russia (Commission Regulation (EC) No 1264/2003 of 16 July 2003 initiating an investigation concerning the alleged circumvention of anti-dumping measures imposed by Council Regulation (EC) No 2320/97 and making such imports subject to registration, OJ L 178 , 17/07/2003 P. 0009 - 0012)

[242] Regulation 384/96, Art 14 (5)

[243] Regulation 384/96, Art. 6 (9)

cepted at the time the 15-month period expires.[244] The conclusion of the investigation means either imposition of definitive measures, i.e. duties in virtue of Art. 9, or acceptance of undertakings in virtue of Art. 8 of the Basic Regulation; or termination without measures.

The proceeding is terminated without imposition of measures in following cases:

➢ The complaint is withdrawn, unless termination would not be in the Community interest;[245]

➢ Protective measures are unnecessary since no dumping has been found, the imports have caused no injury or either the dumping margin or the import volume is de minimis;[246] or

➢ It would not be in the Community interest to apply protective measures.

Table 13. New investigation against Russian exports concluded by imposition of definitive duties (1996-2003)		
Year	Product	Council Regulation Nr.
1996	Grain-oriented electrical sheets (big)	Com. Dec. (ECSC) 303/96, L42, 20.02.96
	Unwrought magnesium	1347/96, 2.07.96, L174, 12.07.96
1997	Zinc (unwrought unalloyed)	1931/97, 22.09.97, L272, 4.10.97
	Seamless steel pipes and tubes	2320/97, 17.11.97, L322, 25.11.97
1998	No definitive duties as a result of new investigations	

---

[244] See, e.g. Rubber-grade carbon blacks originating in Egypt and Russia, the procedure was terminated as 15-months deadline to impose definitive duties expired (Anti-Dumping Statistics covering the year 2003, p. 12). Alternatively, interested parties could institute court proceedings on the basis of Art. 232 EC (failure to act)

[245] Regulation 384/96, Art. 9 (1); See e.g. Hollow sections originating, inter alia, in Russia (Commission Decision of 15.12.2003, OJ L 327 , 16/12/2003 P. 0046 – 0047), where the complainant, Defence Committee of the Welded Steel Tube Industry on behalf of producers representing a major proportion of the total Community production of hollow sections, formally withdrew its complaint.

The Commission considered that the present proceeding should be terminated since the investigation had not brought to light any considerations showing that such termination would not be in the Community interest; See also Flat rolled narrow strips originating in Russia, Commission Decision of 12 February 1998, OJ L 40 , 13.02.98 P. 0015; Grain oriented electrical sheets and strips (flat-rolled products) of a width not exceeding 500 mm, (Commission Decision of 7.02.2003, OJ L 033 , 08.02.2003 P. 0041 – 0042)

[246] See e.g. Ferro-silico-manganese originating in inter alia, in Russia, (Council Regulation (EC) No 495/98 of 23 February 1998, OJ L 062 , 03.03.98 P. 0001 - 0018). Examination of Eurostat data showed that only a minimal quantity of 25 tonnes of FeSiMn were imported from Russia into the Community during the investigation period (out of a total consumption in the Community of approximately 538 000 tonnes). In view of the negligible quantity of these imports, it was neither considered necessary nor appropriate to calculate whether they were at dumped price levels.

1999	Hardboard	194/99, 25.01.99, L22, 29.01.99, p.16
2000	Solutions of urea and ammonium nitrate	1995/00, 18.09.2000, L238, 22.09.00, p.15
2001	Aluminium foil	950/01, 14.05.01, L134, 17.05.01, p.1
	Steel ropes and cables	1601/01, 2.09.01, L211, 04.08.01, p.1
2002	Tube and pipe fittings, of iron and steel	1514/02, 19.08.02, L228, 24.08.02, p.1
2003	Silicon metal	2229/03, 22.12.03, L339, 24.12.03, p.3

Source: European Commission, the Community's Anti-dumping and anti-subsidy and safeguard activities, annual reports from the Commission to the European Parliament

Table 14. New investigation against Russian exports terminated without the imposition of measures (1996-2003)			
Year	Product	Commission Decision Nr.	Reason for Termination
1998	Flat-rolled narrow strips	98/141/EC, 12.02.98, L40, 13.02.98, p.15	Withdrawal of a complaint
2003	Grain-oriented electrical sheets and strips (small)	2003/84/EC 7.02.03, L33 8.02.03, p.41	Withdrawal of a complaint
	Rubber-grade carbon blacks		15-month deadline to impose definitive measures expired
	Hollow sections	2003/808/EC, 15.12.03, L327, 16.12.03, p.46	Withdrawal of a complaint
1996-1997, 1999-2002	No terminations		

Source: European Commission, the Community's Anti-dumping and anti-subsidy and safeguard activities, annual reports from the Commission to the European Parliament

III. Reviews

Anti-dumping measures, including price undertakings, may be subject, under the basic Regulation, to five different types of reviews:
  1. Expiry review (Article 11(2)),
  2. Interim review (Article 11(3)),
  3. Newcomer review (Article 11(4)),

4. Anti-absorption review (Article 12)
5. Anti-circumvention review (Article 13).

As it have already been mentioned supra, the amendments of Basic Regulation of March 2004 reformed some provisions regarding anti-dumping reviews with the aim to increase transparency, efficiency and predictability of such reviews. The mandatory deadlines of such reviews were introduced and therefore the applicant is aware how long it will last. Before many exporters were unwilling to initiate, e.g. interim review, because they could not calculate the date of outcome of a review. However, the rules concerning deadlines will enter into force two years after the entry into force of amending Regulation, i.e. on 20th march 2006. On the separate note should be admitted that rules regarding anti-circumvention investigation were completely reformed and became more precise, whereas before the discretion of the Commission played the decisive role in interpretation of vague definitions.

1. Expiry review

Article 11(2) and Article 18 of the Basic Regulations provide for the expiry of measures after five years, unless an expiry review demonstrates that they should be maintained in their original form.

The Commission must inform the interested parties of the impending expiry of the measures by publication of a notice in the Official Journal. This notice of impending expiry must be published "at an appropriate time" during the final year of application of the measures in question.[247] An expiry review can be initiated on the initiative of the Commission, or upon request made by or on behalf of Community producers where the request contains sufficient evidence that the expiry of the measures would be likely to result in a continuation or recurrence of dumping and injury. The Community producers may lodge a request for an expiry review after the notice of impending expiry has been published but at least three months before the normal expiry date of measure.[248] The anti-dumping measure remains in force pending the outcome of such review.

In accordance with the Art. 11 (6) at the outcome of an expiry review, measures shall either be repealed or maintained.

The amendments to the Regulation 384/96 of March 2004 introduced the mandatory deadline for expiry review. In accordance with the new redaction of Art. 11 (5), which is applicable from 20th March 2006, expiry review shall normally be concluded within 12 months of the date of initiation of the review and in all cases within 15 months of initiation. The same rule is also applicable to interim reviews, which will be examined infra. In accordance with the new rules, if the investigation is not completed within the above deadlines, the measures shall

---

[247] Regulation 384/96, Art. 11 (2)
[248] Regulation 384/96, Art. 11 (2)

expire. Table gives an outline of the expiry review investigations concerning Russian exports concluded in the period between 1996 and 2003,[249] which shows that the cases of confirmation of duty are more common.

Table 15. Expiry reviews (1996-2003)		
1. Concluded by confirmation of duty		
Year	**Product**	**Council Regulation Nr.**
1996-1999	No outcome	
2000	**Potassium chloride***	969/00, 08.05.00, L112, 11.05.00, p.4
	Silicon carbide	1100/00, 22.05.00, L125, 26.05.00, p.3
2001	**Urea**	901/01, 7.05.01, L127, 09.05.01, p.11
2002	**Ammonium nitrate***	658/02, 15.04.02, L102, 18.04.02, p.1
2003	**Grain oriented electrical sheets**	151/03, 27.01.03, L25, 30.01.03, p.7
*Parallel interim review		
2. Concluded by termination		
Year	**Product**	**Commission Decision Nr.**
2000	**Ferro-chrome (low carbon)**	2000/242/EC, 24.03.00, L76, 25.03.00, p.23
2001	**Ferro-silicon**	2001/230/EC, 21.02.01, L184, 23.02.01, p.36
1996-1999, 2002-2003	No terminations	
Conclusion: 5 conformations of duty, 2 terminations		
Source: European Commission, the Community's Anti-dumping and anti-subsidy and safeguard activities, annual reports from the Commission to the European Parliament		

2. Interim review

Many exporters make use of the possibility to initiate an interim review, where the need for the continued imposition of final anti-dumping measures may be reviewed during the normal period of validity of measures. Interim review may be initiated on the initiative of the Commission, at the request of a member state, at the request of exporters, importers or the Community producers concerned by the measures.[250] Requests for an interim review may be only accepted provided at least one year has elapsed since the imposition of the measures. However, this

---

[249] Source: Anti-dumping Reports for Years 1996-2003
[250] Regulation 384/96, Art. 11(3)

one-year waiting period does not apply to reviews initiated on the Commission's own initiative or following the request by a member state.[251]

Interim reviews may bring advantage for exporter, because in the best case it is possible that the anti-dumping measure would be repealed before the expiry of 5-year period of validity. On the other side, it is possible that the level of duties would be increased even though the request contains evidence that there have been a decrease in dumping and/or injury margin.[252] It can be explained by the practice of the Commission, where the outcome of the review is not necessarily determined by the grounds on which it was initiated. There have been many cases where such reviews worsened the position of exporters.[253] Moreover, many Russian exporters are unwilling to initiate reviews because their duration, high fees of foreign advisers (as a rule exporters hire law firm in Brussels, which works in one team with in-house lawyers), paperwork connected with replying to questionnaires and preparing all evidential materials, which may disorganize daily activity of the company for the months.

The Article 11 (3) of the Basic regulation provides that the request for interim review must contain sufficient evidence justifying that:

➤ the continued imposition of the measure is no longer necessary to offset dumping and/or

➤ the injury would be unlikely to continue or recur if the measure were removed or varied, or

➤ that the existing measure is not, or is no longer, sufficient to counteract the dumping, which is causing injury.

At the outcome of an interim review measures shall be repealed, maintained or amended.[254]

According to the new rules of March 2004, if the interim review investigation is not completed within the mandatory deadline within 15 months of initiation, he measures remain unchanged. However this provision shall enter into force on 20th March 2006 as in case of expiry review.

Table gives an outline of the interim review investigations concerning Russian exports concluded in the period between 1996 and 2003,[255] which shows that the cases of confirmation/amendment of duty are more common. Only in 2 cases of 6 during the period in question the measures were repealed.

---

[251] Regulation 384/96, Art. 11(3)

[252] Van Bael/Bellis, EC Anti-dumping Laws, p. 305

[253] See e.g. Potassium chloride or originating in Russia (Council Regulation (EC) No 643/94 of 21 March 1994, OJ L 080 , 24/03/1994 P. 0001 – 0007), review was initiated on the initiative of the Commission and amended the duty, introducing the combination of duties.

[254] Regulation 384/96, Art. 11(6)

[255] Source: Anti-dumping Reports for Years 1996-2003

Table 16. Interim reviews (1996-2003)		
1. Concluded by confirmation/amendment of duty		
Year	**Product**	**Council Regulation Nr.**
1998	**Potassium chloride**	449/98, 23.02.98, L58, 27.02.98, p.15
1999	**Calcium metal**	733/99, 30.03.99, L94, 09.04.99, p.1
	Ferro-chrome (low carbon)	1976/99, 13.09.99, L245, 17.09.99, p.1
2000	**Seamless pipes and tubes of iron or non-alloy steel**	190/00, 24.01.00, L23, 28.01.00, p.1
	Potassium chloride*	969/00, 08.05.00, L112, 11.05.00, p.4
2002	**Ammonium nitrate***	658/02, 15.04.02, L102, 18.04.02, p.1
1996-1997, 2001, 2003	No outcome	
*Parallel expiry review		
2. Concluded by termination		
Year	**Product**	**Council Regulation Nr./ Remarks**
1998	**Ferro-silico-manganese**	495/98, 23.02.98, L62, 03.03.98, p.1/ the Council requested the Commission to initiate a review, measures were repealed after 3 years as export volumes were de minimis
	Hematite pig iron	Com. Dec. 962/98/ECSC, 07.05.98, L135, 08.05.98, p.7/ review initiated by the Commission, measures were been repealed after 4 years.
2003	**Urea**	2228/03, 22.12.03, L339, 24.12.03, p.1/ partial interim review, was initiated by the Commission to examine the appropriateness of measures in force. Procedure is terminated without amending the duty in force
1996-1997, 1999-2002	No terminations	
Conclusion: 6 confirmation/amendment of duty, 3 terminations, thereof in 2 cases the duty was repealed		
Source: European Commission, the Community's Anti-dumping and anti-subsidy and safeguard activities, annual reports from the Commission to the European Parliament		

3. Combined expiry and interim review investigation

The Commission often carries out interim and expiry review simultaneously[256] (see e.g. Potassium chloride and Ammonium nitrate originating in Russia in Tables 18 and 19 above). Although the Regulation provides that measures will remain in force pending the outcome of an expiry review, it does not contain a similar provision relating to interim reviews. This would seem to indicate that measures will lapse at the end of their normal period of validity even where an interim review is in progress at that time, unless simultaneous expiry review is initiated However, Art. 11(7) provides that where an interim review is in progress at the end of the period of application of measures, the interim review will also cover the circumstances set out in the paragraphs dealing with expiry reviews.

It is unclear to what extent this provision is sufficient to justify the continuation of the measures pending the outcome of the interim review. It would appear unjustified to rely on this provision to transform interim reviews into expiry reviews where the interim review was, for instance, initiated following a request by exporters alleging the absence of dumping and/or injury.[257] In the absence of evidence which would justify the initiation of an expiry review, the measures should be allowed to expire.[258]

The new amending Regulation introduced the deadline for combined expiry and interim review, which enters into force from 20th March 2006. Thereunder, if an expiry review is initiated while an interim review is ongoing in the same proceeding, an interim review shall be concluded at the same time as foreseen for the expiry review [in all cases 15 months of initiation]. If the investigation is not completed within the mandatory deadline of 15 months, the measures shall expire in case when expiry and interim reviews were carried out in parallel, where either the expiry review was initiated while an interim review was ongoing in the same proceeding or where such reviews were initiated at the same time.

4. New exporter review

Article 11(4) of the basic Regulation allows for a review ("newcomer" review) to be carried out in order to determine individual margins of dumping for new exporters located in the exporting country in question, which did not export the product during the investigation period.

Such parties have to show that they are genuine new exporters, i.e. that they are not related to any of the exporters or producers in the exporting country, which

---

[256] 21st Anti-dumping report, 2002, p.35

[257] Van Bael/Bellis, EC Anti-dumping Laws, p. 314

[258] This follows from the Judgment of the Court of 7 December 1993, Case C-216/91, (Rima Eletrometalurgia SA v Council), ECR 1993, I-06303

are subject to the anti-dumping measures, and that they have actually started to export to the Community following the investigation period, or that they have entered into an irrevocable contractual obligation to export a significant quantity to the Community.

When a review for a new exporter is initiated, the duties are repealed with regard to that exporter, though its imports are made subject to registration under Article 14(5) of the basic Regulation in order to ensure that, should the review result in a determination of dumping in respect of such an exporter, anti-dumping duties may be levied retroactively to the date of the initiation of the review.

New exporter review shall in all cases be concluded within nine months of the date of initiation. This deadline is applicable from 20th March 2006.

It should be noted, that the newcomer review was introduced to the EU law by Regulation 384/96 and since then there has not been any review concerning Russian exporter.

5. Anti-absorption review

The possibility of absorption reviews is included in Article 12 of the Basic Regulation. Thereunder, "where the Community industry or any other interested party submit, normally within two years from the entry into force of the measures, sufficient information showing that, after the original investigation period and prior to or following the imposition of measures, export prices have decreased or that there has been no movement, or insufficient movement in the resale prices or subsequent selling prices of the imported product in the Community, the investigation may, after consultation, be reopened to examine whether the measure has had effects on the abovementioned prices."[259]

Where a reinvestigation shows increased dumping the measures in force may, after consultation, be amended by the Council, acting on the proposal from the Commission in accordance with the new findings of export prices.[260] The Commission may impose an additional anti-dumping duty to the extent the original duty was absorbed. The amendments of March 2004 introduced limitations regarding additional anti-dumping duty. Thereunder, the amount of the anti-dumping duty imposed in anti-absorption investigation shall not exceed twice the amount of duty imposed initially by the Council. It is a revolutionary provision, because until now in practice means the anti-dumping duty imposed as a result of anti-absorption investigation could be higher than twice the amount of initial duty.[261] The amount of the duty shall be determined on the same basis as the definitive duty as provided by Art. 9 (2).

---

[259] Regulation 384/96, Art. 12 (1)

[260] Regulation 384/96, Art. 12 (3)

[261] See e.g. Ammonium nitrate originating in Russia (Council Regulation (EC) No 663/98 of 23 March 1998, OJ L 093 , 26.03.1998 p. 0001 - 0007), where the new level of anti-dumping

The amendments of March 2004 also introduced deadlines for anti-absorption investigation. In accordance with the new redaction of Art. 12(4) of Regulation 384/96 such reinvestigation shall normally be concluded within six months of the date of initiation and in all cases within nine months of initiation. This deadline, as all deadlines introduced in the recent amendments, will be applicable from 20th March 2006. The rest changes of anti-absorption procedure are applicable to all investigations initiated after 20th March 2004.

6. Anti-circumvention review

The amendments to the Anti-dumping legislation of March 2004 reformed rules concerning anti-circumvention investigations. These rules are applicable from 20th March 2004.

Under the modified Art. 13 (1) circumvention is defined as "a change in the pattern of trade between third countries and the Community or between individual companies in the country subject to measures and the Community, which stems from a practice, process or work for which there is insufficient due cause or economic justification other than the imposition of the duty, and where there is evidence of injury or that the remedial effects of the duty are being undermined in terms of the prices and/or quantities of the like product, and where there is evidence of dumping in relation to the normal values previously established for the like product." Further paragraph 2 introduced clarifications that the practice, process or work referred to in paragraph 1 of Art. 13 (1) includes, "inter alia, the slight modification of the product concerned to make it fall under customs codes which are normally not subject to the measures, provided that the modification does not alter its essential characteristics; the consignment of the product subject to measures via third countries; the reorganization by exporters or producers of their patterns and channels of sales in the country subject to measures in order to eventually have their products exported to the Community through producers benefiting from an individual duty rate lower than that applicable to the products of the manufacturers; and, in the circumstances indicated under Article 13(2), [262]

---

duty was determined by adding to the previous level of the duty (minimum import price less export price at the Community frontier in the original investigation period) the difference between the export prices in the original investigation and those of the current reinvestigation.

[262] Art. 13 (2) provides conditions under which assembly operations in the EU or a third country will be considered to circumvent the measures in force: (a) the operation started or substantially increased since, or just prior to, the initiation of the anti-dumping investigation and the parts concerned are from the country subject to measures; and (b) the parts constitute 60 % or more of the total value of the parts of the assembled product, except that in no case shall circumvention be considered to be taking place where the value added to the parts brought in, during the assembly or completion operation, is greater than 25 % of the manufacturing cost, and (c) the remedial effects of the duty are being undermined in terms of the prices and/or quantities of the assembled like product and there is evidence of dumping in relation to the normal values previously established for the like or similar products.

the assembly of parts by an assembly operation in the Community or a third country."

Article 13(3) of the Basic Regulation provides that the relevant procedural provisions of the Regulation with regard to initiations and the conduct of investigations are applicable to anti-circumvention investigations. Article 13 (3) gave precise indications regarding the parties entitled to initiate investigations: Commission, Member States or any interested party. Furthermore, initiations shall be made by Commission Regulation, which may also instruct the customs authorities to make imports subject to registration in accordance with Art. 14 (5) or request guarantees. Before the amendments, the initiation of an anti-circumvention investigation was automatically accompanied by registration of imports, a step that is taken in regular anti-dumping investigations only when certain conditions are met in exceptional circumstances. Now the Regulation just uses the permissive language "may". It should be noted that that initiation of anti-circumvention investigations made by Commission Regulation differs from regular investigation which is initiated by a mere notice.

The new rules of Art. 13 (3) also introduce deadline for anti-circumvention investigation – nine months nine months from initiation.

Art. 13 (3) finally provides that "when the facts as finally ascertained justify the extension of measures, this shall be done by the Council, acting on a proposal submitted by the Commission, after consultation of the Advisory Committee." The extension will have retroactive effect from the date on which registration of imports was imposed pursuant to Article 14 (5) or on which guarantees were requested.

Modified Art. 13 (3) will be applicable also to pending investigation at the moment of entry of amendments to force. It has advantage for Russia, as at the moment of entry of amendments into force one investigation was pending. It is the case Seamless pipes and tubes of iron or non-alloy steel originating in Russia where the anti-absorbance investigation was initiated on the ground of the request, which "contained sufficient evidence, that the anti-dumping measures on imports of certain seamless pipes and tubes of iron or non-alloy steel originating in Russia and Ukraine are being circumvented by means of adding minimal quantities of other substances to the product concerned, thus allowing these products to be classifiable under other CN codes not subject to anti-dumping measures". [263]

---

[263] See Commission Regulation (EC) No 1264/2003 of 16 July 2003 initiating an investigation concerning the alleged circumvention of anti-dumping measures imposed by Council Regulation (EC) No 2320/97 on imports of certain seamless pipes and tubes of iron or non-alloy steel originating in Russia and of anti-dumping measures imposed by Council Regulation (EC) No 348/2000 on imports of certain seamless pipes and tubes of iron or non-alloy steel originating in Ukraine by wrong declaration of imports of the same product and by imports of certain

IV. Refund procedure

The rules governing refund proceeding are set out in Art. 11 (8) of the Basic Regulation. Pursuant to this provision, an importer may request reimbursement of duties collected where it is shown that the dumping margin, on the basis of which duties were paid, has been eliminated or reduced to a level below the level of the duty in force.

Refund applications have to be submitted by the importer to the authorities of the Member State where the importation took place and, accordingly, the duty was paid. The Member State will then transmit the request to the Commission. The application has to be supported by evidence on normal value and export prices, using the same methodology as used during the original investigation. This information will be verified by the Commission services. In practice, a refund proceeding is almost identical to an interim review and is likely to take between twelve to eighteen months before completion. Moreover, the chances of obtaining a refund are extremely limited due to the Commission practice of deducting the anti-dumping duties as a cost of the importer, in case the export price has to be reconstructed or is on a duty paid basis. This effectively requires the exporter to make a so-called "double jump" to eliminate the dumping margin. The first "jump" consists in an increase of the export price (or a reduction in normal value) sufficient to eliminate the dumping margin determined in the original investigation. In addition, the exporter has to compensate the extra dumping margin created by the deduction of the anti-dumping duty paid (and for which a refund is claimed) from the export price during the reconstruction of the ex-works export price in the framework of the refund proceeding.

The following example may clarify this practice:

Example 5. Refund proceedings		
	Initial investigation	**Refund investigation**
Normal value	$ 100	$100
Export price (CIF, duty paid)	$108	$118
- Customs duty	$8	$8
- Anti-dumping duty	0	$10
- Ocean freight	$3	$3
- Inland freight	$2	$2
- Commission	$5	$5
Ex-factory export price	**$90**	**$90**
Dumping margin	**$10%**	**$10%**

seamless pipes and tubes of alloy steel, other than stainless steel, originating in Russia and Ukraine, and making such imports subject to registration
(OJ L 178 , 17/07/2003 P. 0009 - 0012), rec.7.

In the above example, the exporter, after the imposition of a ten per cent anti-dumping duty, increased his export prices sufficiently to offset the dumping margin found. However, due to the deduction of the anti-dumping duty as a cost in the refund proceeding, his dumping margin remains unchanged, i.e. ten per cent. In order to obtain a refund, he would have had to increase the export prices to $128, i.e. $108 plus $10 (dumping margin) plus $10 (anti-dumping duty).

The above example explains why, in the past, refunds have been granted only exceptionally. There have been no case of granting a refund for a Russian exporter until now. However, the Art. 11(10) contains a provision, which could change this situation. Art. 11(10) provides that in refund proceeding and in interim reviews the anti-dumping duty should no longer be deducted as a cost "when compulsive evidence is provided that the duty is duly reflected in resale prices and the subsequent selling prices in the Community". However, due to lack of practice it remains unclear how this provision will be implemented in practice.

The Commission published in 2002 the updated guidelines for potential applicants of refunds,[264] the purpose of which is to indicate Commission practice in the treatment of applications for refunds of anti-dumping duties.

V. Judicial review

Acts of the Commission and the Council are subject to judicial review by the Court of justice of the European Communities, either directly, or in the context of a preliminary reference from a national court. Direct challenges to anti-dumping measures fall within the jurisdiction of the Court of First Instance since 15 March 1994.[265] The European Court of Justice retains jurisdiction in all preliminary rulings.[266]

1. Direct actions

The direct actions that are of special relevance in the context of the enforcement of the EU anti-dumping laws are following.

---

[264] Commission notice concerning the reimbursement of anti-dumping duties, OJ C 127 of 29.05.02, p. 10

[265] From 15 March 1994 the Jurisdiction of the Court of First Instance was extended to include direct actions in anti-dumping and anti-subsidy cases. See 94/149/ECSC, EC: Council Decision of 7 March 1994 amending Decision 93/350/Euratom, ECSC, EEC amending Decision 88/591/ECSC, EEC, Euratom establishing a Court of First Instance of the European Communities, OJ L 066 , 10.03.1994 p. 0029 - 0029

[266] Art 225(1) of the EC Treaty

a) Action for annulment

Judicial review of the EU anti-dumping measures is most frequently sought through an action for annulment under Art. 230 of the EC Treaty. In addition, Art. 241 of the EC Treaty permits applicants to challenge, during the course of such an action, the provisions of the Basic Regulation.

aa) Acts reviewable under Art. 230 of the EC Treaty

Art. 230 of the EC Treaty provides that:

"the Court of Justice shall review the legality of acts... of the Council [and] of the Commission... other than recommendations or opinions..."

Art. 249 of the EC Treaty provides that acts of the Council or the Commission, other than recommendations or opinions, may be regulations, decisions or directives.

Definitive anti-dumping duties are adopted, modified or repealed by the Council.[267] The EU practice is to enact such measures by way of regulation. The reasoning for this practice appears to be that the acts are intended to be binding, directly applicable and of general application by virtue of the Art. 249 of the EC Treaty. Provisional duties are generally adopted by the Commission, although they may also be adopted by the Council.[268] As in the case of definitive duties, the act will be in the form of a regulation.

A proceeding is terminated without measures[269] or undertaking accepted[270] by either the Commission or Council. The act will generally be in the form of a decision. The reasoning for this choice of form would appear to be that the acts in question are not intended to be a general application. Although such decisions do not formally state the addressee, the Community apparently takes the view that they concern a limited class of natural or legal persons.[271]

Accordingly, all regulations or decisions of the Commission or Council adopted under the Basic regulation will be acts capable of review under Art. 230 of the EC Treaty.

The question of whether or not certain preparatory acts of the Commission (such as initiation of an investigation or the decision to verify a sample of companies) would be subject to review remains an open question, to be decided in accordance with the Court's established case law. The Court has ruled, for example, that a rejection by the Commission of an offer of an undertaking may not be challenged. Such a rejection was considered by the Court as an intermediate

---

[267] Regulation 384/96, Art. 9(4)

[268] Regulation 384/96, Art. 7

[269] Regulation 384/96, Art. 9

[270] Regulation 384/96, Art. 8

[271] Van Bael/Bellis, EC Anti-dumping Laws, p. 329

measure the purpose of which is to prepare for the final decision.[272] On the other hand, the Court has ruled that a decision of the Commission to refuse access to the non-confidential file is an act capable of review under Art. 230 of the EC Treaty.[273]

bb) Grounds for review under Art. 230 of the EC Treaty

The grounds for review under Art. 230 of the EC Treaty are lack of competence, infringement of an essential procedural requirement, infringement of the EC Treaty or of any rule of law relating to its application, and misuse of power.

The wording of the grounds for reviews is therefore sufficiently wide to cover most if not all of the arguments that an applicant may wish to raise.

As far as the standard of review is concerned, it would appear that actions before the Court will be successful only if the EU authorities have failed to observe the procedural guarantees provided for in the Basic Regulation, have committed manifest errors in the assessment of the facts, or have based the reasons for their decisions on considerations amounting to misuse of powers.[274] One of the most fruitful grounds of application has tended to be infringement of essential procedural requirements.[275] This have a consequence that the EU anti-dumping measures are under very limited scope of judicial review. This was summarised in the Ferchimex case: "The Court of Justice has consistently held that the Community judicature cannot intervene in assessments reserved to the Community authorities but must restrict its review to verifying whether the procedural rules have been complied with, whether the facts on which the contested choice is based are accurate or whether there has been a manifest error of appraisal or a misuse of powers".[276]

In addition, the Court has shown itself willing to have regard to provisions of the WTO Anti-dumping Agreement which the EU Basic Regulation implements, and to ensure that Community acts are in compliance with the WTO law.[277] The latter will be actual in view of the Russian accession to the WTO.

b) Action for failure to act

A direct action may also be brought against the Council or the Commission for failure to act by a Member State, another Community institution or a natural or

---

[272]Judgment of the Court of 14 March 1990, Joined cases C-133/87 and C-150/87, (Nashua Corp. v Commission and Council) ECR 1990 Page I-00719

[273]Judgment of the Court of 28 November 1991, Case C-170/89 (Bureau Europeen des Unions de Consommateurs (BEUC) v Commission), ECR 1991 P. I-05709, rec. 11

[274] Van Bael/Bellis, EC Anti-dumping Laws, p. 335

[275] Commission of the European Communities, 21st Anti-dumping report, 2002, p. 48

[276] Judgment of the Court of First Instance of 28 September 1995, Case T-164/94 (Ferchimex v Council), ECR 1995, II-02681, rec. 67.

[277] Commission of the European Communities, 21st Anti-dumping report, 2002, p. 49, Van Bael/Bellis, EC Anti-dumping Laws, p. 335

legal person under Art. 232 of the EC Treaty. A private party may bring such an act, which would have been of direct and individual concern to him. An action brought under Art. 232 is admissible only if the institution has first been called upon to act. After the request for action has been made, the institution must define its position within two months. If the institution fails to define its position within this period – either by accepting – or rejecting the request – an action may be brought within a further period of two months.

c) Action for damages
Actions for damages may be brought under the provisions of Art. 215, second paragraph, of the EC treaty. Unlike the actions discussed above, there are no limitations on the persons who may bring an action for damages.

2. Preliminary rulings
Under Art. 234 of the EC Treaty, the European Court of Justice has jurisdiction to give preliminary rulings at the request of national courts on questions concerning the interpretation or validity of provisions of Community law. Any national court or tribunal may request a preliminary ruling if it considers that a decision on a question of Community law is necessary to enable it to render a judgement. A court or tribunal from which there is no appeal must take such a request. When such a request is made, the proceedings in the national court are generally suspended until the European Court of Justice gives a ruling. In the context of a preliminary reference, the European Court of Justice has the power to interpret the EU law, but not to apply it to the facts of the case. After the European Court of Justice has issued a ruling, the case is sent back to the national court, which applies the ruling to the facts of the case. Until the Extramet case[278], preliminary rulings provided the only possibility for unrelated importers to challenge regulations imposing anti-dumping measures.

Table 17. EU Anti-dumping proceeding timetable (for market economy countries)		
Date	**Legal Framework-Regulation 384/96**	**Legal steps**
15January 2005	Art.5 (1)	Filing of the complaint with the EU Commission. Examination of the Complaint by the Commission and consultation of the anti-dumping advisory committee.

---

[278] Judgment of the Court of 16 May 1991, Case C-358/89 (Extramet Industrie SA v Council),ECR 1991 P. I-02501

1 March 2005	Art.5 (9) Art.6 (9)	Initiation of the anti-dumping proceeding (maximum within 45 days of the filing of the complaint) Investigation is, whenever possible, to be concluded within one year (in any event within 15 months) of initiation.
10 April 2005	Art.6 (2)	Submission of the questionnaire responses of exporters, importers and EU producers (maximum within 40 days of initiation): ➢ The time limit for exporters – 30 days counted from the date of receipt of the questionnaire (deemed to have been received one week from the day on which it was sent). ➢ Extension to the 30 day period deadline may be granted (usually maximum one week)
	Art.6 (10)	Submission of arguments on injury and community interest by all interested parties
April 2005	Art.16	Verification visits
July-August 2005	Art.6 (3),(4)	Verification of exporters (and related importers) + EU produces + other importers
	Art.6 (5)	Hearing at the Commission by interested parties (injury and dumping issues) – usually after verifications
November 2005	Art.7	Imposition of provisional measures by the Commission after consultation of the advisory committee (no earlier than 60 days but not later than 9 months from the initiation of the proceedings.) Duration: ➢ 6 months (further 3months extension is possible) or ➢ 9 nine months.
	Art.9 (1), 9 (2)	Termination with no measures (maximum within 9 months after initiation)
May 2006	Art.9, Art. 11	Maximum within 9 months following the imposition of the provisional measures and maximum within 15 months following the initiation of the proceeding: ➢ Imposition of definitive measures by the Council after consultation of the advisory committee

		Duration five years from its imposition or five years from the date of the conclusion of the most recent review. or Termination with no measures
2007-2011	Art.11 (3)	Interim review (upon a request by any exporter/importer/Community producers – 1 year since the imposition of the definitive measure, on the initiative of the Commission or a Member State – any time) ➤ Amendment of duties or ➤ Confirmation or ➤ Repeal Shall normally be concluded within 12 months of the date of initiation, and must in all cases be concluded within 15 months of initiation (Mandatory deadline from 20th March 2006).
	Art.11 (2)	Expiry review (sunset) (the Community producers are entitled to lodge a review request no later than 3 months before the end of the 5-year period) ➤ Confirmation of duties ➤ Repeal Shall normally be concluded within 12 months of the date of initiation, and must in all cases be concluded within 15 months of initiation (Mandatory deadline from 20th March 2006).
	Art.12	Anti-absorption investigation ➤ Additional anti-dumping duty Shall normally be concluded within 6 months of the date of initiation, and must in all cases be concluded within 9 months of initiation. (Mandatory deadline from 20th March 2006).
	Art.13	Anti-circumvention investigation ➤ Extension of anti-dumping duty Shall normally be concluded within 9 months of initiation. (Mandatory deadline from 20th March 2006).
	Art.11 (8)	Refund proceedings Refund of anti-dumping duty paid in excess

	Judicial re-view	Actions before the Court of First Instance and the Court of Justice ➢ Art.230 (Action for annulment) ➢ Art. 241 (Action to invoke the inapplicability of the Regulation) ➢ Art. 232 (Action for failure to act), ➢ Art. 288 Abs.2 (Action for damages) ➢ Art. 234 (Preliminary ruling)

D. Anti-dumping measures

The EU legislation provides for two legal forms of anti-dumping measures:
1. Anti-dumping duties;
2. Undertakings.

I. Anti-dumping duties

Art. 14(1) of the Basic Regulation prescribes the Regulation to be the legal form of imposition of anti-dumping duties. Any such Regulation must be published in the Official Journal of the European Communities.[279]

1. Amount of duty

The amount of the anti-dumping duty shall not exceed the margin of dumping established but it should be less than the margin if such lesser duty would be adequate to remove the injury to the Community industry.[280] This rule is known in the doctrine as a "lesser duty rule".[281]

As the level of anti-dumping duties need not necessarily correspond to that of the dumping margin, the Community authorities enjoy in practice considerable flexibility in determining the level of duty, vary often not in favour of exporters.[282] The absolute maximum is the dumping margin, irrespective of the injury suffered by the Community injury. The minimum amount is whatever is needed to eliminate injury.

Injury margins can be calculated either according to the "price undercutting" taking place, or according to the "target price" method.

When injury is calculated according to price undercutting, the Commission services simply assess by how much the Community producers' price are undercut by the dumped imports, and injury is determined on the basis of this difference.

Target prices are used in situation where price depression has already occurred, and therefore the current price level will not compensate the Community indus-

---

[279] Regulation 384/96, Art 14 (2)
[280] Regulation 384/96, Art 9 (4)
[281] Anti-dumping Handbook for Russian Exporters, p. 22
[282] Van Bael/Bellis, EC Anti-dumping Laws, p. 214

try for their injury. The Commission in these cases sets a price at a level deemed to represent what the price would be without the influence of the dumped imports. Subsequently, the injury margin is calculated at the price level thus found. The duty is then limited to the so-called injury margin, i.e. margin by which prices must be raised in order to allow the EU domestic industry to cover its cost of production and earn a "reasonable" profit.

Below are the formulas of calculation of injury margin based on the actual prices (price undercutting) or target price (price underselling).[283]

Example 6. Determination of injury margin
Formula 1. Price undercutting
(injury margin determined by comparing the weighted average resale prices of the imports into the EU with the weighted average sale prices of the same or similar models of the EU producers.)

$$(A-B)/C \times 100 = \text{injury margin (\%)}$$

A: the weighted average price of the comparable model sold by the Community producers
B: the exporter's weighted average resale price;
C: the CIF export price (duty unpaid) EU frontier

Formula 2. Determination of target price
(in cases where it is impossible to compare the exporter's prices with those of the Community producers because the latter has been depressed as a result of the dumped import and are no longer made at a profitable level.

$$\text{Target price} = A + B + C$$

A: the cost of manufacturing by the Community producer;
B: the selling, general and administrative expenses of the Community producer;
C: a reasonable profit

Example 7.[284] Calculation of injury margin in accordance with a lesser duty rule (for Market economy countries)

1. Representatives of the EU sell goods at a price $97 for a unit. (not a steady price).
2. Level of the price which remove the injury = $100.
3. Export price of a unit, duty paid = $95+$1(duty)=$96. Therefore, price undercutting = $100-$96=$4.
4. **Dumping margin** as a percentage on the basis of the CIF export price (duty unpaid) EU frontier = 4/95×100=4,2%
5. Result: application of a lesser duty rule lead to injury margin = 4,2% instead of 12,6% (see Example 4 at. P.73), because injury margin is lesser.

---

[283] Formulas from Van Bael/Bellis, EC Anti-dumping Laws, p. 215
[284] Anti-dumping Handbook for Russian Exporters, p.22

2. Form of duty

Anti-dumping duty can be imposed in a following variety of forms:

1.A percentage of the import price, i.e. ad valorem, which are used in majority of cases, including against Russian export. This kind of duty has a practical disadvantage for an exporter, which increases export price in order to terminate the anti-dumping practice but practically this has a consequence that he must pay higher duty.[285]

2.The difference between the import price and a certain minimum or floor price[286]. Depending on the circumstances and the products involved, it may be to the exporter's advantage if the duties are set by reference to a floor price because, in such a case, the payment of duties can be avoided by raising the export price. In all other instances, the payment of the duty is unavoidable and the exporter selling the product without dumping can only seek redress by having the importer file a claim for refund.

3. A specific duty, i.e. a fixed amount per unit, weight or measure, imported;

4. A combination of (1) and (2)[287] or (2) and (3), the purpose of such a combination is to avoid the circumvention. It is actually the worst case for an exporter, which under the circumstances can lose the EU for many years.

The EU institutions chose the appropriate measures.[288] Some authors suggest that, in view of the Commission wide discretion, it should be under an obligation to explain the reason for choosing a particular form of duty.[289] However, the EU is not under a legal obligation to make such explanations.

II. Undertaking

1. Notion and conditions for accepting an undertaking

The modified in March 2004 Art. 8 (1) of the Basic Regulation provides that "upon condition that a provisional affirmative determination of dumping and injury has been made, the Commission may accept satisfactory voluntary undertaking offers submitted by any exporter to revise its prices or to cease exports at

---

[285] Nettesheim, in: Grabitz/von Bogdandz/Nettesheim, p.230

[286] Urea originating in Russia (Council Regulation No 901/2001 of 7 May 2001, OJ L 127 , 09/05/2001 P. 0011 – 0019), Art. 1 (2) : "the amount of the definitive anti-dumping duty shall be the difference between the minimum import price of EUR 115 per tonne and the net, free-at-Community-frontier price, before duty, in all cases where the latter is less than the minimum import price."

[287] See e.g. Potassium chloride originating in Russia (Council Regulation No 449/98 of 23 February 1998, OJ L 058 , 27/02/1998 P. 0015 – 0026), Art 1(2): The amount of duty shall be equal to the fixed amount in ECU per ton of KCl shown below per type and grade, or the difference between the minimum prices in ECU shown below and the net, free-at-Community-frontier price per ton KCl, before customs clearance for the corresponding type and grade, whichever is the higher

[288] Wenig, KII, rec. 139

[289] Van Bael/Bellis, EC Anti-dumping Laws, p. 613

dumped prices, if, after specific consultation of the Advisory Committee, it is satisfied that the injurious effect of the dumping is thereby eliminated." It further provides that "in such a case and as long as such undertakings are in force, the provisional duties imposed by the Commission or the definitive duties imposed by the Council as the case may be shall not apply to the relevant imports of the product concerned." Actually the Article 8 (1) was not modified a lot, except that the formulation is more clear now. However the formulation "the provisional duties imposed by the Commission or the definitive duties imposed by the Council shall not apply" is not clear enough. It can be understood that the duties will be imposed and just will not be applied, whereas in case of breach or withdrawal of undertaking they shall automatically apply.[290] In the redaction of Basic Regulation before March 2004 in case of acceptance of an undertaking investigation would just be terminated without impositions of measures.

The legal nature of undertaking is contract under public law.[291] It is not entirely clear if it is an unilateral or bilateral undertaking. In literature the legal commitment of EU institutions in undertaking is sometimes rejected. These authors claim that undertakings are binding only for exporters.[292]

The only substantive condition for an undertaking to be acceptable is that the Commission must be satisfied that the dumping margin or the injurious effect of the dumping is eliminated by the undertaking.[293] The Commission may seek or accept undertakings only after "a provisional affirmative determination of dumping and injury caused by such dumping has been made."[294] The EU authorities enjoy a wide discretion in accepting or rejecting undertakings offered by exporters. Art. 8 (3) provides that "undertakings offered need not be accepted if their acceptance is considered impractical, if such as where the number of actual or potential exporters is too great, or for other reasons, including reasons of general policy." This discretion has been questioned by some authors.[295] However, the Court confirmed the level of discretion of the EU institution regarding the acceptance of undertakings from exporters, emphasizing that there is no any provision in the EU anti-dumping law which can compel EU Commission to accept an undertaking.[296]

---

[290] See Regulation 434/96, Art. 8(9)

[291] Friedrichs, EGV/Antidumpingrecht, p. 212

[292] Beseler/Williams, Antidumping and antisubsidy law, Rn. 9.2.2.

[293] See Regulation 434/96, Art. 8(1), which provides that :
"Price increases under such undertakings shall not be higher than necessary to eliminate the margin of dumping and they should be less than the margin of dumping if such increases would be adequate to remove the injury to the Community industry."

[294] See Regulation 434/96, Art. 8(2)

[295] Van Bael/Bellis, EC Anti-dumping Laws, p. 615

[296] See e.g. Judgment of the Court of 7 May 1987, Case 255/84, (Nachi Fujikoshi Corp. v Council), ECR 1987, 01861, rec. 4 : "No provision of the Regulation compels the Community institutions to accept price undertakings offered by traders concerned by an investigation

Art. 8 (3) of the Basic Regulation provides that "the exporter concerned may be provided with the reasons for which it is proposed to reject the offer of an undertaking and may be given an opportunity to make comments thereon", the wording of the provision being permissive. It provides further that "the reasons for rejection shall be set out in the definitive decision."

The most common reasons to justify rejection of undertaking, the following grounds have been given:

> The exporter did not cooperate during the period of investigation.[297]
> The price would not be increased to an appropriate level within an acceptable period of time.
> The breach of previous undertaking.[298]
> The conditions of the undertaking offered would not permit adequate monitoring of compliance with the terms of undertaking.[299]
> Due to the absence of sufficient guarantees by the exporter and the government, undertaking cannot be effectively monitored or enforced.[300]
> The fact that the party offering an undertaking is not an exporting producer, but an intermediate trader.[301]

It should be noted that Art. 18 of partnership and Cooperation agreement between EU and Russia contains the following provision: "before definitive anti-dumping duties are imposed, the Parties shall do their utmost to bring about a constructive solution to the problem." This article can be applied, inter alia, to acceptance of undertakings from Russian exporters. It is emphasised, that the both parties must seek constructive solution to the problem, whereas the Com-

---

prior to the imposition of anti-dumping duties. On the contrary, it is clear from the Regulation that it is for the institutions , in the exercise of their discretionary power to determine whether such undertakings are acceptable. The refusal to accept undertakings which have been given individual consideration cannot, if it is accompanied by a statement of reasons satisfying the requirements of Art. 190 of the Treaty, be criticised by the Court, unless the reasons on which it is based exceed the margin of discretion. " See also Judgment of the Court (Fifth Chamber) of 7 May 1987, Case 240/84, (Toyo v Council), ECR 1987 Page 01809, rec. 4; Judgment of the Court (Fifth Chamber) of 7 May 1987, Case 260/84, (Minebea v Council), ECR 1987 Page 01975

[297] See e.g. Ammonium nitrate originating in Russia (Council Regulation (EC) No 663/98 of 23 March 1998, OJ L 093 , 26/03/1998 p. 0001 – 0007)

[298] See e.g. Ammonium nitrate originating in Russia (Council Regulation (EC) No 663/98 of 23 March 1998, OJ L 093 , 26/03/1998 p. 0001 – 0007) , rec. 35

[299] See e.g. Silicon originating Russia (Council Regulation (EC) No 2229/2003 of 22 December 2003, OJ L 339 , 24/12/2003 P. 0003 – 0013), rec. 93-95

[300] See e.g. Potassium chloride originating in, inter alia, Russia (Council Regulation (EC) No 969/2000 of 8 May 2000, OJ L 112 , 11/05/2000 P. 0004 – 0026), rec. 128

[301] See e.g. Solutions of urea and ammonium nitrate originating in, inter alia, Russia (Council Regulation (EC) No 1995/2000 of 18 September 2000, OJ L 238 , 22/09/2000 P. 0015 – 0023), rec.48

mission continues its practice of rejection of undertakings from Russian exporters.

2. Advantages and drawbacks of undertakings for exporters

Undertaking has following advantages for an exporter:
- ➤ The additional income resulting from the price increase ends up in their pockets, whereas anti-dumping duties goes straight to the Community.[302]
- ➤ Undertakings can be terminated on short notice if the situation on the market changes, whereas duties remain in force for at least five years unless a review procedure is successful.
- ➤ The geographical scope of an undertaking may be limited to a particular region of the EU.[303]

However undertaking has also several disadvantages for exporters:
- ➤ Undertakings have a direct effect on the price of the exported product, which have to be increased. In contrast, the effect of an anti-dumping duty is less immediate.
- ➤ It is possible to reduce the price only after the approval of the EU Commission, i.e. time consuming.
- ➤ It takes more effort to comply with undertaking (the obligation to file undertaking reports, to provide information on undertaking, etc[304]), whereas the collection of duties is automatic. In case if the report is not provided in time, as a rule it will be considered as a breach of he undertaking.

3. Monitoring of undertakings

As undertakings have to provide the same remedial effect as the alternative duties would do, the examination, adaptation and drafting of undertaking offers has to be based on a double assessment of risk and effectiveness. In order to allow the Commission to monitor whether or not the undertakings are being respected, the parties concerned have to submit regular sales reports, normally every quarter. They also have to provide the Commission with any other information that is considered necessary, and to allow verification of such data and any other rele-

---

[302] In theory, it is possible for an importer to obtain a refund of anti-dumping duties paid if it can show that the amount of duty collected exceeds the dumping margin. In practice, the refund procedure under the Art.11 of Regulation 384/96 is cumbersome, as it requires importers to make a request to the customs authorities of the member state into which the goods were imported within three months of the time of importation. (See Van Bael/Bellis, EC Anti-dumping Laws, p. 239)

[303] Regulation 434/96, Art. 8(3)

[304] See Art 8 (7) which provides that: The Commission shall require any exporter from which an undertaking has been accepted to provide, periodically, information relevant to the fulfillment of such undertaking, and to permit verification of pertinent data. Non-compliance with such requirements shall be construed as a breach of he undertaking.

vant information at their premises, even at short notice.[305] In case of breach or withdrawal of undertakings, a duty is imposed.

The amendments of March 2004 modified the rules concerning withdrawal of undertakings, which are applicable to all investigations initiated after the entry of amendments into force. In accordance with Art. 8 (9) in cases where the exporter does not respect the engagement and price undertakings need to be withdrawn, the Commission by a single act will withdraw the price undertaking and will replace it with duties. Before two legal acts were needed, one to withdraw the undertaking and a second one to re-impose an anti-dumping duty.

The amendments introduced also paragraph 2 of Art. 8 (9) providing that "any interested party or Member State may submit information showing prima facie evidence of a breach of an undertaking. The subsequent assessment of whether or not a breach of an undertaking has occurred shall normally be concluded within six months, but in no case later than nine months following a duly substantiated request." This means that the company whose undertaking was accepted from now on is under double control: of the Commission and of interested parties, i.e. potential competitors.

At the moment of writing there are 5 undertakings of Russian exporters in force.

III. Imposition of different forms of duties on the examples of cases of Russian exporters

In order to show how lengthy anti-dumping measures against some products can be the author will examine 3 cases of export of Russian fertilizers to the Community. As a rule the measures are in force much longer than normal 5 years due to the active use of review investigations by the Community industry. In practice this means that some Russian products are excluded from the EU market for more than a decade. Regarding the case Urea originating in Russia, the author would like to emphasize, that if the EU will let the measure expire on 10.15.2006 without continuation of measures, the anti-dumping measures against this product would have been in force for 20 years. This fact proves that anti-dumping measures are used to protect some sensitive sectors of market. In two examined cases, i.e. Ammonium nitrate and Urea, as well as in case Solutions of urea and ammonium nitrate originating in, inter alia, Russia[306] the European Fertilizer Manufacturers' Association, representing the major producers of nitrogen-based fertilizers in Europe,[307] was a complainant. Its mission is to identify, support and manage the common interests of its members, which are carried out mostly by initiating successive and mostly successful anti-dumping cases

---

[305] Commission of the European Communities, 21st Anti-dumping report, 2002, p. 46

[306] Commission Regulation (EC) No 617/2000 of 16 March 2000, OJ L 075 , 24.03.2000 p. 0003 – 0017

[307] Detailed about EFMA activities at: http://www.efma.org. The major news and price releases are dedicated Anti-dumping.

against foreign competitors. In this context it is no wonder that the "Fortress Europe" theme,[308] concerning the possible protectionist implications of anti-dumping measures, which started at the end of 80-s is still at the centre of public debate. Regarding the decade-long protection of the EU fertilizer market through anti-dumping measures there is an expression "Fertilizer Fortress Europe".

The Case Potassium chloride will be examined in detail, whereas cases Ammonium nitrate and Urea will be described in the form of tables, showing in chronological order all legal actions concerning the anti-dumping investigations against these products.

1. Potassium chloride

Potassium chloride demonstrates a very complicated case. In general Russian export of potassium chloride has been under EU anti-dumping measures since 1992. The EU anti-dumping measures in form of combined duties in period from 1994 to 2000 had practically excluded the imports of Potassium chloride to the Community. The only possibility of exports for years had been an inward processing. In 2000 the form of measures was changed but not repealed.

Originally anti-dumping measures against potassium chloride originating in, inter alia, in Russia were imposed by the Council Regulation Nr. 3068/92.[309] The duty was equal to the difference between the minimum prices and the net, free-at-Community-frontier price before customs clearance. However, less than one year after imposition of measures, by a notice published on 26 June 1993[310] the Commission initiated an interim review. As a result Council Regulation Nr. 643/94[311] amended the duty as a combination of minimum price and fixed duty. This type of measure was warranted because circumvention of the original duties had been taking place. The further ground for amendment of the form of duty was the findings of the Commission that due to the high overcapacity for the production of potash in the exporting countries concerned, the lack of domestic purchasers and the corresponding availability of large quantities for export and, on the other hand, the relative attractiveness of the Community market compared with other export markets, there could be a possibility that the exporters would further lower their export prices.

In four years measures were amended by Council Regulation Nr. 449/98.[312]

---

[308] See e.g. Van Bael/Bellis, EC Anti-dumping Laws, p. 57, Egeln/Klann, Antidumpingpolitik der EG, p.80

[309] Council Regulation (EEC) No 3068/92 of 23.10.1992, OJ L 308 , 24.10.1992 P. 0041 – 0045

[310] OJ No C 175, 26. 6. 1993, p. 10.

[311] Council Regulation (EC) No 643/94 of 21 March 1994, OJ L 080 , 24.03.1994 P. 0001 - 0007

[312] Council Regulation (EC) No 449/98 of 23.02.1998,OJ L 058 , 27.02.1998 P. 0015 - 0026

This time the interim review was initiated by the International Potash Company, a Russian exporter of potassium chloride on behalf of the Belarusian and Russian producers. The applicant claimed that the EU Enlargement of 1995 had resulted in a change in the circumstances on the basis of which the measures in force had been established. It also submitted that in 1994, export prices had to be based on facts available whereas it was now prepared to cooperate. Finally, it argued that the form of the measures should be re-examined since it disproportionately impeded its normal trading activity with the Community. However, the form of the measures remained a combination of a minimum price with a specific duty, but was adapted in accordance with the findings of the investigation.

8 June 1998 the International Potash Company (the applicant) brought the action for annulment of Article 1 of Regulation Nr.449/98 before the Court of First Instance. [313] The applicant contested the legality of combination of a form of duty as a combination of a fixed duty and a variable duty. The applicant claimed, that, by imposing a duty, which is variable or fixed, whichever is the higher, the Council introduced a duty in excess of the dumping margin and therefore infringed Art. 9(4) of the Basic Regulation. Moreover, the applicant claimed breach of the principle of proportionality laid down in Article 5 of the EC Treaty because the imposition of a variable duty alone would have been sufficient to achieve the objectives of the Basic Regulation.

The Court stated that, in the present case, it was precisely the fact that the variable duty had been circumvented, which led the Community Institutions to impose a combination of fixed and variable duties. Consequently, the action was dismissed in its entirety.

In March 1999, following a request lodged by the European Association of Potash Producers representing the Community Industry, the investigation was initiated as a combined expiry and interim review (limited to the form of the duty).[314] At the outcome of the investigation the form of measures was at last amended.[315] It was considered to amend the form of the measures by eliminating the minimum-price component while retaining the fixed duty element.

In accordance with the rec. 125 of the Regulation, "since the current form of anti-dumping measures has had the effect of practically excluding imports of the product concerned, other than those destined for inward processing, and consequently of eliminating a significant source of supply on this market, it is concluded that there are no compelling reasons against the prolongation of the exist-

---

[313] Judgment of the Court of First Instance of 29 September 2000, Case T-87/98, (International Potash Company v Council), ECR 2000 Page II-03179

[314] OJ C 80, 23.3.1999, p. 9.

[315] Council Regulation (EC) No 969/2000 of 8 May 2000 imposing a definitive anti-dumping duty on imports of potassium chloride originating in Belarus, Russia and Ukraine, OJ L 112 , 11/05/2000 P. 0004 - 0026

ing anti-dumping measures, but that it is in the interest of the Community to change the form of measures".

Proposals for an undertaking offered by Russian exporter were rejected by the Commission on the grounds that "in the absence of sufficient guarantees by the exporter and the Russian government, they could not be effectively monitored or enforced and that furthermore the risk of compensatory pricing of the product concerned imported into the Community under the inward processing regime could not be excluded."

It is interesting to note, that the Regulation, which amended the form of duty is dated earlier (8 May 2000) than the Judgement of the Court (29 September 2000), which confirmed the combination of duties.

Table 18. Form of anti-dumping duties Case Potassium chloride originating in, inter alia, in Russia (anti-dumping measures in force since 23.04.1992)		
Date	Law/Legal action	Form of Duty
31. 10.1990	Notice of Initiation of anti-dumping investigation pursuant the complaint of European Potash Producers' Association, acting on behalf of producers accounting for the Community's entire potash output, OJ C 274, 31. 10. 90	
23.04.1992	Commission Regulation No 1031/92, OJ L 110 , 28.04.92 (Imposing Provisional duties)	Difference between the minimum prices and the net free-at-Community-frontier-price, not cleared through customs.
23.10.1992	Council Regulation Nr. 3068/92, OJ L 308 , 24.10.92 (Imposing Definitive duties)	Confirmation of provisional duties
26.06.1993	Notice of initiation of interim review by the Commission, OJ C145, 26.06.93	
21.03.1994	Council Regulation No 643/94, OJ L 080, 24.03.94 (Imposing Definitive duties)	Amendment of form of duty. Combination of a minimum price with a specific duty.
5.08.1996	Notice of initiation of interim review pursuant to request of Russian exporter, OJ C 201, 5.08.95	
23.02.1998	Council Regulation No 449/98, OJ L 058, 27.02.98 (Imposing Definitive duties)	Amendment of measures. The form of the measures remained, but the minimum

		prices and fixed duties were adapted in accordance with the findings of the investigation.
08.06.1998	International Potash Company challenged the legality of combined duty of Regulation 449/98 before the Court, Case T-87/98	
23.3.1999	Notice of initiation of an expiry review pursuant the request of the European Association of Potash Producers on behalf of producers, acting on behalf of producers accounting for the 99% of Community's entire potash output and an interim review (limited to the form of the duty) on the Commission's initiative, OJ C 80, 23.3.99	
8.05.2000	Council Regulation No 969/2000, 8.05.00	Amendment of the form of the measures by eliminating the minimum-price component while retaining the fixed duty element. Valid duty – EUR 19,61-40,63 per tonne (specific)
29.09.2000	Judgment of the Court of First Instance of 29 September 2000, Case T-87/98, (International Potash Company v Council)	The action was dismissed in its entirety. The combination of measures in Regulation 449/98 was not considered illegal.

2. Ammonium nitrate

Table 19. Form of anti-dumping duties Case Ammonium nitrate originating in, inter alia, in Russia (Anti-dumping measures in force since 13.04.1994)		
Date	**Law/Legal action**	**Form of duty**
24. 11. 1992	Notice of initiation of anti-dumping investigation pursuant the complaint of the Fertilizer Manufacturers' Association on behalf of the producers representing the whole production of ammonium nitrate in the UK, OJ No C 306, 24. 11.92	

13.04.1994	94/293/EC: Commission Decision of 13.04.94, OJ L 129, 21.5.94 (regional anti-dumping proceeding – UK market)	Quantitative undertaking limiting exports to UK to 100 000 tonnes (breached within the first year of operation)
09.06.1994	Notice of initiation of anti-dumping investigation pursuant the complaint of European Fertilizer Manufacturers' Association (EFMA) on behalf of producers representing major proportion of Community production. OJ No C 158, 9.06.94 (Community-wide investigation)	
23.08.1995	Council Regulation No 2022/95 of 16.08.95 OJ L 198, 23.08.95	The variable anti-dumping duty: the difference between ECU 102,9 per tonne net of product and the net CIF price, Community frontier before customs clearance, in all cases where this is lower.
29.05.1997	Notice of initiation of Anti-absorption investigation pursuant the request of EFMA, OJ C 162, 29.05.97, p. 5.	
23.03.1998	Council Regulation No 663/98 of 23.03.98, OJ L 93, 26.03.98	Amendment of duty. Specific duty ECU 26,3 per tonne
23.8.2000	Notice of initiation of expiry and interim review pursuant to the request of EFMA, OJ C 239, 23.8.00	
15.04.2002	Council Regulation No 658/2002 of 15.04.02, OJ L 102, 18.04.02	Amendment of duty. Valid duty - EUR 47,07 per tonne (specific)

3. Urea

Table 20. Form of anti-dumping duties Case Urea in Russia (Anti-dumping measures in force since 08.05.1987)		
Date	**Law/Legal action**	**Form of duty**
11. 10. 1986	Notice of initiation of anti-dumping investigation pursuant the complaint of Common Market Committee of	

	the Nitrogen and Phosphate Fertilizer Industry, OJ No C 254, 11. 10. 1986	
8.05.1987	Commission Regulation No 1289/87 of 8.05.87, OJ L 121, 09.05.87	Provisional duty (minimum price)-the amount by which the price per tonne net, free-at-Community-frontier, before duty, is less than 133 ECU
04.11.1987	Council Regulation No 3339/87 of 4.11.87, OJ L 317, 07.11.87	Undertaking
21.02.1989	Commission Decision of 21.02.89, OJ L 052, 24.02.89	Undertaking confirmed
27.03.1993	Notice of initiation of interim review on the Commission's initiative, OJ No C 87, 27.03.93	
16.01.1995	Council Regulation No 477/95 of 16.01.95, OJ L 049, 04.03.995	Definitive duty (variable duty on the basis of a minimum import price) is the difference between ECU 115 per tonne and the net, free-at-Community frontier price, before customs clearance, if this price is lower
12.05.1995	European Fertilizer Manufacturers Association (EFMA) brought an action for annulment of duties imposed by Regulation No 477/95 in order to adopt more stringent measures	
17.12.1997	Judgment of the Court of First Instance of 17.12.97, Case T-121/95 (EFMA v. Council)	Application dismissed
4.3.2000	Notice of initiation of expiry review pursuant the request of the EFMA, OJ C 62, 4.3.2000	
07.05.2001	Council Regulation No 901/2001 of 7.05.01	Continuation of measures Valid duty - the difference between ECU 115 per tonne and the net, free-at-Community frontier price, before customs clearance, if this price is lower (variable duty on the basis of a minimum import price)

7.05.2001	Council Regulation No 901/2001 of 7.05.01, OJ L 127 , 09.05.01	
13.06.2002	Notice on the initiation of partial interim review on the Commission' initiative in order to examine the appropriateness of the form of the measures in force, OJ C 140, 13.6.02	
22.12.2003	Council Regulation (EC) No 2228/2003 of 22.12.03, OJ L 339, 24.12.03	The partial interim review terminated without amending duty in force

Conclusion of Part two

Anti-Dumping law has always been, and it still is, by far the most important instrument Community authorities may use to secure protection against unwanted imports. On 31 December 2003 156 EU anti-dumping measures were in force, 12 of which were against Russian exports. Russia along with China, India, Taiwan, Thailand and Republic of Korea is the country most targeted by the EU anti-dumping measures. In general more than 60 products from 34 countries are covered by the EU anti-dumping measures. Anti-Dumping actions tend to be favoured over other trade remedies because they offer the possibility for a selective approach and it does not entitle the exporting country to any compensation. Furthermore, the methodology used in anti-dumping law can give rise to high dumping margins and duties unrelated to the actual market situation. As the legal analysis of the present Chapter has shown, the EU anti-dumping law is very flexible in interpretation of definitions of dumping and injury. The rules are so vague, that the discretion of the EU Commission plays the decisive role. The majority of rules provide for calculating weighted average and constructed prices instead of prices in the real course of trade. In addition to the many options in terms of methodology expressly provided for under the Regulation, the Community authorities have further amplified their discretionary powers by way of a "creative" interpretation of the Regulations. The only consistency in the Community's "ad hoc" interpretation of the Regulation would appear to be that higher dumping margins are thus being arrived at. It has a consequence that very often unfavourable outcome for exporters is produced.

Therefore, anti-Dumping proceedings, instead of aiming solely at restoring prices in the market to fair levels, are now being used to give European industry a chance to get its act together in the face of global competition. It can be seen that due to the possibility of selection of protected industries, some of them, for example fertilizer industry, are protected by anti-dumping measures for decades. The worst case is the urea market, which has been protected for almost 20 years. Logically, the wide discretion enjoyed by the EU Commission presupposes the existence of a system of checks and balances to make sure that the discretion is not abused. However in the absence of a meaningful control by the European Parliament over the discretionary powers of the Commission and Council, it remains for the European Court of Justice to provide the necessary checks and balances. Unfortunately, the Court of Justice has thus far refused to interfere with the considerable discretion enjoyed by the Community authorities when interpreting the Anti-Dumping Regulation, limiting the scope of review to procedural issues. Almost all cases brought by the Russian exporters in anti-dumping were lost. Therefore, it makes the possibility of review of anti-dumping measures almost impossible within the EU system.

In addition to the exporters and importers, the obvious victims of this state of play in the EU are the users and consumers that pay higher prices. Their interests tend to suffer from being neglect. Furthermore, one may rightly wonder whether in the end even European industry's interests are being served by the kind of protection resulting from anti-dumping activities.

It has often been stated that anti-dumping proceedings act as a guarantee of safety and fairness in a liberal trade order. However, this thesis is only valid if all interested parties can have full faith and confidence in the ultimate fairness of the system. The system's credibility presupposes transparent procedures, objective findings and a comprehensive judicial review instead of today's obscure results of backroom computations, which tend to remain unchecked by the Court in issues beyond procedural. In practice this state of play on the eve of the EU enlargement only proves the fears of building of "Fortress Europe".

Table 21.

Number of EU anti-dumping measures against Russian exports (1996-2003)			
Year	Measures against Russian exporters	Total EU measures	Share in total EU measures
1996	12	144	8,3%
1997	14	138	10,4%
1998	12	139	8,6%
1999	11	151	7,3%
2000	11	175	6,3%
2001	11	175	6,3%
2002	11	174	6,3%
2003	12	156	7,7%
Average	11,7	156,5	7,5%
Source: European Commission, the Community's Anti-dumping annual reports from the Commission to the European Parliament			

Table 22.

EU anti-dumping measures against Russian exports[316]				
State: 01.03.2004				
Product	**Measure**	**Level**	**Law**	**Normal expiry**
1. Aluminium foil (Аллюминиевая фольга)	Duties (ad-valorem)	14,9%	Council Reg. (EC) No 950/2001 14.05.2001, L 134, 17.5.2001, p. 1	18.05.06
	Undertakings		Commission Dec. No 2001/381/EC 16.05.2001, L 134 17.05.2001, p. 67	
2. Ammonium nitrate (Нитрат аммония)	Duties (specific)	47,07EUR/T	Council Reg. (EC) No 658/2002 15.04.2002, L 102 18.04.2002, p. 1	19.04.07
3. Grain-oriented electrical steel sheets (Трансформатор-ная сталь)	Duties (ad valorem)	40,10%	Council Reg. (EC) No 151/2003 27.01.2003, L 25 30.01.2003, p.7	31.01.08
	Undertakings (are parallel to definitive du-ties)			
4. Potassium chloride (Хлористый калий)	Duties (specific)	19,61-40,63 EUR/T	Council Reg. (EC) No 969/2000 08.05.2000, L 112 11.05.2000, p. 4	12.05.05

[316] Source: a list updated weekly of all anti-dumping and anti-subsidy measures either in force and or under current investigation
http://europa.eu.int/comm/trade/issues/respectrules/anti_dumping/stats.htm

5. Seamless steel pipes and tubes (Бесшовные трубы)	Duties (ad valorem)	26,80%	Council Reg. (EC) No 2320/97 17.11.97, L 322 25.11.97, p. 1 as last amended by Council Reg. (EC) No 190/2000 24.01.2000, L 23 28.01.2000, p. 78	an expiry and an interim review on-going
	Undertakings accepted for 3 exporters		Commission Dec. No 2000/70/EC 22.12.1999	
	Anti-circumvention		L 178 17.07.2003, p.9	On-going
6. Silicon carbide (Карбид кремния)	Duties (ad valorem)	23,30%	Council Reg. (EC) No 1100/2000 22.05.2000, L 125 26.05.2000, p. 3.	27.05.05
	Undertaking		Commission Dec. No 94/202/EC 09.03.94 prolonged by above Council Reg., L 94 13.04.94, p. 32	
7. Solutions of urea and ammonium nitrate (Раствор мочевины и нитрата аммония)	Duties (specific)	17,90 - 20,11EUR/T	Council Reg. (EC) No 1995/2000 18.09.2000, L 238 22.09.2000, p. 15 at last amended by Council Reg. (EC) No. 1675/2003 22.09.2003, L.238 25.09.2003 p.4	23.09.05

8. Steel ropes and cables (Стальные тросы и канаты)	Duties (ad valorem)	36,1% - 50,7%	Council Reg. (EC) No 1601/2001 02.08.2001, L 211 04.08.2001, p. 1 as last amended by Council Reg. (EC) No 1268/2003 15.07.2003, L 180 18.07.2003, p. 23	05.08.06
	Undertaking		Commission Dec. No 2001/602/EC 26.07.2001, L 211 04.08.2001, p. 47	
9. Tube and pipe fittings, of iron or steel (Фиттинги)	Duties (ad valorem)	43,30%	Council Reg. (EC) No 1514/2002 19.08.2002, L 228 24.08.2002, p. 1 At last amended by Council Reg. (EC) No. 778/2003 05.05.2003	25.08.07
10. Urea (Мочевина)	Duties	Minimum export price	Council Reg. (EC) No 901/2001 07.05.2001, L 127 09.05.2001, p. 11	10.05.06
11. Silicon metal Металлический кремний	Duties (ad valorem)	22,7-23,6%	L339, 24.12.2003, p. 3	25.12.08

Table 23.

Definitive anti-dumping measures in force against Russian exports Years 1996-2003. As on 31 December of each year (D for Duties, U for Undertaking)								
Product/ Year	1996	1997	1998	1999	2000	2001	2002	2003
Aluminium foil						D/U	D/U	D/U
Ammonium nitrate	D	D	D	D	D	D	D	D
Calcium metal	D	D	D					
Ferro-chrome (low carbon)	D	D	D	D				
Ferro-silico-marganese	D	D						
Ferro-silicon	D	D	D	D	D			
Grain-oriented electrical steel shits (big)	D/U	D/U	D/U	D/U	D/U	D/U	D/U	D/U
Hardboard				D	D	D	D	D
Isobutanol	D	D	D					
Magnesium, un-wrought	D	D	D/U	D/U	D/U			
Pig iron	D	D						
Potassium chloride	D	D	D	D	D	D	D	D
Seamless pipes and tubes		D	D	D	D/U	D/U	D/U	D/U
Silicon carbide	D	D	D/U	D/U	D/U	D/U	D/U	D/U
Silicon metal								D
Steel ropes and cables						D/U	D/U	D/U
Tube and pipe fitting, of iron or steel							D	D
Urea	D	D	D	D	D	D	D	D
Urea and am-monium nitrate solutions					D	D	D	D
Zinc (un-wrought, unal-loyed)		D	D	D	D	D		
Total measures	12	14	12	11	11	11	11	12

PART THREE. RUSSIA'S STATUS AS A MARKET ECONOMY COUNTRY GRANTED BY THE EU IN 2002

A. Historical Analysis

I. Background
In May 2002, the European Union took a decision to grant a full and unconditional market economy status to the Russian Federation. In response to that decision the Commission Services prepared a new amendment to the Basic Anti-dumping Regulation[317], which was subsequently adopted by the Council and published in the Official Journal of the European Communities on 7 November 2002[318]. The amendments of the EU anti-dumping legislation mean, that for the calculation of dumping margins, costs and prices will in the first place be taken from the Russian market. This is supposed to give Russian exporters a better possibility to have their individual situation accurately reflected as compared to the so-called analogue country approach[319], which used to be normally applied and which refers to a substantial part to prices and costs in a third country markets. For the purpose of anti-dumping proceedings, Russia, had, up to entry of the abovementioned amendment into force, not been considered as having a market economy because of the extent of State influence on individual companies. In these cases a single dumping margin was calculated for the whole country using data from a third country with a market economy.

The market economy status of Russia could favour the establishment of positive image of the country and was a big step towards the Russian accession to the WTO.

The problem of market economy status was raised for the first time as far back as in the late 1980s; it was also actively discussed during the conclusion of the Partnership and Cooperation Agreement of 1994, which actually laid down the trade regime between Russia and the EU according to market economy criteria. Since then Russia's non-market status had the only real implication for the EU-Russia trade: application of special provisions of anti-dumping procedures against products originating in Russia.

Russian officials regularly raised the problem of the market economy status in 1994–98. These claims were supported by the argument that in the period of major economic reforms, the Russian economy greatly suffered from the EU anti-

---

[317] Proposal for a Council Regulation further amending Council Regulation (EC) No. 384/1996 on the protection against dumped imports from countries not members of the European Communities (presented by the Commission), 19.08.2002, COM (2002) 467 final.
[318] OJ L 305 of 7.11.2002, p.1
[319] More detailed on the concept of analogue country in the EU anti-dumping law see Chapter III 2. "The concept of analogue country in the EU Anti-dumping legislation".

dumping duties[320]. At last some amendments were made in anti-dumping regulation of the EU in 1998 under the pressure of Russian diplomacy. Thereunder individual Russian companies were eligible to be granted market economy status
on an individual basis, if they could show that they operated under normal market economy conditions. EU officials tried to present these amendments as the
definitive solution of the problem and as de facto rendering of market economy
status for Russia[321]. In practice, the status of the Russian producers did not
change considerably[322]. Thus, EU anti-dumping policy towards Russia and the
problem of market economy status of Russia remained very important for Russia
after the changes in the EU anti-dumping legislation in 1998. Besides, since
1994, the EU anti-dumping policy towards Russia did not correspond to economic and political reality; it was a survival of the past used as an instrument of
closing western markets for Russian producers, which could by any reason make
a competition for western commodities[323]. So, since 1994 non-market status of
Russia according to EU legislation had only one practical consequence – an application of special treatment during the anti-dumping proceeding against Russian producers. Annual losses for the Russian economy from EU anti-dumping
duties were about 200-250 million US dollars in period 1994-1998[324]. EU anti-
dumping duties were imposed on 10% of Russian industrial export, primarily
chemical and metallurgical, to the EU and established appreciable obstacles for
the development of potential points of growth in these industries.

One may find strange that such attention is paid to the history of the problem,
because after the EU statement at the May 2002 EU-Russia Summit about the
intention to grant Russia market economy status all these claims seemed to lose
their urgency. First of all, let us try to investigate the reasons for such a cardinal

[320] Kaveshnikov, Three stories about Strategic Partnership between Russia and the European
Union, p. 3

[321] For example, Deputy Head of the Delegation of the European Commission in Russia Gil-
bert Dubois expressed this point of view on some conferences in 1998-99, see Kaveshnikov,
Three stories about Strategic Partnership between Russia and the European Union, p. 4.

[322] MacLean, The impact of the EC's conditional market economy principle in Chinese and
Russian AD cases, p. 65

[323] This fact was evident even for many officials of the Commission. For example, a high official of the EU in an unofficial conversation with a Russian diplomat in the autumn 2001 expressed the idea to make market economy criteria for Russian producers much softer. (See:
Kaveshnikov, Three stories about Strategic Partnership between Russia and the European Union, p.3. Author's interview with a high official of Russian Delegation to the European Communities, December 2001.)

[324] According to the unofficial calculation, the damage was about 200 million US dollars in
1998 (Kaveshnikov N. EU Antidumping Policy Goes on Damaging Russian Economy, Euro,
5, 1999, p. 29. Deputy Minister of economic development and trade Maxim Medvedkov
evaluated it at the level of $230-240 million in 2002 (On the press-conference of Deputy Min-
ister of economic development M. Medvedkov, communication of 30 May 2002, available
online at: www.mid.ru).

change in the EU's position. During last years the EU related granting of market economy status for Russia with the low oil and gas prices at the Russian domestic market, considering these low prices as a hidden subsidy to Russian producers. Low energy prices at the domestic market are conditions sine qua non not even for the development but for the existence of the Russian economy. Romano Prodi's decision at the May 2002 summit in the absence of any significant concessions from the Russian side was unexpected for foreign ministry officials of the Member States[325]. It is evident that EU principal decision to grant Russia the market economy status was taken not because the EU devoted much attention to the interests of its strategic partner, but because the EU did not want to be stay behind the USA[326].

EU activity after the May 2002 Summit gave another argument for this thesis. The EU anti-dumping amendments 2002 introduced certain changes to EU general anti-dumping regime, which expressly empower the Commission services to apply non-market economy treatment techniques in respect to countries, which, although enjoying full market economy status under EU anti-dumping law, may have certain "non-market" features. The Commission's practice to date and opinions of practitioners suggest that these changes are essentially tailor-made for Russian exporters.[327] Although these amendments are applied to all countries, but evidently they will act primarily against countries that are not members of the WTO, because WTO members can contest these provisions in the WTO judicial bodies. One should not be surprised that the amendment to the anti-dumping legislation became an object of sharp criticism. For example, Deputy Minister of economic development and trade of the Russian Federation and Head of Russia WTO accession team Maxim Medvedkov said that the proposal was an attempt to implement double standards and was aimed to deprive Russia of its "natural advantages like cheap energy, labor and raw materials.[328]" He added, that in fact the 2002 amendments to the European anti-dumping legislation mean the continuation of the previous EU trade regime towards Russia, when it was a non-market economy country.

---

[325] Moreover, this decision was meet by many member states with sharp discontent. For example, an official of Russian Embassy in France, interviewed by Mr. Kaveshnikov in July 2002, told about such a reaction of the French diplomats. (See Kaveshnikov, Three stories about Strategic Partnership between Russia and the European Union, p.4)

[326] At the Russia-US summit President George W. Bush proclaimed that the United States "expects to make its final decision on whether Russia should be treated as a market economy no later than June 14, 2002."

[327] See e.g. Borovikov/Evtimov, EC treatment of non-market economies in anti-dumping law, p.4

[328] On comments on amendments proposed to EU antidumping legislation, communication of 30 May 2002, loaded from the site of MFA RF – www.mid.ru

However, given the universal scope of application of the amendments of 2002, one cannot exclude the possibility that one day they could affect the interests of other WTO members exporting to the EU. Furthermore, Russia will very soon become a fully-fledged member of WTO. Should that happen, the issue of consistency of the new amendments with WTO rules will inevitably arise.

The objective of the present Chapter is to analyse the history and state of play of the EU anti-dumping treatment of Russia in light of the rules of the multilateral trading system. The author takes as a starting point the relevant WTO rules currently in force. The following part of the present study will demonstrate how the EU anti-dumping practice towards Russia as a past "non-market economy" country developed trough the years. The author will examine the essence of the 2002 amendments to the EU Basic Anti-dumping Regulation 384/96 and their consistence with the WTO rules. It will be shown, whether the present and anticipated practice of the implementation of those amendments would be in line with WTO Agreements, in particular when applied to exporters from WTO members. This is especially acute in view of the Russian accession to the WTO.

II. Market and non-market economies in the context of GATT/WTO anti-dumping rules

As an ideal a market economy could be defined as a national economy in all sectors of which supply and demand determine all production and price levels, the government does not intervene in trade, subsidies do not exist, etc. Undoubtedly, it is obvious that such an economy does not exist in reality. Therefore, it is virtually impossible to draw a precise distinction between market economies and non-market economies without some discretion, based also on political considerations.

The GATT, or now the WTO, never attempted to define non-market economies or market economies or to distinguish between the two categories. Instead, GATT/WTO rules merely state that for anti-dumping purposes only, concepts such as domestic market price or cost of production may have little relevance in the context of a state-run economy. It is worth noting in this respect that GATT 1994 and its predecessor have resolved this issue in as much as a "non-political" manner as possible[329].

In the GATT Review Session of 1954-55, a proposal by Czechoslovakia was considered to amend sub-paragraph 1(b) of GATT Article VI to deal with the special problem of establishing comparable prices in the case of a country whose trade is operated by a state monopoly. GATT members were not prepared to amend Article VI in this respect, but agreed on a respective interpretative note to address the case. As follows from the text of the interpretative note, it is no more than a statement of fact providing no specific indications as to what course of

---

[329] Borovikov/Evtimov, EC treatment of non-market economies in anti-dumping law, p.5

action investigating authorities should take in dealing with centrally planned economy dumping. In practice, the issue was left to the discretion of the national administrations. As subsequent developments have shown, the room for flexibility has been widely used.

Thus, the second Supplementary Provision to Paragraph 1 of Article VI GATT (hereinafter "Note 2")[330], which can be found in Annex I to the GATT, provides for the only multilateral rule allowing the disregard of domestic data in an exporting country by reasons of absence of market economy conditions, in the context of anti-dumping proceedings.

It states as follows:

"It is recognized that, in the case of imports from a country which has a complete or substantially complete monopoly of its trade and where all domestic prices are fixed by the State, special difficulties may exist in determining price comparability for the purposes of paragraph 1, and in such cases importing contracting parties may find it necessary to take into account the possibility that a strict comparison with domestic prices in such a country may not always be appropriate."

Therefore, GATT/WTO rules expressly provide for a set of two cumulative criteria to be applied by WTO members in their own anti-dumping regimes with respect to other WTO members, namely:

1. The existence of a State monopoly over trade; and
2. State regulation of all domestic prices.

Moreover, the disregard of data is not to be applied automatically in the case of a country meeting the two criteria. The provision leaves scope for taking into account domestic prices and costs in the state-managed economy. Naturally, with respect to countries, which are not GATT/WTO members, these criteria could be applied in a different, i.e. in a less favourable, manner.

The GATT did not suggest which alternative methods might be used to establish normal value where all domestic data is not reliable for the reasons of State control. Under these circumstances, GATT Contracting Parties developed their own approaches, at their own discretion[331]. The USA was the first to apply the so-called "analogue" (surrogate) third country method. This method was later introduced into the practice of GATT Accession Working Parties, and, in 1979, was codified in the plurilateral Tokyo Round Subsidies Code[332]. Following the Tokyo Round, that method was introduced into EU anti-dumping law as well.

---

[330] It is binding on all WTO members in itself and by virtue of Art. 2.7 of the WTO Anti-dumping Agreement

[331] Czako/Human/Miranda , A Handbook on Anti-dumping investigations, p. 35

[332] See Article 15 (applicable to both anti-dumping and anti-subsidy proceedings) of the 1979 Agreement on the Interpretation and Application of Articles VI, XVI and XXIII of GATT (hereinafter "1979 Subsidies Code"). The Tokyo Round Subsidies Code was a plurilateral accord agreed upon mainly by OECD members. Article 15 thereof did not withstand the test of

The essence of such developments in the national anti-dumping laws intended to implement the GATT is that, for the purposes of dumping calculations for non-market economy countries, a market economy third country's domestic price and cost data is used for comparison with non-market economy country's export price. The non-market economy's domestic data is therefore totally disregarded, with rare exceptions for natural comparative advantages.

Many GATT Contracting Parties initially developed their anti-dumping policies in full conformity with Note 2 and the GATT. Their lists of non-market economies consisted of communist countries with centrally planned economies, which met the two criteria of Note 2. The only questionable element in those developments, in terms of GATT/WTO consistency, was that the possibility of disregarding prices was generally replaced by a mandatory prescription.

The national anti-dumping rules were GATT-consistent and economically sound until the end of 1980s. At that time, unprecedented political and economic reforms were launched in almost all of the former communist countries, including Russia.

Obviously, Note 2 is of particular importance to the entire international trading system as the only WTO clause, which contains two non-market economy criteria. The reference to the two criteria set out by Note 2 in order to distinguish between non-market economies and market economies can ensure that the principle of legal certainty in international trade is actually respected. If not constrained by Note 2, WTO Members could (and in fact some of them do, including the EU) apply their own definitions of non-market economies and market economies and consequently qualify or re-qualify third countries as non-market economies or market economies with discretion, according to their political and/or practical interests. The negative consequences of such different national trade practices might lead to undermining the credibility in the multilateral trading system.

In practice, the anti-dumping law and practices of certain WTO members such as EU so far has been evolving with the disregard of GATT/WTO regarding the determination the market and non-market economy status.

III. The concept of analogue country in the EU Anti-dumping legislation

1. Background

For better understanding of the achievements of 2002 amendments to the EU anti-dumping legislation the author finds that it is necessary to analyze the so called "analogue country concept" which used to be applied to Russian exports until 8 November 2002 and actually is still applying to investigations that were

---

multilateral consensus during the Uruguay Round, as its text or substance have not been included in any of the WTO agreements.

initiated even one week before the entry of amendments into force[333]. This concept is very important as the abovementioned amendments carry some resemblance with the concept of the analogue country and it appears that this practice could continue in future in spite of the new market economy status of Russia (see infra).

In present Art. 2 (7) of Regulation 384/96 lays down the three following rules concerning the selection of the analogue country:

1. The analogue country is to be selected in a reasonable manner, with due account taken of any reliable information made available at the time of selection.

2. Where appropriate, a market economy third country, which is subject to the same investigation, is to be used and account will also be taken of time limits.

3. The analogue country should preferably be third country. Art. 2 (7) of the Basic Regulation makes it clear that the Community may be selected as an analogue country only if the use of price or constructed value as established in a third country is not possible. The use of Community prices is clearly a solution of last resort.

However the cases where Community was chosen to be analogue county did occur, for example in Pure silk typewriter ribbon fabrics from China[334], where the Community producer and the Chinese producer were the only producers of the product in question in the world, therefore the Community was chosen as an analogue country. This practise is very dangerous as the European producers could in fact manipulate the dumping case by raising the own prices, which would entail the normal value of exporters and as a result the fair price would turn out to be a dumping price[335].

The selection of analogue countries is in many cases arbitrary and may, therefore, reflect non-representative high normal values, which significantly impact on the dumping margin calculations[336]. In a number of cases, countries, including the United States and Canada, with vastly different levels of development have been chosen[337]. From a Russian as well as Chinese perspective for exam-

---

[333] See e.g. Grain oriented electrical sheets from Russia 2003 – Brasil was chosen as analogue country in spite of opposition of Russian exporting producers (Council Regulation (EC) No 151/2003 of 27 January 2003 imposing a definitive anti-dumping duty on imports of certain grain oriented electrical sheets originating in Russia OJ L 025 , 30/01/2003 P. 0007 – 0020)

[334] Pure silk typewriter ribbon fabrics originating in the people's Republic of China, Commission Regulation (EEC) No 1937/90 of 4 July 1990, OJ L 174 , 07.07.1990 p. 0027

[335] Wessely, Antidumping- und Kartellrecht in der EG, S.51

[336] Rydelski, The Community's New Anti-Dumping Practice towards China and Russia, p. 587

[337] See e.g. Council Regulation (EC) No 969/2000 of 8 May 2000 imposing a definitive anti-dumping duty on imports of potassium chloride originating in Belarus, Russia and Ukraine, OJ L 112 , 11/05/2000 P. 0004 – 0026, analogue country - Canada; Council Regulation (EC)

ple, the very choice of such comparators totally nullified all of the most obvious advantages enjoyed by Russian companies, such as access to natural resources, cheap energy prices and cheap labor (leading, in turn, to the ability to produce low-end, labor – intensive goods cheaply) since those benefits could not be used to assist penetration of export markets when an analogue country with high, or relatively high production costs are chosen[338]. A conclusion that dumping has taken place becomes almost inevitable in these circumstances.

The European Court of Justice (ECJ) in case "Nölle"[339] has emphasized that "the choice of reference country is a matter falling within the discretion enjoyed by the institutions in analysing complex economic situations. However, the exercise of that discretion is not excluded from review by the Court." European Court of Justice has made it clear that the European Commission should take into account various factors relating to the volume and methods of production, to conditions of access to raw materials and to the prices on the domestic market in its determination of an analogue country. Following the Judgement "Nölle" the following elements governing the choice of analogue country were codified in an internal note issued by the Commission services at the end of 1992[340]:

1. the nature of the domestic market of the analogue country and, in particular, whether market forces prevail in the setting of prices and whether the market is not isolated with resulting price distortion;
2. the existence of a production of a like product to that under investigation;
3. the conditions of access to raw materials in the analogue country envisaged should be comparable to those in the country under investigation;
4. the volumes of product concerned sold on the domestic market of the envisaged analogue country should exceed the quantities exported to the EU by the third country concerned.

A review of the cases dealt with by Community authorities gives rise to a number of general comments.

2. Empirical selection process

The selection process under which analogue countries are chosen by Community authorities has been essentially empirical. EU authorities have tried to select as the analogue country a market economy country in which the like product is

---

No 658/2002 of 15 April 2002 imposing a definitive anti-dumping duty on imports of ammonium nitrate originating in Russia, OJ L 102 , 18/04/2002 P. 0001 – 0011, analogue country - USA

[338] Pouncey, 4 (1997) International Trade Law &Regulation 143.

[339] ECJ, Case C-16/90, (Detlef Nölle, trading as "Eugen Nölle" v Hauptzollamt Bremen-Freihafen), Judgment of 22 October 1991, European Court reports 1991 Page I-05163

[340] Van Bael/Bellis, EC Anti-dumping Laws, p. 316

produced with the same manufacturing processes and technical standards and on the same scale as in the non-market economy country concerned[341].

The major problem is that the choice of the analogue country takes place not in accordance with rigid rules, but mostly on case-by-case basis. It depends on very many factors. The fact is that only producing and exporting the product in questions market economy countries, in which prices are built in the process of competition, can be used as analogue country. These factors have a consequence that the choice is limited to only small circle of countries.

However, the EU Commission practice shows, that very often an analogue market economy is chosen, in which the prices are not built in accordance with market economy forces, which rises a serious doubt in an appropriateness of the analogue country concept. For example, in Sodium carbonate from the Soviet Union the European Commission chose Austria as an analogue country because "price controls in Austria ensure that price levels stand in a reasonable proportion to production costs[342]". In some other cases the countries in which the only one producer had a dominant position on the relevant market were chosen, the circumstance, which makes every reasonable person doubt that the prices are results of normal market forces[343]. For example, this issue was a ground for the reference to the European Court of Justice for preliminary ruling[344]. The Court ruled that "the mere fact that there is only one producer in the reference country does not in itself preclude the prices there from being the result of genuine competition, since such competition may just as well result, in the absence of price controls, from the presence of significant imports from other countries. Similarly, the choice of a reference country with a market economy cannot be called into question merely because that country makes imports from certain other countries subject to anti-dumping duties. The mere fact that the reference coun-

---

[341] Van Bael/Bellis, EC Anti-dumping Laws, p. 316

[342] Commission Regulation (EEC) No 2599/79 of 22 November 1979 imposing a provisional anti-dumping duty on certain sodium carbonate originating in the Soviet Union, OJ L 297 , 24/11/1979 P. 0012

[343] Wessely, Antidumping- and Kartellrecht in der EG, S. 52

[344] See Judgment of the Court (Fifth Chamber) of 29 May 1997, Case C-26/96 (Rotexchemie International Handels GmbH & Co. v Hauptzollamt Hamburg-Waltershof, Reference for a preliminary ruling: Finanzgericht Hamburg – Germany), ECR 1997 P. I-02817, OJ C 212 12.07.1997. The reference to the Court resulted from a proceeding before a German Court, which had been brought by Rotexchemie, an importer of potassium permanganate. Rotexchemie had raised objections against the application of the anti-dumping Regulation imposing definitive duties on its imports from China. The USA was selected as a reference country. The applicant considered this country to be an inappropriate choice by the reason that the U.S. market for potassium permanganate consists of only one producer, which is protected from foreign competition by anti-dumping duties. In the opinion of the Applicant, the consequences of these factors were that the prices charged in the United States were not the result of normal market forces. Therefore the inflated normal value led to an artificially high dumping margin.

try imposes anti-dumping duties on imports from certain other countries does not, therefore, support the conclusion that the prices charged in that country do not result from genuine competition." This has a clear consequence that choice of reference country falls within the very wide discretion enjoyed by the EU institutions. The further example confirming this fact and escalating the EU Commission concerns about the Russian energy prices would be a choice of Slovak Republic for Russian urea[345]. An importers' association objected to the choice of the Slovak Republic as analogue country for the following reasons: the Slovak Republic, unlike Russia, has no natural gas production. Since gas is the basic raw material for the production of urea, it is the main element in the cost of the final product. Moreover, it was claimed that the Slovak Republic is totally dependent on Russian gas and pays a very high price for it. It was therefore claimed that the use of the Slovak Republic as analogue country would artificially inflate normal value and thus result in an artificially high dumping margin. Secondly, the importers' association submitted that, given the importance of gas in the production of urea, any analogue country in this case should be a gas-producing country. The importers' association proposed Norway, Canada or Saudi Arabia as alternative analogue countries.

With regard to the first argumentation, the EU Commission emphasised, that Russian gas prices are heavily discounted on the Russian market and are not determined by market forces. Saudi Arabia was considered inappropriate because this country's legislation allows for artificially low raw material prices for the national industry using natural gas and provides investment incentives for its fertiliser industry. Therefore the choice of Slovak Republic as an analogue country was confirmed, emphasising that "prices of natural gas in the Slovak Republic were competitive and not higher than gas prices in other market economies".

In a number of cases, the analogue country was said to be "the only market economy third country producing and exporting the relevant product in substantial quantities[346].

In a number of other cases, the analogue country was selected by common agreement between the parties, most often expressed tacitly[347]. This occurred, for instance, where the analogue country suggested by the complainant was not objected to by other interested parties[348] or suggestions made by the Commis-

---

[345] Urea originating in Russia, Council Regulation (EC) No 901/2001 of 7 May 2001, OJ L 127 , 09.05.2001 P. 0011 – 0019

[346] See e.g., Lithium hydroxide from, inter alia, USSR, OJ (Council Regulation (EEC) No 191/80 of 29 January 1980, OJ L 023, 30.01.80 P. 0019). See also Potassium permanganate from, inter alia, USSR (Commission Regulation (EEC) No 1537/90 of 28 May 1990, OJ L 145 , 08/06/1990 p. 0009), where the US was chosen as analogue country as it was the only non-EEC market economy with considerable production.

[347] Van Bael/Bellis, EC Anti-dumping Laws, p. 316

[348] See e.g., Photographic enlargers from, inter alia, USSR (Commission Regulation (EEC) No 1958/82 of 16 July 1982, OJ L 212 , 21/07/82 P. 0032)

sion in the course of the proceeding were not objected to or no acceptable alternative proposal was offered by either side[349].

In cases involving both market economy and non-market economy countries, Community authorities have tended to use as an analogue one of the market economy countries already involved in the proceeding explaining it by the so-called principle of "avoidance of an additional administrative burden".[350] From this point of view it is appropriate to compare the choice of an analogue country with a lottery or a Russian roulette: the normal value and the dumping margin would depend on the fact, what country is involved in the investigation in question[351].

An analysis of recent cases confirms the above. Indeed, in almost all cases initiated since 1990, the analogue country has been selected among the market economy countries also subject to the proceedings[352]. A preference for a market economy third country which is subject to the same investigation is now expressly included in the text of art. 2 (7) of the Basic Regulation.

A following factor that plays an important role in the selection of the analogue country is whether producers in the country in question are willing (or are legally authorised) to co-operate with the investigation. In Mechanical wrist-watches and movements from, inter alia, USSR, the Commission rejected Switzerland as an analogue country on the ground that "it is not possible, by virtue of Swiss law, for officials of the Commission to carry out inspections at the premises of Swiss watch producers[353]". The Hong Kong was the only possible third country in spite of the fact that Hong Kong watch manufacturers bought parts or sub-assemblies from an outside firm whereas Soviet manufacturers produced them internally. In case when producers from suggested analogue country are not ready to disclose EU Commission prices, costs and conditions of manufacture, the EU Commission is forced to reject the suggested third country. Very often the non-cooperating parties are manufacturers from countries with low prices that are rejecting to co-operate because out of a pure and explicable fear, that disclosed data can be a reason for initiating a later EU anti-dumping investigations against themselves. For example, in Ammonium nitrate from Russia[354],

---

[349] See, e.g., Ball bearings II from, inter alia, USSR (81/406/EEC: Commission Decision of 4 June 1981, OJ L 152, 11/06/81 P. 0044.) See also Certain iron or steel ropes and cables from, inter alia, Russia (Council Regulation (EC) No 1601/2001 of 2 August 2001, OJ L 211 , 04/08/2001 P. 0001 – 0019)

350 See e.g. Urea originating , inter alia, in the USSR, Commission Regulation (EEC) No 1289/87 of 8 May 1987, OJ L 121 , 09/05/1987 p. 0011

[351] Wessely, Antidumping- and Kartellrecht in der EG, p. 54

[352] Van Bael/Bellis, EC Anti-dumping Laws, p. 316

[353] Mechanical wrist-watches originating in the USSR, Commission Regulation (EEC) No 84/82 of 14 January 1982, OJ L 011, 16/01/82 P. 0014

[354] Ammonium nitrate originating in Russia, Council Regulation (EC) No 658/2002 of 15 April 2002, OJ L 102 , 18/04/2002 P. 0001 - 0011

neither the Polish producers nor the sole Lithuanian producer were willing to cooperate. Consequently, the USA was selected as the most appropriate analogue country, in spite of the fact that European Fertiliser Import Association proposed Lithuania on the grounds of its close proximity and similar manufacturing conditions to Russia, its absence of barter trade and the fact that the sole Lithuanian producer purchases gas from a Russian supplier. In the latest case Grain oriented sheets from Russia[355] the fact that neither Czech Republic nor Poland were willing to cooperate led to the choice of Brazil, the only producer of the relevant product on the market with completely different conditions of manufacture then that on the Russian market.

From the practice of the Commission Services, described supra, one can draw a conclusion, that the concept of an analogue country has a big level of an abstraction side by side with an administrative arbitrariness[356]. The meaning and the irrational consequences of the choice of an analogue country can be shown on an example of the case brought before European Court of Justice[357]. In an anti-dumping investigation against imports of multi-phase electric motors from, inter alia, USSR the European Commission chose Sweden as an analogue country for calculation of provisional duty[358]. On this ground the dumping margin varied between 192% and 283%. Shortly after the provisional duties were imposed, the parallel proceeding on Yugoslav imports took place. On this ground the European Commission chose Yugoslavia for calculation of definitive anti-dumping measures[359]. The dumping margin reduced consequently to the amount between 121% and 146%.

3. Conclusion

One can point out two issues concerning the concept of analogue country. Firstly, this concept has a consequence that the exporter from non-market economy country cannot predict which prices has he to offer in order to avoid an anti-dumping investigation, because it is absolutely impossible to predict which analogue country would be chosen in the concrete case. In opposite to the ex-

---

[355] Certain grain oriented electrical sheets originating in Russia, Council Regulation (EC) No 151/2003 of 27.01.2003, OJ L 025 , 30.01.2003 P. 0007 – 0020

[356] Wessely, Antidumping- and Kartellrect in der EG, S. 49

[357] Judgment of the Court (Fifth Chamber) of 11 July 1990, Joined cases C-305/86 and C-160/87, (Neotype Techmashexport GmbH v Commission and Council of the European Communities), European Court reports 1990 Page I-02945

[358] Standardized multi-phase electric motors having an output of more than 0,75 kW but not more than 75 kW, originating, inter alia, in the USSR, Commission Regulation (EEC) No 3019/86 of 30 September 1986 OJ L 280 , 01.10.1986 p. 0068 (provisional anti-dumping duties)

[359] Standardized multi-phase electric motors having an output of more than 0,75 kW but not more than 75 kW, originating, inter alia, in the USSR, Council Regulation (EEC) No 864/87 of 23 March 1987, OJ L 083 , 27/03/1987 p. 0001 – 0013 (definitive anti-dumping duties)

porters from market economy country they cannot even prevent dumping by cutting the prices, because the domestic prices would be completely disregarded.

The second point against the concept of analogue country is that this concept contradicts the protective purpose of anti-dumping law, namely the promotion of international competition, because it deprives the companies in question of comparative advantages, such as cheap energy prices, access to raw materials, cheap labour and etc. This questions the whole concept of anti-dumping law.

Even western scholars recognize that the calculation of normal value on the basis of third country is inadequate and may violate WTO antidumping provisions. The application of this procedure deprived Russian producers of their rights to use available natural concurrency advantages, despite that the Joint Declaration in Relation to Article 18 of Partnership and Cooperation Agreement provide that these advantages should be taken into account. Consequently, the anti-dumping margin increased and the higher anti-dumping duties were imposed. Moreover, as the actual costs of the non-market country producer are not taken into account, Russian export to the EU was often considered as dumping even when the export price of the product was higher then the price at the home market. Anti-dumping duties imposed on Russians products were and remain to be often of a prohibitive character.

IV. Market and non-market economies in the EU anti-dumping law. Historical overview

1. The period 1968-1994 – Russia as a State trading country

The special rules for the determination of normal value applicable to imports from "non-market economy" countries first appeared in the anti-dumping Regulation No. 1681/79, without, meanwhile, providing any definition of the term.[360] Instead, complimentary regulations set out an explicit list of countries to which a special procedure was to apply.[361] It is interesting to note, that the very first anti-dumping legislation of the European Community, Council Regulation Nr. 459/68 specifically indicated that the special procedure with regard to normal value determinations had to apply in respect of countries "where trade is on a basis of near or total monopoly and where domestic prices are fixed by the

---

[360] Council Regulations (EEC) 1681/79 of August 1979 (OJ L 196, 02.08.1979, p. 0089-0103) and 3017/79 of 20 December 1979 (OJ L 339, 31.12.1979) on protection against dumped or subsidised imports from countries not members of the EEC.

[361] List of state trading countries of that period of time can be found in Council Regulation (EEC) Nr. 925/79 of May 1979 on common rules for imports from State trading countries, OJ L. 131, 29.05.1979, p.0001 and the following Council Regulation (EEC) Nr. 1756/82, OJ L 195, 05.07.1982, p.0001-0020 and included besides Soviet Union also Bulgaria, Hungary, Poland, Romania, Czechoslovakia, German Democratic Republic, North Korea, Mongolia

State",[362] i.e. almost verbally (the word "all" dropped) reproduced the relevant text of the Note 2.

The lack of any substantive criteria for distinguishing market economy from non-market economy in EU legislation have nearly been admitted by the European Court of Justice. The European Court of Justice has relied (although without reference to the GATT) on the two criteria set by the GATT's Note2, using the wording of old anti-dumping regulation 459/68. It can thus be claimed, that Note 2 is the single legal yardstick enabling a meaningful distinction between non-market economies and market economies.[363] In considering whether former Yugoslavia was an appropriate market economy third country, the European Court of Justice held:

"It must therefore be examined whether in that country trade in electric motors is subject to a total or near monopoly or whether all domestic prices are fixed by the State. The two conditions are not satisfied in case of Yugoslavia...[364]".

However, one can notice the modifications to the scope of application of the two criteria, which the European Court of Justice brought into his judgment. The GATT's "complete or substantially complete monopoly" over trade in a country was turned into monopoly of trade in a single economic sector. Moreover, the cumulative application of the two criteria, prescribed by the GATT, was changed to alternative.

Nonetheless, until the early 1990s, in spite of the EC's legislative departure from GATT rules in terms of terminology and conditions for disregard of exporters' domestic data, the EU anti-dumping practice remained generally consistent with the GATT. This was due to the fact that those countries listed and treated as non-market economies had remained countries with state-run economies[365].

Indeed, upon the perestroika processes initiated by President Gorbachev, the Soviet Union was indeed a state-planned country. In the Soviet Union the state monopoly of external trade was legislatively fixed by the Decree of people's commissars of 22 April 1928 "On the nationalization of external trade".[366]

2. The period 1994-1998 - Era of economic changes in Russia and sighing of Partnership and Cooperation Agreement

By 1994, however, significant political and economic changes took place in almost all non-market economy states including Russia, which became an inde-

---

[362] OJ L 093, 17.04.1968, p.0001

[363] Borovikov/ Evtimov. EC treatment of non-market economies in anti-dumping law, p.12

[364] Judgment of the Court (Fifth Chamber) of 11 July 1990, Joined cases C-305/86 and C-160/87, (Neotype Techmashexport GmbH v Commission and Council of the European Communities), European Court reports 1990 Page I-02945

[365] Borovikov/Evtimov . EC's treatment of non-market economies in anti-dumping law

[366] Shepenko R.A., Anti-dumping procedure, p. 288.

pendent state at the end of 1991. Those processes coincided with the Uruguay Round negotiations, which led to the establishment of the WTO.

The EU realized that nearly all former Communist Bloc countries were no longer state-trading countries, in spite of the fact that neither of those countries including Russia had achieved a market economy by western standard. In any event, those of former "state-trading countries" which were already members of GATT, and/or which eventually became members of the WTO (e.g. the Czech Republic, Hungary, Poland, Romania, the Slovak Republic) could no longer remain under the EU's non-market economy treatment, which moreover was inconsistent with GATT's Note 2.

Thus, in 1994, the EU adopted a new trade policy approach with regard to the former non-market economy /state trading countries.

The EU simply replaced the term "state-trading country" by the term "certain third countries"[367]. This term included some new countries, as China, never previously referred to as a state-trading country, in the same list as the states of the former Soviet Union.

According to the doctrine, "while the old term "state-trading country" provided economic rationale to the different treatment, which the EU accorded to the countries designated as state-trading countries, the new term "certain third countries" seems to be inherently devoid of meaningful yardsticks as regards its economic content"[368]. The text of the relevant Regulation Nr. 519/94 determines the group of the "certain third countries" merely by reference to "the particular features of the economic system in the third countries in question..."[369]. The definition "particular features of the economic system" is so vague, that it is clear that its content can be determined solely according to political considerations and discretion of the EU institutions. Therefore, after this change of the legislation the scope of the notion of non-market economy in the Basic Regulation of 1994 became potentially even more dependant on the EU's discretionary policy. The analogue country method and all its negative consequences affected: "non-market economy countries and, in particular, those to which Regulation 519/94 on rules for imports from certain third countries applies[370].

The current Council Regulation (EC) Nr. 384/96 (Basic Regulation)[371], which was intended to take account of the results of the Uruguay Round, did nothing to

---

[367] Council Regulation (EC) 519/94 of 07.03.1994 on common rules for imports from certain third countries and repealing Regulations (EEC) 1765/82, 1766/82 and 3420/83, OJ L 67, 10.03.1994. The Regulation 519/94 was last amended by Regulation (EC) 427/2003.

[368] Borovikov/Evtimov, EC treatment of non-market economies in anti-dumping law, p.13

[369] See Preamble of the Regulation 519/94, cited supra

[370] Article 2 (7) of Council Regulation (EC) 3283/1194 of 22 December 1994 on protection against dumped imports from countries not members of the European Community (OJ L 349, 31.12.1994)

[371] Council Regulation (EC) Nr. 484/96 of 22.12.1995 (OJ L. 56, 6.3.1996, p.1), at last amended by Council Regulation (EC) Nr. 461/2004 of 8.03. 2004 (OJ L.77, 13.3.2004, p.12)

bring the EU's anti-dumping treatment of non-market economy countries in line with Note 2 of WTO Rules, regardless of the fact that the most non-market economy countries including Russia were on the way of the significant economic reforms. The doctrine pointed out, that "by such inaction, the EU made another critical step away from GATT/WTO Rules. When in 1979 the EU anti-dumping legislation first abandoned the two criteria of Note 2, it could justify its move with the state-run economic system of all countries the non-market economy treatment applied to. In 1996 such a justification would not have been applicable to a large part of the non-market economy countries, including Russia. The EU did not violate WTO rules in law merely because in 1996 there were no GATT/WTO members among "listed" non-market economy countries."[372]

With regard to Russia, it has been clear for some time that the legality of the EU's continued treatment of it as a non-market economy country is questionable, as the WTO definition of a centrally planned economy has become increasingly less applicable to its changed circumstances. Indeed, the EU has recognised at a political level that "Russia is no longer a state trading country, [and] that it is now a country in transition"[373] while continuing to treat Russia as a non-market economy country for anti-dumping purposes. This is one of the grounds on which the EU's decision in September 1997 to impose an anti-dumping duty on Russian exports in Unwrought, unalloyed zinc[374] was challenged before the Court of First Instance[375]. However, in this case, the Court of the First Instance dismissed the application as inadmissible on the ground that the applicant, a company established in Switzerland, was not able to show direct and individual concern[376].

3. The period from 1998 to 2002 - Conditional market economy treatment towards Russian exports

a) Background

On 1 July 1998, 7 month after entry into force of Partnership and Cooperation Agreement between Russia and the EU, the first "market economy status" amendment to the 1996 Basic Regulation entered into force[377]. The Preamble of

---

[372]Borovikov/Evtimov, EC treatment of non-market economies in anti-dumping law, p.14

[373] Preamble to Partnership and Cooperation Agreement between the EC and the Member States and Russia of 24 June 1994 which came into force 1 December 1997.

[374] Horowitz/Goddard, EU regulation on Russian Metal Trade, p. 10. (Mr.Horowitz represented the applicant before the Court of First Instance as an advokat)

[375] Action brought on 17 December 1997 by Euromin S.A. against the Council of the European Union (Case T-597/97), OJ C 72, 07.03.1998, p.17

[376] Case T-597/97 (Euromin S.A. v. Council), Judgement of 20 June 2000

[377] Council Regulation (EC) Nr. 905/98 of 27 April 1998 amending Regulation (EC) Nr. 384/96 on protection against dumped imports from countries not members of the European Community, OJ L. 128, 30/04/1998, p. 0018-0019

the Regulation 905/98 provided, that changes to the anti-dumping law were needed because "the process of Reform in Russia and the People's Republic of China has fundamentally altered their economies and has led to the emergence of firms for which market economy conditions prevail" and, most notably, because "both countries have as a result moved away from the economic circumstances which inspired the use of the analogue country method".

The change in EU anti-dumping policy meant namely that, if relevant conditions were satisfied, Russian and Chinese producers and exporters, that had traditionally been handicapped in EU anti-dumping investigations by the analogue country rule, would be able to take advantage of the prospect of securing individual dumping margins based on their own domestic sale prices as opposed to those of analogue producers in third countries.

Having recognised the successful reforms in Russia and China, the EU lawmakers still did not accord unconditional market economy treatment to that countries. Instead, they offered Russian and Chinese exporters "hybrid" treatment on case-by-case basis. Thereunder if exporters can prove that they operate in an environment where market conditions prevail, they will be treated like companies in market economy countries. If they don't wish to claim market economy treatment, or cannot prove that they qualify for it, the exporters will receive the non-market economy treatment they would have received before 1 July 1998 (i.e. normal value based on costs and prices in analogue country).

b) Five market economy criteria

The market economy status could be achieved solely after convincing the EU anti-dumping authorities that five following market economy criteria provided in Article 2 (7) (c) of the Basic Regulation are satisfied:

➢ decisions of firms regarding prices, costs and inputs, for instance, raw materials, costs of technology and labour, output, sales and investment, are made in response to market signals reflecting supply and demand, and without significant State interference in this regard, and costs of major inputs substantially reflect market values;

➢ firms have one clear set of basic accounting records which are independently audited in line with international accounting standards and are applied for all purposes;

➢ the production costs and financial situation of firms are not subject to significant distortions carried over from the former non-market economy system, in particular in relation to depreciation of assets, other write-offs, barter trade and payment via compensation of debts;

➢ the firms concerned are subject to bankruptcy and property laws which guarantee legal certainty and stability for the operation of firms, and

➢ exchange rate conversions are carried out at the market rate.

The list is not exhaustive and is only provided as an indication. It should be added, that these five conditions have been made cumulative; apparently all must be satisfied before market economy treatment can be extended. So, for example, an exporter, who establishes beyond doubt that it operates completely independently from the influence of Russian government, and which takes commercial decisions solely in accordance with market forces, could still find its market economy treatment application rejected because it fails to maintain accounting records in accordance with required standards[378]. Actually, the inability to satisfy the first and the second market economy criteria is the most common cause of applications for market economy status were rejected[379].

c) Impact of market economy treatment on dumping margins

One of the principal rationales for the introduction of the possibility for Chinese and Russian enterprises being eligible for market economy treatment was to facilitate the possibility of a fairer comparison for the purposes of establishing dumping margins. Generally speaking, the use of actual domestic and export prices, as opposed to analogue prices or constructed values, should lead to lower dumping margins as a result of the removal of arbitrary elements applied by the EU institutions in determining individual anti-dumping duty-levels.

The widespread and relatively common rejection of applicants for market economy treatment shows that it is very difficult to compare dumping margins determined by reference to analogue country prices to those calculated through the market economy approach.

The table below, however, attempts to summarise the results from investigations, which have lead to the acceptance of at least one market economy treatment application. However it should be noted again, that the lack of sufficient market economy treatment cases prevents a more rigorous analysis.

---

[378] See e.g. Solutions of urea and ammonium nitrate from, inter alia Russia, where the two applicant companies were deemed not to have maintained accounting records that were sufficiently independently audited in line with international standards. Moreover, the accounting principles applied allegedly deviated from those standards in several areas including e.g. depreciation and fixed asset revaluation rates. Furthermore, the Commission came to the unexplainable conclusion, that "the basic purpose of the accounts was to meet the requirements of the tax authorities and not to provide a complete picture of the company's situation at the end of the accounting period." (Commission Regulation (EC) No 617/2000 of 16 March, OJ L 075 , 24.03.2000 p. 0003 – 0017)

[379] See e.g. MacLean, The impact of the EC's conditional market economy principle in Chinese and Russian AD cases, p.71

Table 24. Comparison of dumping margins for market economy treatment and analogue price determinations.[380]			
Investigated product	Lowest analogue margin	Highest analogue margin	Market economy treatment applicants
CD boxes from China	8,3%	10,4%	6,6%
Stainless steel fasteners	13,6%	24,2%	18,5%
Aluminium foil from Russia and China[381]	26,8%	26,8%	14,9%
Compact fluorescent lamps from china	6,0%	59,6%	0%+61,8%

d) The 2000 "conditional market economy" amendments to the Basic Regulation

The subsequent amendments to the Basic Regulation in 2000 simply extended the conditional market economy treatment to Ukraine, Kazakhstan and Vietnam, which were not WTO members[382]. Moreover, conditional market economy treatment was also provided automatically, i.e. without considering whether those countries meet the criteria of Note 2, with regard to any non-market economy country, "which is a member of the WTO at the date of the initiation of the anti-dumping investigation"[383]. The latter novelty is indeed intriguing in that it expressly provides that a country can join the WTO on general, "commercially viable" terms acceptable to WTO Members, i.e. become a full-fledged party to this international institution and still not be treated as such on the basis of unilateral considerations. The far-reaching negative implications of such an approach for the integrity and smooth operation of the WTO system are hard to overestimate. In the legal sense such an Orwellian "all-animals-are-equal, but some-are-more-equal-than-others" stance is indeed unique[384]. It appears to be the first precedent in the GATT/WTO history when members that have assumed all obligations under the WTO Agreement and its Annexes are openly denied their

---

[380] MacLean, The impact of the EC's conditional market economy principle in Chinese and Russian AD cases, p.71

[381] only Russian exporter was granted a market economy treatment

[382] Council Regulation (EC) 2238/2000, OJ L 258, 11.10.2000, p. 0002-0003

[383] Art. 2 (7)(b) of the Basic Regulation as amended by Council Regulation (EC) 2238/2000

[384] Polouektov, Non market Economy Issues in the WTO Anti-Dumping Law, Journal of World Trade, 1-37, 2002, p. 25

rights for non-discriminatory treatment Future dispute settlement panels may well be expected to look into this and other similar cases.

e) Results of application of a "hybrid" market economy status towards Russia

As a result of nearly five years of application of the five Market economy status criteria by the EU, less than 10 per cent of all applications for market economy status have been successful[385]. Prima facie, at least, something is deficient with a system that only allows a fraction of applications to be successful.

For example, in the EU anti-dumping investigation concerning imports of aluminium foil from, inter alia, Russia, it was decided to grant market economy treatment to Russian exporting producer[386]. Indeed it is the only out of nearly 20 completed anti-dumping investigation targeting Russian imports in 1 July 1998 - 8 November 2002, the period in which the "hybrid" market economy status applied to Russia[387], in which a market economy treatment of sorts was permitted. However this market economy treatment was even not unconditional as the energy cost of a Russian producer was rejected.

The five "market economy status" criteria cited supra, have been strongly criticised by Russia and China, the largest affected exporters of the EU. And indeed, practitioners agree on the view that the 1998 amendments introducing "hybrid" treatment have in fact worsened the situation of exporters from the countries concerned[388].

As already noted supra, the Basic Regulation specifies that market economy status is to be granted to exporting producers, which can establish, in accordance with the five market economy status criteria, that "market economy conditions

---

[385] See e.g. MacLean, The impact of the EC's conditional market economy principle in Chinese and Russian AD cases, p.73

[386] Aluminium foil originating in Russia, Council Regulation (EC) Nr. 950/2001 of 14 May 2001, OJ L. 134, 17.05.2001, p. 0001-0017, rec. 24: "the investigation showed that the decisions regarding costs and inputs were made in response to market signals without significant state interference and the costs of major inputs reflected market values. The company had one clear set of basic accounting records, which were independently audited in line with international accounting standards. The production costs and the financial situation of the company were not subject to significant distortions carried over from the former non-market economy system and the company was subject to bankruptcy and property laws which guaranteed stability. Finally, exchange rate conversions were carried out at the market rate. On the basis of the foregoing it was concluded that the criteria in Article 2 (7) (c) of the Basic Regulation were met and that the company (Joint Stock Company United Company "Siberian Aluminium") should therefore be granted market economy status".

[387] See speech of Richard Luff on the Adam Smith Conference "Russian Accession to the WTO", October 2002 "Russia's proposed status as "market economy" country: a way forward or a status quo?"

[388] See e.g. MacLean, The impact of the EC's conditional market economy principle in Chinese and Russian AD cases, at p. 65-66, Borvikov/ Evtimov, op. cited supra note , at p. 22

prevail for this producer or producers in respect of the manufacture and sale of the like product concerned"[389]. The anti-dumping practice has shown, that the Commission, instead of focusing on weather market economy conditions prevail in the exporters activities, has de facto applied the five criteria with the aim of finding perfect market conditions. Moreover, the five criteria themselves are drafted in an ambiguous and "catch-all" fashion, providing the Commission with sufficient flexibility to deny market economy status to any applicant. It may well be argued the Russian exporters in 1998-2002 were required to establish market conditions, which are of higher standard than the conditions in which companies from traditional market economies, including EU, operate.

Three, rather discouraging, conclusions can be gleaned from the above analysis, namely:

➢ During the period in question, i.e. 1st July 1988 – 8th November 2002 only one Russian enterprise have managed to successfully prove its entitlement to market economy status, which however cannot be considered to be a fully fledged market economy status, as the energy cost of a Russian producer was rejected.

➢ The conditions for achieving market economy status, both as stated in the Council Regulation introducing conditional market economy treatment and, more importantly, as applied in practice, have proved hugely onerous to satisfy;

➢ In terms of individual dumping margins awarded to applicant enterprises who have successfully established their eligibility for market economy treatment, there is little evidence of a significant decline in individual dumping margins than would otherwise have been the case (See Table 24 p.153).

In fact the Community anti-dumping policy during the period in question penalised Russian exporters far more than gave them any tangible reward. Far from encouraging economic reform, if anything, the development in the EU's anti-dumping policy towards Russia and China may even had a negative impact.

Table 25. Status of Russia (correspondingly former Soviet Union) in the EU Anti-dumping Law		
Period	Status	Applicable Law
1968 - 1994	State-trading country	Soviet Union was included in the list of state-trading countries of Council Regulation (EEC) Nr. 925/79 and subsequent Council Regulation 1756/82 (EEC) on common rules for imports from state trading countries

---

[389] Art 2 (7) (b) of the Basic Regulation.

23.12.1991	Recognition of the Russian Federation as a legal successor of the Soviet Union	Declaration of the EC on the legal status of Russia, Bull. EC 1991 Nr. 12 Point 1.4.10
07.03.1994 – 1.07.1998	Certain third country (simply replacing the term "state trading country" by "certain third country")	Council Regulation (EC) Nr. 519/94 on common rules for imports from certain third countries
24.06.1994	Recognition that Russia is no longer a state trading country, but a "country with an economy in transition" on political level	24 June 1994 – signing Partnership and Cooperation Agreement between the EU and Russia
1.12.1997	Entry into force of the EU recognition of Russia as a "country with an economy in transition"	1 December 1997 entry into force of Partnership and Cooperation Agreement between the EU and Russia
1.07.1998 – 8.11.2002	Conditional "market economy status" – i.e. "hybrid" treatment on case-by-case basis. Granting of market economy status if an exporter/producer can prove "that market economy conditions prevail for this producer in respect of the manufacture and the sale of the like product concerned". If this is not the case, the rules for non- market economy countries shall apply.	Council Regulation (EC) 905/98 of 27 April 1998
29 .05.2002	Announcing Russia as a fully-fledged market economy country on political level	Ninth EU-Russia Summit in Moscow
8.11.2002 till present	Granting Russia a fully-fledged market economy status regarding EU anti-dumping law	Council Regulation (EC) 1972/2002 of 5 November 2002

B. The 2002 amendment to the Basic Regulation - The granting of Market Economy Status to Russia

I. Background

During the Ninth EU-Russia Summit held on 29 May 2002 in Moscow, President of the European Commission Romano Prodi announced that the EU would be granting Russia the formal status and treatment of a fully-fledged market economy, in recognition of the major reforms it has successfully undertaken in recent years.

Days following the formal recognition of Russia as a market economy country by EU, the United States also announced their decision to grant market economy status to Russia. Commentators have advanced views that the twin decisions of the EU and the USA were largely political, being a "diplomatic pay-off" to Russia for its course in foreign policy following September 11th events, and also possibly an invitation for Russia to make concessions on market access in goods and services in the ongoing negotiations on Russia's accession to the WTO.

It is relevant to note that the EU and the United States, in addition to applying similar trade policy approaches towards Russia, share similar trade concerns with respect to Russia. One major example of such concern is the so-called "dual pricing" applied on energy in Russia- the fact that Russian companies charge higher freely-negotiated prices on their energy exports than the State-controlled prices they charge to domestic energy consumers. This example is relevant in particular since the concern for Russia's dual pricing, is reflected in the 2002 amendments to the Anti-dumping Basic Regulation 384/96, as will be seen infra. Consequently, one should expect, that the United States would strongly support those amendments to the EU anti-dumping law. There were some arguments in literature[390] and in Russian and International press, which are shown infra, that some of the 2002 amendments are likely to violate a number of WTO provisions. However, such possible violations of WTO rules are also likely to be promoted by a number of major trading powers in the WTO.

II. Legal framework of the Russian market economy status

5th November 2002, in response to the EU's political decision to grant market economy status to Russia, the appropriate amendments to the Basic Regulation were adopted[391]. Entitlement to market economy treatment in practice has only been applied prospectively, i.e. to all investigations initiated pursuant to Basic Regulation No. 384/96 after 8 November 2002, date of entry into force of amendments to the Basic Regulation[392]. The European Commission has consistently declined to allow the change in methodology to be invoked as a ground for reviewing anti-dumping measures in place at the time the amendment came into force. It is ironical that three cases, affecting about 50 million euros worth

---

[390] See, e.g. Borovikov/Evtimov, EC treatment of non-market economies in anti-dumping law, p.23

[391] Council Regulation (EC) No. 1972/2002 of 5 November 2002 amending Regulation (EC) No. 2026/1997 on the protection against dumped imports from countries not members of the European Communities, OJ L305, 07.11.2002, p.1

[392] The Regulation shall enter into force on the day following that of its publication in the Official Journal of the European Communities, i.e. on 08.11.2002

of goods[393] were filed in 2002, two of them since Prodi made his promise in May[394] but before the legislative fixing of a market economy status and one three weeks before[395]. To these investigations applies the old "hybrid" treatment. A reasonable person can only doubt if this timing, which allows to apply an old anti-dumping regime to three investigations in spite of a promise given on the highest level, was a coincidence.

In Case Grain oriented electrical sheets,[396] initiated three weeks before amendments, Brazil was chosen as analogue country. In Case Silicon metal,[397] initiated less that one month before entry of amendments into force, exporters received market economy treatment in accordance with "hybrid" rules, which means that companies satisfied five market economy criteria and underwent though the process of application for the market economy treatment.

III. The 2002 amendments to the Basic Anti-dumping Regulation
1. Legal analysis

As already mentioned supra, by amendments 2002 Russia was deleted from the list of countries granted "hybrid" treatment[398]. As it is stipulated in the Preamble: "in view of the very significant progress made by the Russian Federation towards the establishment of market economy conditions, as recognized by the conclusions of the Russia-European Union Summit on 29 May 2002, it is appropriate to allow normal value for Russian exporters and producers to be established in accordance with the provisions of Article 2 (1) to (6) of Regulation (EC) Nr. 384/96 [i.e. according to the procedure for market economies]". Moreover, the Basic Regulation saw the introduction of certain modifications to the rules applicable to market economies. As appears from the amendment and will be shown infra, the deliberative practice of the Commission is very likely to continue in spite of a newly granted market economy status for Russia[399].

---

[393] EU grants Russia market economy status, the Moscow times, 11/11/2002.

[394] See Notice of initiation of an anti-dumping proceeding concerning imports of silicon metal originating in Russia, OJ C 246 , 12/10/2002 P. 0012 – 0013 and Notice of initiation of an anti-dumping proceeding concerning imports of hollow sections originating in Russia and Turkey, OJ C 249 , 16/10/2002 P. 0005 - 0008

[395] See Notice of initiation of an anti-dumping proceeding concerning imports of certain grain oriented electrical sheets and strips (flat-rolled products) of a width not exceeding 500 mm originating in Poland and Russia, OJ C 111 , 08/05/2002 P. 0005 - 0007

[396] Council Regulation (EC) No 151/2003 of 27.01.2003, OJ L 025 , 30.01.2003 P. 7 – 20, rec. 20-28

[397] See Commission Regulation No 1235/2003 of 10 July 2003, OJ L 173 , 11.07.2003 P. 14 – 34, rec. 15-18

[398] Art. 1 (4) of Council Regulation (EC) No. 1972/2002 of 5 November 2002

[399] See e.g. Luff, Russia's proposed status as "market economy" country: a way forward or a status quo?

As a result of deletion of Russia from the list of Article 2 (7)(b), Russian exporters are no longer forced to complete market economy questionnaires and attempt to convince the Commission services that they satisfy the five market economy criteria. However, the other amendments to the Basic Regulation clearly show that the EU does not have the resolve to accord exactly the same treatment to Russian (as well as other exporters from former non-market economies) as that enjoyed by exporters from "traditional" market economy countries in anti-dumping. In fact, according the opinions of practicing lawyers and articles in Russian and international press, these amendments appear to be tailor-made for "new market economy" exporters, which can no longer be "caught" under traditional non-market economy treatment.[400] The 2002 amendments can be applied in a way to achieve effects in terms of disregard of domestic costs and prices similar to those applied under non-market economy or "hybrid" treatments.

The latter statement will be explained by way of discussion of the main features of the 2002 amendments with the help of some hypothetical examples.[401]

The Amendment to Article 2 (3) of Basic Regulation, which allows disregard of domestic price data, introduced the term "particular market situation" for the product concerned, which may be deemed to exist, inter alia, under following circumstances:

> ➤ when prices are artificially low;
> ➤ when there is significant barter trade;
> ➤ when there are non-commercial processing arrangements.

It codifies past Commission practice in respect of Russian exporters that have occasionally satisfied the five market economy status criteria. The big advantage of the new status is that the burden of proof is no longer on the side of exporter. The Commission has to demonstrate that certain exporters do not meet market standards. However, practicing lawyers in charge of Russian anti-dumping cases before 2002 amendments in practice expect little to change for Russia after gaining market economy status[402].

The irony therefore is that although Russia received full market economy status, at the same time it will become easier to reject an exporting company's domestic prices because of its "particular market situation". In case domestic prices are rejected and constructed normal value is used, the Commission will be free to reject cost data that do not reasonably reflect the actual costs. Instead, "information from other representative markets" (one may ask, does this not bear a strong

---

[400] Borovikov/Evtimov, EC treatment of non-market economies in anti-dumping law, p.23

[401] Following hypotetical examples from Borovikov/Evtimov, EC treatment of non-market economies in anti-dumping law, p.23 ff.

[402] See e.g. statement of Richard Luff in Moscow Times, 11/11/2002 or Borovikov/Evtimov, EC treatment of non-market economies in anti-dumping law. Mr. Luff (van Bael &Bellis) and Mr. Borovikov (Hammonds) are attorneys in Brussels in charge of different Russian anti-dumping cases for many years.

resemblance to the term "analogue markets"?) may be used. Under the amendment, the Commission could resort to "relevant data pertaining to the world market or other representative markets, where appropriate." Since currently in Russia (partial)-government monopolies still provide many inputs, and barter trade is still quite common, it will be easy for the Commission to argue that a special market situation exists, that reported costs are not reasonably reflecting actual costs and that, therefore, information relating to another representative market must be used.

In other words, the 2002 amendments to the Basic Regulation is clearly an attempt to take back with the "technical arm" what the "political arm" is giving as it basically reintroduces the analogue country methodology through the backdoor.[403]

It is not difficult to imagine a situation reflecting past Commission practice, in which a Russian exporter, otherwise enjoying market economy status by virtue of the 2002 amendments, would have made some sales under barter arrangements in its domestic market. Under the amendment to Article 2 (3), the Commission will have the legal basis to disregard data on the exporter's domestic sales (those made under barter arrangements, if no more) because of the existence of a "particular market situation". The effects would be similar to a situation in which the Russian exporter would have been granted market economy status individually under the old "hybrid" regime. It should be noted, that it is very difficult to understand the approach of the Commission services towards barter trade. The practice of the EU anti-dumping cases shows that it does not distinguish between cost-distorting and non-distorting barter trade[404]. Needless to say, in many cases the Commission also failed to examine whether any distortions caused by barter trade are "significant" or "insignificant". Moreover, in many cases it failed to examine the difference between barter trade and "clearing trade" or "open account trade", commercial transactions which always reflect actual costs and market prices and are appropriately recorded. The alleged existence of barter trade has played a role in the rejection of a number of market economy treatment applications under the "hybrid" regime. In Urea and Ammonium Nitrate from inter alia Russia two applications from Russian companies were rejected, inter alia, on the grounds that the applicant companies had been engaged in barter[405]. The Commission found that "company A, which in fact was found to have purchased Urea and Ammonium Nitrate from a related producer, paid for it on several occasions by delivering a product used by its supplier to produce compound fertilisers. Company B had been instructed by re-

---

[403] See Richard Luff in Moscow Times, 11/11/2002

[404] See, e.g. Borovikov/Evtimov, EC treatment of non-market economies in anti-dumping law, p.21

[405] Solutions of urea and ammonium nitrate originating inter alia, in Russia, Commission Regulation (EC) No 617/2000 of 16 March 2000, OJ L 075 , 24/03/2000 p. 0003 - 0017

gional authorities to deliver Urea and Ammonium Nitrate to farmers, the value of which would be offset against its tax bills. The farmers were to deliver grain to a State-owned agricultural consortium for use by the Regional Food Fund. Nearly half of company B's domestic sales of Urea and Ammonium Nitrate were accounted for in this way." It can be seen that barter trade not on regular basis but even "on several occasions" could cause the disregard of domestic data.

It should be further noted that under previous GATT panel practice, a "particular market situation" can be used to justify disregard of domestic data only to the extent it has had the "effect of rendering the sales themselves unfit to permit a proper comparison".[406] In reference to our hypothetical situation, the GATT interpretation would mean that barter trade can justify disregard of domestic prices only if it has effectively distorted the price values actually applied in the barter transactions.

In applying the amended Article 2 (3), the Commission would also examine whether the Russian exporter's domestic prices are artificially low. To that end, it would verify whether those prices are profitable, by comparing those prices with the respective "cost of production" of the exporter. In doing so, the Commission most likely would not use the actual cost of production, but would adjust them in accordance with the amended Article 2 (5) (see infra). In past Commission practice such adjustments have brought adjusted costs of production way above the level of actual costs and prices charged domestically. Naturally, such Commission practice has always led to fining of "abnormally' or "artificially" low domestic prices of the Russian exporter. As a result, the "artificially low" domestic prices of the exporter are disregarded.

In order to clarify the above, it is necessary to examine the next amendment to the Basic Regulation, i.e. the amendment to the Article 2 (5). The full impact of the amendments in question on Russian exporters can be assessed only by examination of the combined effect of the amendments to Articles 2(3) and 2 (5) of the Basic Regulation 384/96.

The fully-fledged market economy status under the EU anti-dumping regime in principle implies that, even if the exporter's domestically charged prices are disregarded for any reason (for instance, as in the examples above), the normal value should be constructed on the basis of the exporter's actual domestic costs of production. However, the amendment to the Article 2 (5) of the Basic Regulation provides that "if costs associated with the production and sale of the product under investigation are not reasonably reflected[407] in the records of the party

---

[406] EC-Imposition of anti-dumping duties on imports of cotton yarn from Brasil, GATT ADP/137 of 4 July 1995, Report of the Panel

[407] For instance, the Commission service can consider that costs are "not reasonably reflected" even if the exporter's accounts are kept in a complete and correct way, only because the relevant records allegedly do not reflect "the real [market] value" of the cost input. It will be

concerned, they shall be adjusted or established on the basis of the costs of other producers or exporters in the same country or, where such information is not available or cannot be used, on any other reasonable basis, including information from other representative markets". Let us imagine a typical situation in which a large share of a Russian exporter's cost structure consists of payments for gas and electricity supplied by Russian utility companies. In Russia, the energy utilities are vertically integrated monopolists with more or less State shareholding. Most of them are called natural monopolies. The Commission services have always considered that State-regulated prices for gas and electricity in Russia do not reflect fair market values, merely referring to the Russian phenomenon of "dual pricing" of energy. The Commission has failed to understand that energy prices in Russia, albeit controlled by the State, are set at profitable levels. A number of Russian exporters offered the Commission services respective evidence that utilities supplied them with energy inputs at profitable prices. This evidence, however, was turned down as not relevant[408]. Moreover, the Commission services have refused to accept arguments setting out reasons why prices for gas and electricity in the Russian market are currently lower than world market prices.

Thus, the Commission services would invoke the amended Article 2 (5) by asserting that energy costs of the Russian exporter cannot in principle be reasonably reflected in its accounting records. The Commission would then disregard the costs of gas and electricity, and would instead apply third country or world market costs and prices of these energy commodities. Eventually, constructed costs of production of the Russian exporting producer would be absurdly inflated, which automatically leads to:

> ➢ disregard of " artificially low" domestically charged prices under the amended Article 2 (3); and/or
> ➢ finding of higher dumping margin, after the actual export prices are compared to the normal value, constructed on the basis of third country gas and electricity costs.

As a result, the exporters to which the amendment to Article 2 (5) will be applied, most likely Russian, but also possibly other countries' exporters, would not be in a substantially different situation than that of non-market economies or "hybrid" status exporters, as far as disregard of domestic costs is concerned.

The EU official response to the critics of amendments in question by deputy Minister for Economic Development and Trade Mr. Medvedkov (deprive Russia "of its natural competitive advantages arising from inexpensive electricity, la-

---

shown further how domestic energy costs in Russia have become the main target of this aspect of the Commission's anti-dumping practice.

[408] Numerous publications in the Russian press on the Anti-dumping amendments of the Basic Regulation 2002

bour and raw materials[409]) was as following: "by definition, natural or competitive advantages are not adjusted in any shape or form in anti-dumping investigations. Such advantages are not the cause of unfair trade. However, as clearly recognized by Russia at the May 2002 Summit the Russian energy market has not yet been liberalized (although this is the goal). This implies that energy prices in Russia are still subject to state regulation of prices and are not subject to market forces and thus out of line with the true full costs of energy (i.e. with natural advantages). This is further underlined by the existence of dual pricing. In these circumstances WTO rules allow adjustments to be made to energy prices in the calculation of dumping margins.[410]" This statement only proved the EU concern over the Russian energy prices.

2. Practice of the EU Commission

The latest example of imposing the anti-dumping duties on Russian exporters of Silicon metal, already mentioned regarding amendments 2002 supra, can show the concern of the EU in Russian energy prices. In provisional regulation of 10 July 2003 in addition to granting Russian exporters market economy treatment according to the "hybrid" Rules of 1998, on the separate note "with regard to electricity prices it was clearly indicated that, should any distortion appear in the course of the further investigation, this would be corrected by an appropriate adjustment".[411] Further at the calculation of normal value "with regard to the manufacturing costs, and in particular energy costs, it was found that the price charged by Russian electricity suppliers to two silicon producers could not reasonably reflect the costs associated with the production of electricity, when compared to prices of representative electricity producers in the Community, the analogue country and Russia, including those in Russia. It was therefore concluded that the energy cost was not reliable for these two producers and provisionally decided to use the power price charged to another producer in Russia." All exporting producers and Russian government made submissions arguing that the cost of electricity used at provisional stage should be amended. They emphasised that their main electricity supplier is a majority private-owned company and that its low price can be explained by the presence of the world's largest complex of hydroelectric power stations, based on a natural comparative advantage. However, the Regulation of 22 December 2003 imposing definitive duties set out that "since it was found that electricity prices in Russia are regulated and that the price charged by this electricity supplier was very low, even when compared to other suppliers of electricity generated by hydro-electric power stations

---

[409] See Chapter Background

[410] See: Frequently asked questions on Russia market economy status,, Materials of the Delegation of the European Commission in Russia, 2002

[411] Council Regulation (EC) No 2229/2003 of 22.12.2003, OJ L 339 , 24.12/.003 P. 3 – 13, rec. 25

in the analogue country Norway and also in Canada, it was decided to reject this claim and to confirm the provisional decision to use the electricity price charged by another electricity supplier in Russia." [412] No wonder that this case was highly criticised by Russian Ministry of Economical Development and Trade as well as the whole business community. The EU Commission completely ignored all comments both from Russian exporters and from government.[413] Russian government commented this case as "systematical unwillingness of the EU to implement the fully-fledged market economy status of Russia".[414]

Moreover, the previous practice of the Commission services has shown that the low energy prices were the main reason for the rejection of a market economy treatment under the "hybrid" regime. For example, in the already mentioned Solutions of Urea and Ammonium Nitrate from inter alia Russia[415] it was held that the fact that a company received energy supplies at a discounted rate for cash payments was indicative that this particular input was not being provided at market value[416]. This, admittedly combined with other factors, such as inter alia, barter trade, led to the rejection of the application by the company in question. In contrast, in Aluminium Foil from Russia[417], the European Commission first decided the Russian company applying for market economy treatment could succeed since the cost of its major inputs reflected market values. It subsequently adjusted the energy costs in the construction of its normal values because it was found that the company in question was charged an "unusually low price by the majority state-owned electricity company". In light of the fact that the product under investigations was manufactured through energy-intensive processes, this seems somewhat anomalous[418]. However, the Commission was prepared to substitute published worldwide power tariffs and rates as a component in the constructing the relevant normal value.

---

[412] Commission Regulation (EC) Nr. 1235/2003 of 10.07.2003, OJ L. 173, 11.07.2003, rec. 27

[413] Note of Russian Permanent Delegation at EU in Brussels Nr. 75 of 7.05.2003 and Letter of Russian Trade Ministry to Trade Commissioner Mr. Paskal Lamy Nr. 440 of 19.08.2003

[414] See materials of Russian Ministry of Economical Development and Trade to the fifth Russia-EU industrials Round Table on 1st December 2003

[415] OJ L 075 , 24/03/2000 p. 0003 - 0017

[416] For company B, the cost of energy, i.e. a major input for the production of UAN, did not reflect market values. The company reported that, since 1998, a series of discount schemes had been introduced by Presidential decree to encourage customers to pay cash for electricity and gas. For electricity, the cash discounts allowed to range from 30 % to 50 % and for gas, from 25 % to 50 %, the sole proviso being that the discounted energy price should not fall below the full primary costs of the supplier. In other words, and independently of the fact that these discounts were a clear indication of State interference in the market, prices did not reflect the full cost of energy, let alone its true market value (Commission Regulation (EC) No 617/2000 of 16 March 2000

[417] OJ L. 134, 17.05.2001, p. 0001-0017

[418] See MacLean, The impact of the EC's conditional market economy principle in Chinese and Russian AD cases, p.70

3. Critical observations

Generally in respect of the impact of the 2002 amendments on Russia's export trade with the EU, it is appropriate to make the following observations. The granting of market economy status generally decreases the likelihood of initiation of anti-dumping cases against Russian imports to the EU, as the EU complainants will need to establish a dumping margin based on comparison with "analogue country" prices, but with Russian domestic prices. Russian exporters have also been facilitated from the procedural point of view, as they will no longer be forced to make burdensome "analogue country" and "market economy treatment" claim submissions within very short time limits. Moreover, recognition of Russia as a market economy underlines the substantial progress in economic reforms by Russia, and such reforms are a precondition for WTO accession. Therefore, such recognition should facilitate the process of Russia's accession to the WTO. However, most of the other amendments significantly reduce the substantive benefits expected by Russian exporters following the EU's grant of fully-fledged market economy treatment, by providing for numerous opportunities for the Commission services to disregard certain Russian domestic prices and costs. The implementation of those amendments is likely to have a strongly disadvantageous impact on price comparison for dumping calculation purposes, and is likely to lead to excessively inflated dumping margins for Russian exporters. Russia's dual pricing on energy is likely to be the main target of the 2002 amendments.

As a conclusion a cynical person may argue that the Commission service of wishing to treat Russian companies on a fully-fledged market economy standing is a cover-up oriented towards discrimination. Indeed, Russian producers could be discriminated against in a manner whereby products which the Community is in need of will be given the luxury of "market economy status", while sensitive products, which are currently a threat for any number of reasons to the EU industry, will continue to be dolled out the old treatment. Indeed, the two last amendments Commission concern (1) the adjustments that can be made to costs of production where the records of the investigated company do not reasonably reflect the costs associated with the production and sale of the product concerned and (2) the sources of information to which the Commission may resort in case of use of facts available (such use occurs normally when a company is not sufficiently co-operative with the Commission. It normally leads to a higher dumping duty). In both cases, the Commission will be able to resort to "other representative markets" or to the "world market", a terminology that is not too distant from the term "analogue country". Therefore, from a practical point of view, the new rules will allow the Commission to continue to determine normal value for Russian exporters on the basis of costs data in a third country market as is currently the case under the analogue country methodology.

IV. WTO consistency of the 2002 amendments

It is also necessary to touch upon the issue of WTO consistency of the 2002 amendments to the EU's trade defence mechanism. Clearly, the most likely target of the amendments is the Russian Federation, and also the Ukraine and Kazakhstan, which are not yet WTO members, but whose exporters may enjoy market economy status on individual basis. Hence formally on the day of entry of the Basic Anti-dumping Regulation in force, the issue of WTO-consistency of the amendments to the Basic Regulation as regards Russia and these countries was not acute. With regard to China, a WTO member, the situation would not be very different due to the transitional rules in anti-dumping and anti-subsidy matters, which were imposed on it upon WTO accession by major players such as the EU and the USA.[419] Thereunder, for fifteen years following China's WTO accession, Chinese exporters subject to e.g. an EU anti-dumping investigation will need to establish prevailing market conditions in their industry-specific operations, in order to be treated by the EU as exporters from a fully-fledged WTO member country, i.e. the "hybrid" regime is still applicable[420]. One may also question why China, already a member of the WTO, has not been awarded full-fledged market economy treatment, while Russia, not yet acceded, was granted such status. One answer may be that trade from China is perceived as extremely threatening. Chinese products, due to cheap costs of production, have an intrinsic added value in comparison to like products in, for example, the EU.

Another answer is that there is a difference between Chinese and Russian trade to the EU. While the former to a significant extent is concerned with finished goods incorporating high added value (toys, clothing, household appliances), Russian exports largely comprise semi-finished or raw materials, which could be useful to EU industry. One type of trade is therefore perceived as a greater threat than the other. It is, as a result, easier to grant market economy status to Russia than to China, in the whole scheme of things.[421]

Nonetheless, one day Russia and the other above mentioned countries will become fully-fledged WTO members. Moreover, the possibility that EU would find it "appropriate" to apply world market data in anti-dumping and anti-subsidy proceedings against exporters from other countries, which are already WTO members, is not excluded. Therefore, it is important that the international trade community take a thorough view on the 2002 amendments to the EU's trade defence laws in light of WTO rules. Of prime importance is the fact that

---

[419] Borovikov/Evtimov, EC treatment of non-market economies in anti-dumping law, p.26

[420] Protocol on the Accession of the People's Republic of China, WTO document WT/L/432, p. 8-9. In view of the 2002 amendments to the Basic Regulation the expectations for fully-fledged market economy treatment of Chinese exporters are even less likely to be met.
Available at: http://www.wto.org/english/thewto_e/acc_e/completeacc_e.htm#chn

[421] Luff, Russia's proposed status as "market economy" country: a way forward or a status quo?

the EU policy makers have again demonstrated complete disregard of the two WTO criteria for disregard of domestic data due to State interference, namely those of Note 2 as confirmed in Article 2.7 of the WTO Anti-dumping agreement.[422] Moreover, the amendments clearly go way beyond other texts of the Uruguay Round agreements on anti-dumping measures, which set out the sources of cost and price data that may be used by the importing country's anti-dumping authorities. Some international practitioners are of the opinion, that should the implementation of the EU's 2002 amendments undergo a close scrutiny under the respective multilateral rules, it is most likely it would be found WTO-inconsistent.[423] A WTO panel has already condemned the United States for applying a broad interpretation of a price benchmark provided in Article 14 (d) of the WTO Agreement on subsidies and countervailing measures, which had led to the use by the U.S. anti-subsidy authorities of "world market price" data against Canadian imports[424].

Thus it seems that the EU walk on the verge of clear-cut WTO inconsistency in its trade defence policy against non-market economies and new market economy countries as Russia, which have been built upon the departures from GATT/WTO rules from previous years. But the difference at the present time is that now they are a step further away from WTO disciplines, because they attempt to modify the conditions of trade between fully-fledged market economy countries. The EU lawmakers also place exporters from possible "target" countries under uncertainty in their trade with the EU. The most of international practitioners are of the view that the 2002 amendments, but notably the anticipated practice of the Commission services comprising, questionable techniques as described above, would give rise to significant controversies in bilateral and multilateral talks, including in the WTO[425].

V. Ways of bringing the EU treatment of former non-market economies in line with international trade rules

When solutions to the problems of the EU treatment of a former non-market economy country or better to say a "new market economy country" as Russia is sought, there are at least two points of view. One point of view would be of that country, which is a WTO member, the status Russia has been pursuing for years

---

[422] Borovikov/Evtimov, EC treatment of non-market economies in anti-dumping law, p.26

[423] Borovikov/Evtimov, EC treatment of non-market economies in anti-dumping law, p.26

[424] WT/DS236/R of 27 September 2002, United States- Preliminary Determinations with respect to certain softwood lumber from Canada, Report of the Panel, pares. 7.31-7.59, adopted by the DSB on 1 November 2002, from Borovikov/Evtimov, EC treatment of non-market economies in anti-dumping law, p.27

[425] See e.g. Luff, Russia's proposed status as "market economy" country: a way forward or a status quo?; Borovikov/Evtimov, EC treatment of non-market economies in anti-dumping law, p.27

now. Another point of view would be that of the country, which is not yet a member of WTO, but which concluded bilateral Partnership and Cooperation Agreement with the EU. Both WTO members and signatories of Partnership and Cooperation Agreement can insist on the strict implementation of the anti-dumping provisions in the respective multilateral or bilateral agreements.[426]

1. Signatories of Partnership and Cooperation Agreement

It is widely accepted that WTO members are not bound to respect GATT/WTO rules vis-à-vis non-member countries. Therefore, although the post-1996 approach of the EU towards countries like Russia, Kazakhstan and Ukraine has openly disregarded WTO rules, these countries believed they could not do much about it.[427]

However, there is a view in the legal doctrine, according to which the WTO Members apply WTO rules in their trading relationship with acceding countries. This have a purpose of integration of the soon-to-be WTO Members to the international trade order and on the other hand facilitation concessions on market access and other trade commitments. Moreover, trade practitioners are of the opinion, that requirements in respect of candidates for WTO accession which are contrary to existing WTO rules (such as those which were imposed on China in respect to anti-dumping), inevitably would undermine their credibility in the multilateral trading system.[428]

In order to understand the current attitude of non-WTO member countries which are affected by EU's policy, in particular former USSR Republics leading by Russia, it was important to examine the main aspects of their long trade negotiations with the EU over the granting of fully-fledged market economy status in recognition of their market reforms in the 1990s, which was the main topic of this chapter. They considered themselves as being subjected to unfair treatment by the EU, which had kept them in the same "black list" with State-run economies such as North Korea.

As Russia and other CIS countries have signed Partnership and Cooperation Agreements with the EU, they are eligible to know, what rights they acquired by virtue of those agreements.

One fundamental intention of the signing parties of Partnership and Cooperation agreement derives from the legislative history and the text of the Agreement: these agreements should, insofar as possible, adhere to the provisions and tenor of the GATT, subject to strictly specified exceptions.

---

[426] Borovikov/Evtimov, EC treatment of non-market economies in anti-dumping law, p. 27
[427] Borovikov/Evtimov, EC treatment of non-market economies in anti-dumping law, p. 28
[428] Borovikov/Evtimov, EC treatment of non-market economies in anti-dumping law, p. 29

The Art. 18 (1) of the Partnership and Cooperation Agreement between The EU and Russia, dealing with anti-dumping, does not constitute an exception. It reads as follows:

"Nothing in this Title, …shall prejudice or affect in any way the taking, by either Party, of anti-dumping…in accordance with Article VI of the GATT, the Agreement on implementation of Article VI of the GATT [The Anti-dumping Code], …or related internal legislation."

However, the consultations and more than 10 years practice of Partnership and Cooperation Agreement showed that its provisions concerning mutual consultations in virtue of Art. 18 (2) of the Agreement and Russian natural comparative advantages were in the main part disregarded by the EU. Under those circumstances, Russian exporters and government should intensify bilateral consultations with the EU and its Member States, pursuant to the respective provisions of the Partnership and Cooperation Agreement. The aim of these consultations would be to bring the EC anti-dumping treatment of exporters from Russia in line with the text and purpose of the Agreement's anti-dumping provision.

2. WTO members

By way of adopting the 2002 amendments to the Basic Regulation, the EU actually of potentially affected trading interests of several WTO members and acceding countries, i.e. Russia. As discussed supra, the 2002 amendments to Art. 2 (3) and 2 (5) of the Basic Regulation allow the EU authorities to disregard domestic price and cost data of WTO member exporters, which enjoy fully-fledged market economy status, and apply third country data in the dumping calculations affecting them.

As it was discussed below, potential disregard of WTO rules by EU in this respect directly undermines the legal order of the multilateral trading system. It is true that the EU is supported by some other influential players in the WTO, which share EU's concerns for greater protection with regard to cheaper imports from formerly communist economies, as well as from certain resource rich and therefore low cost production countries.[429] Questionable policy of the EU and some other major players such as the USA reconfirmed in WTO accession protocols of newly acceding members such as China. Nonetheless, the affected countries need not be discouraged in their attempts to bring the anti-dumping policy of the EU and other WTO trading powers such as USA and Australia in conformity with WTO rules. The international practitioners dealing with the EU and WTO law strongly believe, that "taking into consideration, that the multilateral trading system is now going through difficult times, there is sustained criti-

---

[429] Borovikov/Evtimov, EC treatment of non-market economies in anti-dumping law, p.28

cism as regards the system's fairness and its credibility is undermined, such attempts have a good potential to test the system."[430]

In order to challenge disregard of WTO rules, WTO members directly affected by the EU anti-dumping policy have right to consultations under the WTO dispute settlement provisions. Other countries – WTO members, which are devoted to promoting the credibility in the multilateral trading system and which also have comparative advantages in natural resources, may also consider joining efforts through WTO mechanisms.

Desirable solutions would include new amendments to the Basic Regulation ensuring application of the standard market economy treatment, which excludes disregard of domestic costs and use of third country data in respect of all WTO members and acceding countries.

---

[430] Borovikov/Evtimov, EC treatment of non-market economies in anti-dumping law, p.32

PART FOUR. PERSPECTIVES

A. The impact of EU Enlargement 2004 on anti-dumping measures against Russia

I. Background

The Russian business representatives have some concerns in view of the EU enlargement from EU-15 to EU-25 in May 2004, which will be a topic of this sub-Chapter. The author will try to analyse the concerns of Russian exporters and show the estimated impact of the EU expansion on EU-Russia trade, precisely speaking on EU anti-dumping measures, bearing in mind the latest accession of Austria, Finland and Sweden in 1995, Finland being a direct Russian neighbour and a traditional trading partner. The EU expansion and its impact on the bilateral trade has been a very hot topic for discussions in Russian and international press and it remains to be seen if it will be solved ever at all without the breach of interests of any party. It is an issue where the compromise and common sense both of the EU officials and Russian government is needed. The author has to admit that the problem is highly political, but millions of dollars are on stake.

Russia along with other third countries, including USA, expressed strong reservations about the European Union's plan to automatically extend existing anti-dumping measures to the 10 new Member States in 2004. For example, the United States, the major trade partner of the EU, declared that "extension of the measures to the new members will disrupt long-established commercial relationships that have benefited exporters and importers alike"[431] and called the EU in a statement delivered to a 1-2 May meeting of the WTO Anti-dumping committee to undertake reviews of the injury determinations of all current trade remedy measures, including price undertakings, before taking the action.

According to the preliminary estimations of Russian Ministry of economical development and trade, the Russian trade with the EU will decrease by "hundreds of millions dollars"[432] due to the automatic expansion of trade restrictive measures on the new members.

II. Legal framework of the extension of the EU anti-dumping policy on new Member States

In accordance with the Treaty of Accession to the European Union of the Czech Republic, Estonia, Cyprus, Latvia, Lithuania, Hungary, Malta, Poland, Slovenia

---

[431] International Trade Reporter, 8 May 2003
[432] news on www.wto.ru, called 02.12.2002

and Slovakia, signed in Athens on 16 April, 2003[433] "From the date of accession, the provisions of the original Treaties and acts adopted by the institutions
and the European Central Bank before accession shall be binding on the new
Member States".

This provision means that upon accession on 1 May 2004, the 25 Member States
of the enlarged EU will constitute one single market with a Common Commercial Policy, which includes the uniform EU-wide application of trade policy instruments, including anti-dumping.

As a result, like with all the other aspects of the EU Common Commercial Policy, as of 1 May 2004, the current EU trade defence law and measures will
automatically apply in Cyprus, Czech Republic, Estonia, Hungary, Latvia,
Lithuania, Malta, Poland, Slovakia and Slovenia.

Anti-dumping measures currently applicable in the EU-15 will be extended
automatically to the 10 new Member States, and therefore will be applicable on
EU-25 level, while existing measures in the 10 new Member States will disappear.[434]

In practical terms, this means that if a company exports to the new Member
States it will become subject to trade defence measures that are in force in the
EU-15 upon enlargement.

At the same time exporters will not any longer be subject to the anti-dumping
which are in force in the new Member States against third countries, as, upon
enlargement, these measures will automatically lapse.

The memos circulated by the EU Commission on 27th March 2003 "Trade and
Enlargement-Why is enlargement good news for third countries" and "Trade
and Enlargement-Sectoral Overview"[435] just confirmed the abovementioned,
what raised the concerns of all affected third countries. Infra the author analy-
ses what it will mean in practice and which economical losses it would entail.

III. Partnership and Cooperation Agreement and the new EU Member States

In accordance with the Article 6 (6) of the Treaty of Accession,

"as from the date of accession, and pending the conclusion of the necessary protocols, the new Member States shall apply the provisions of the Agreements
concluded by the present Member States and, jointly, the Community with, inter
alia, the Russian Federation as well as the provisions of other agreements concluded jointly by the present Member States and the Community before accession.

---

[433]http://www.europa.eu.int/comm/enlargement/negotiations/treaty_of_accession_2003/index.
htm
[434] http://europa.eu.int/comm/trade/issues/respectrules/tdi_enlarg/exporters.htm
[435]trade-info.cec.eu.int/doclib/docs/2003/may/trdoc_113015.pdf

Any adjustments to these Agreements shall be the subject of protocols concluded with the co-contracting countries. Should the protocols not have been concluded by the date of accession, the Community and the Member States shall take, in the framework of their respective competences, the necessary measures to deal with that situation upon accession."

Article 6 (2) provides the procedure of accession of new members to the EU international Agreements. The accession of the new Member States to the agreements or conventions, which have been concluded or signed by the Community and its Member States jointly [including the Partnership and Cooperation Agreement with Russia] shall be agreed by the conclusion of a protocol to such agreements between the Council, acting unanimously on behalf of the Member States, and the third country concerned. This procedure is without prejudice to the Community's own competences and does not affect the allocation of powers between the Community and the Member States as regards the conclusion of such agreements in the future or any other amendments not related to accession. The Commission shall negotiate these protocols on behalf of the Member States on the basis of negotiating directives approved by the Council, acting by unanimity, and in consultation with a committee comprised of the representatives of the Member States. It shall submit a draft of the protocols for conclusion to the Council. In accordance with the Article 6 (3) of the Treaty of Accession, upon acceding to the Partnership and Cooperation Agreement, the new Member States shall acquire the same rights and obligations under the agreement as the present Member States.

In their turn the new members undertook an obligation to bring their agreements with third countries with those by the EU, and, when necessary, withdraw such agreements. This fact is also not the best news for Russian business. This obligation is provided in Art 6 (10) of the Treaty of Accession, which reads as follows: "to the extent that agreements between one or more of the new Member States on the one hand, and one or more third countries on the other, are not compatible with the obligations arising from this Act, the new Member State shall take all appropriate steps to eliminate the incompatibilities established. If a new Member State encounters difficulties in adjusting an agreement concluded with one or more third countries before accession, it shall, according to the terms of the agreement, withdraw from that agreement."

It should be noted that the provisions of Treaty of Accession described supra, do not take into account provisions of the letters on the consequences of EU enlargement that Russia and the EU had exchanged when signing the Partnership and Cooperation Agreement[436]. These letters provide that "if, as a result of an enlargement of the Community, any amendments to this Agreement would be

---

[436] Exchange of letters on the consequences of Enlargement. Documents concerning relations between the EU and Russia, p. 207

required, that would be the subject of consultation between the Parties. In this context the character of bilateral trade and economic relations between Russia and an acceding country will be taken into account as far as possible". In spite of the fact that the formulation "as far as possible" can be interpreted broadly by the EU, it is not a ground for Russia to give up. Therefore, Russia do not exclude the possibility of the suspension of signing of the accession protocol to the Partnership and Cooperation Agreement in case the EU would not take into account the character of bilateral trade and economic relations between Russia and 10 acceding countries[437].

If Russia would refuse to extend the Partnership and Cooperation Agreement to the new member states upon enlargement, the relationship between Russia and the EU would suffer major disruption. The principle of equality applying to all member states would prevent the EU from continuing meetings with Russia within the present framework, which only covers current 15 member states. With a view to a timely consideration of the Russian side's concerns over the implications of the European Union enlargement and to preventing the origination of a "legal vacuum" in relations with the EU entrant states in the period before the signing and ratification by Russia's Federal Assembly of protocols extending to these countries the Russia-EU Partnership and Cooperation Agreement, it is borne in mind to touch upon the dynamics in dialogue with the future members of the European Union on this problem and the role of the Commission of the European Communities.

IV. The previous experience of the extension of EU Anti-dumping measures upon accession of Austria, Finland and Sweden in 1995

In order to try to estimate the possible consequences of the EU Enlargement the author will show the resent practice of the accession of three Western European Countries to the EU, one of them, Finland, being one of the most important Russian trading partners.

1 January 1995 Austria, Finland and Sweden acceded to the EU. The Protocol Agreement to the Partnership and Cooperation Agreement was signed by Parties in Brussels 21 May 1997 and entered into force on 1 December 2000[438]. It was ratified by Russia 18 July 1998 by the Federal Law[439].

---

[437] This Statement was already made and has been actively discussed by Russian business press. See e.g. "Hundreds million dollars", Vedomosti (Russian business newspaper), 02.12.2002

[438] Protocol Agreement to the Partnership and Cooperation establishing a partnership between the European Communities and their Member States, of the one part, and the Russian Federation, of the other part, OJ L 283 , 09/11/2000 p. 0019 - 0025

[439] Federal Law of the Russian Federation of 18.07.1997 Nr. 103-FZ, published in Rossiiskaja Gazeta (Russian Newspaper) 28.07.1998.

Upon the accession of Finland, a historically important Russian trade partner, to the EU all anti-dumping measures were automatically extended upon it. The one of biggest Russian companies RAO UES of Russia (Russian Joint Stock Company - Unified Energy System of Russia) paid for the research of the impact of the accession of Finland to the EU on Russian-Finnish trade. The researched showed that only the automatic extension of the EU anti-dumping measures on Finland entailed the loss of 27 Mio. Finnish marks for Russia [440].

To the author's state of knowledge, only one Russian exporting company initiated the interim review of the anti-dumping measures, which did not result in abolition of measures. By a notice published on 5 August 1995[441], the Commission initiated an interim review pursuant to a request by the International Potash Company (IPC, Moscow), a Russian exporter of potassium chloride on behalf of the Belarusian and Russian producers. The applicant claimed, inter alia, that the accession of Austria, Finland and Sweden had resulted in a change in the circumstances on the basis of which the measures in force had been established. However, the Commission found that "there is no evidence that the accession of the three new Member States has given rise to any reason to alter the Commission's findings regarding the interest of the Community in these reviews proceedings.[442]" The review shown that the inclusion of the three new Community Member States does not alter the analysis of, nor the conclusions on, the dumping practised by the exporters in the countries subject to investigation; indeed, the dumping margin has changed little since the last examination. Therefore, the anti-dumping duty was just adjusted to the new circumstances, which in practice closed the market of three new EU members for the exporter of potassium chloride.

V. Provisional evaluation of economical impact of the EU enlargement on EU Anti-dumping measures against Russia

In opposite to the EU the acceding countries have so far used anti-dumping measures to only a limited extent, probably because these measures are complicated to apply and require qualified staff[443]. The anti-dumping measures against Russian exports were a very limited practice of Poland, Lithuania and Hungary[444]. In the period before accession only Poland and Lithuania had anti-

---

[440] Discussion "EU Enlargement: a threat or a chance for Russia", Committee "Russia in the United Europe", p. 13

[441] Notice of initiation of an interim review of the anti-dumping measures applicable to imports of potassium chloride originating in Belarus, Russia and Ukraine, OJ C 201 , 05/08/1995 P. 0004 - 0005

[442] Potassium chloride originating in Belarus, Russia and Ukraine, Council Regulation (EC) No 449/98 of 23.02.1998, OJ L 058 , 27.02.1998 P. 0015 - 0026

[443] Hamilton, Russia's European economic integration: escapism and realities, p.11

[444] Safonov, Foreign economical relations of Russia with European countries in view of EU Enlargement, p.79

dumping measures against Russian commodities in force (see table 3), Hungarian anti-dumping measures against Russian mineral fertilizers expired in 2003. However, as EU members, the new member countries' firms can exploit the experience and staff of the Commission to secure protection of their markets through anti-dumping measures. The extension of the EU anti-dumping measures currently in force can cause real economical loss to Russia. In accordance to calculations of All-Russia market research institute VNIKI, the application of the EU anti-dumping measures against Russia by new members can cause Russia annual loss of 105 millions dollars. Some exporters will be forced to leave the markets in question, which will cause the following loss: $13,5 Mio. for leaving market of Hungary, $1,2 Mio.-Cyprus, $13,6 Mio.- Poland, $0,1 Mio-Slovenia, $3,9 Mio. - Czech Republic, $13,4 Mio. – Estonia. If Turkey will become a EU Member one day, it will cost Russian business 111,6 Mio. Dollars annually[445].

At the provisional estimates of Russian Ministry of Economic Developments and Trade, losses from extension of EU anti-dumping policy might be as high as 150 Mio. Dollars annually. This figure covers both automatic extension of measures and initiation of new investigation at the initiative of new members.

The following Table gives an overview of anti-dumping measures in force in acceding countries on 1st March 2004 which lapse on 1st May 2004. Only three products from two countries are covered by such measures. This shows the drastic difference in use of anti-dumping policy in EU-15 and new members.

Table 26. Anti-dumping measures of the EU acceding countries against Russia [due to disappear on 1 May 2004] as of 1.03.2004[446]

	Product	Measure	Initiation/expiry
Poland	Synthetic butadiene rubber (Синтетический каучук)	AD duties: Russia 30,1%	08.05.03/ 12.11.2007
Lithuania	Brunt lime Негашеная известь	Specific AD duty 45 Lt/t	19.03.2000/ 18.01.06
	Grey Portland Cement Портланд-цемент	Specific AD duty	10.01.2002/Review ongoing From 13.05.03

---

[445] Safonov, Foreign economical relations of Russia with European countries in view of EU Enlargement, p. 80

[446] See Trade defense measures applied against Russian exports as on 1 September 2003 and data on the Site of DG Trade
http://europa.eu.int/comm/trade/issues/respectrules/tdi_enlarg/measures/index_en.htm

VI. Defending the interests of exporters in the enlarged EU

In the EU memo circulated in the EU delegation in Russia "Russia and EU Enlargement: Selected Issues"[447] the EU ensured Russia, that the European Commission is prepared, as in previous enlargements, to carry out reviews of specific anti-dumping measures on request to examine if the anti-dumping measures would have been significantly different if they were based on information including new Member States. It will do this in line with EU legislation[448].

The EU system offers some solutions for reviewing unwarranted measures upon enlargement:

➢ The exporter may lodge a request for an interim review[449] of the existing measures, which may lead to modifications or abolition of the measures. In addition, it will also be possible to launch enlargement-specific re-examination of the existing trade defence measures. The example of such request was described supra in case of International Potash Company in 1995 Enlargement.

➢ If an exporter can demonstrate that the company was not exporting the product concerned to the EU during the investigation period of the anti-dumping measure, it can request a newcomer review.

Additionally, there are other mechanisms in the EU trade law which address situations where measures are not warranted:

➢ The EU trade defence legislation also provides for a possibility to request a suspension of a trade defence measure. A measure will be suspended, if it is established that the market conditions have changed and that the suspension will unlikely cause an injury to the EU industry.

➢ Importers have a possibility to request refunds of the duties previously collected if it is proved that their transactions were not dumped or subsidised. However analysis in Part two of the present paper showed that the EU is very unwilling to grant refunds.

Due to the big level of deliberation of the European Commission it remains unclear whether the interim reviews would be limited to a re-determination of the duty levels like in case of enlargement 1995 or involve a more in-depth analysis of the injury suffered by the affected EU-wide industry.

Moreover there are some worrisome uncertainties as to how the reviews will be conducted. First, the notice for reviews will not be published until after enlargement, meaning that duties will be collected for some time after enlargement until the requested reviews are completed. Second, the burden will be placed squarely on exporters to establish the need for a review.

---

[447] Enlargement questionnaire 24.09.2203 http://www.eur.ru/ru/p_302.htm

[448] See Chapter EU anti-dumping procedure against Russian exporters

[449] Procedure of reviews see in Chapter: EU anti-dumping procedure against Russian exporters

In other words, enlargement itself is not sufficient grounds for a review, even though enlargement per se calls into question the injury determination. Moreover, the EU is prepared to require foreign exporters to come forward with evidence that the overall condition of EU producers with whom they compete has changed substantially as a result of enlargement. Needless to say, gathering such sensitive information about foreign competitors will not be an easy task.

Under WTO rules, the EU has an international obligation to ensure that trade does not become more restrictive as a result of enlargement, but this obligation is limited to WTO Members only. As a result the EU will enter into compensatory negotiations with any concerned WTO partners that will suffer overall adverse effects. As long as Russia has not become a member of the WTO, it will not have any formal rights to compensation. However the GATT rules on compensation do not concern the application of anti-dumping measures since such measures can be imposed notwithstanding the provisions concerning bound duty rate, thus, the WTO criterion to obtain compensation would, in any event, not be met.

VII. Conclusion

Although the EU expansion has many advantages for Russia-EU bilateral trade, it can make difficulties and cause losses for certain Russian sectors. It is not an easy task to evaluate the consequences of the greatest EU Enlargement on anti-dumping measures on Russian exports to EU. The provisional calculations show that in spite of the assurance of Brussels that the enlargement will go smoothly for both partners, Russian potential losses from extension of anti-dumping duties on its certain exports are very high. The acceding countries are strategic trading partners of Russia without a big practice in anti-dumping issues. After enlargement they will be armed with a very good-oiled anti-dumping mechanism of the EU, which may lead to the increase of the anti-dumping claims in following sectors: aluminium, metal, mineral fertilizers.

In this view Russia should use the potential of Partnership and Cooperation Agreement and to intensify the negotiations with the EU in this field. Moreover, in view of the EU expansion the Russian accession to the WTO is of highest priority, as Russian exporters will have an access to WTO trade dispute mechanisms.

B. Accession to the WTO – The use of WTO Dispute Settlement Mechanism

1. Background

Once the fully-fledged WTO member, Russia will be able to use the WTO dispute settlement mechanism in anti-dumping cases. It is one of the main reasons of Russia's accession to the WTO.

In line with the conclusions of the Uruguay Round, the WTO provides for a strengthened procedure for the settlement of disputes between WTO Members on the application of the WTO agreements. This was a major development for international trade law. The dispute settlement mechanism, which came into being with the World Trade Organisation in 1995, is one of the cornerstones of the Organisation. It gives all 146 Members of the WTO confidence that the agreements negotiated and agreed will be respected. It does not impose new obligations, but it does enforce those already agreed. The rationale behind the Dispute Settlement Understanding (DSU) of the WTO is to provide Members with a clear legal framework for solving disputes, which may arise in the course of implementing WTO agreements. If a Member does not comply with WTO recommendations on bringing its practice in line with WTO rules, then trade compensation or sanctions, for example in the form of duty increases or suspension of WTO obligations may follow. WTO Members, including the EU, are consistently making use of the mechanism. The system has, so far, worked well to solve very important disputes and avoiding 'trade wars'. For this reason, overall, the system is functioning well and has helped to ensure real market opening. Moreover, it compares extremely well with other international dispute settlement systems in terms of speed and efficiency. By providing a multilateral forum for settling disputes, the mechanism guards weaker Members against unilateral action by the strongest.

II. Legal framework

In addition to the general rules governing the dispute settlement[450] there are additional special procedures applicable to anti-dumping disputes, set out in Art. 17 of the WTO Anti-dumping Agreement. In Appendix 2 to the Dispute Settlement Understanding Articles 17.4 through 17.7 of WTO Anti-dumping Agreement mentioned as "special or additional rules contained in the covered agreements". General provisions of Dispute Settlement Understanding and Art. 17 of WTO Anti-dumping Agreement are not concurrent, but complimentary to each other and build together an integral and comprehensive dispute resolution system.[451]

---

[450] Understanding on rules and procedures governing the settlement of disputes, available at: http://www.wto.org/english/docs_e/legal_e/legal_e.htm#dispute

[451] See Appelate Body WT/DS60/AB/R Guatemala-Cement from Mexico, rec. 58ff., quoting from the Panel Report on Guatemala – Cement I, para. 7.16. The Appellate Body in Guatemala – Cement I rejected the finding by the Panel that "the provisions of Article 17 provides for a coherent set of rules for dispute settlement specific to anti-dumping cases, ... that replaces the more general approach of the DSU (emphasis added).(336)" The Appellate Body first held that the special or additional rules within the meaning of Article 1.2 shall prevail over the provisions of the DSU only "to the extent that there is a difference between the two sets of provisions". The Appellate Body then found that Article 17 of the Anti-Dumping Agreement does not replace the "more general approach of the DSU".

III. The scope of dispute settlement

Art. 17.4. sets out the scope of dispute settlement. Thereunder, the matter may be referred to the Dispute Settlement Body if final action has been taken by the administering authorities of the importing Member to levy definitive anti-dumping duties or to accept price undertakings and where a provisional measure has a significant impact and the Member that requested consultations considers that the measure was taken contrary to the WTO provisions.

IV. Challenging the legislation

The Anti-dumping legislation as such can also be challenged at the Dispute Settlement Body, which was confirmed by the WTO Appellate Body in the US-Anti-dumping 1916 Act.[452] In 2000, the WTO condemned the 1916 Anti-Dumping Act for allowing sanctions against dumping not permitted under the WTO agreements. Consequently, benefits accruing to the EU under the WTO Agreement have been nullified or impaired. As a result of this condemnation, the US had to bring the 1916 Act into conformity with its obligations under the WTO Agreement by December 2001. But more than 3 years after the WTO ruling, the 1916 Anti-Dumping Act was still in force threatening EU companies with business activities in the US.

The WTO on 24 February 2004[453,] concluded that the EU may suspend trade obligations against the United States, subject to certain specified limits, after the failure of the latter to bring its Anti-Dumping Act of 1916 into conformity with the WTO. In parallel to the reactivation of the arbitration, the Council adopted on 15 December 2003 a Regulation to provide relief to the EU companies facing

---

[452] See e.g. WTO documents WT/DS136/AD/R US-Anti-dumping Act 1916 (Complaint by of Japan)of 31 march 2002 and WT/DS/162/ABR US-Anti-Dumping Act of 1916 (Complaint by the European Communities), Appellate Body Report on US – 1916 Act,

Para 64-65: In considering whether Article 17 contains an implicit restriction on challenges to anti-dumping legislation as such, the Appellate Body, in US – 1916 Act, noted the following: "Article 17.1 refers, without qualification, to 'the settlement of disputes' under the Anti-Dumping Agreement. Article 17.1 does not distinguish between disputes relating to Anti-Dumping legislation as such and disputes relating to anti-dumping measures taken in the implementation of such legislation. Article 17.1 therefore implies that Members can challenge the consistency of legislation as such with the Anti-Dumping Agreement unless this action is excluded by Article 17.Similarly, Article 17.2 of the Anti-Dumping Agreement does not distinguish between disputes relating to anti-dumping legislation as such and disputes relating to anti-dumping measures taken in the implementation of such legislation. On the contrary, it refers to consultations with respect to 'any matter affecting the operation of this Agreement'.

[453] WT/DS136/ARB, United States-Anti-dumping Act of 1916 (original complaint by the European Communities) Recourse to Arbitration by the United States under Article 22.6 of the DSU.

claims based on the 1916 Anti-Dumping Act.[454] This Regulation entered into force on 9 January 2004 and merely seeks to neutralise the effects of the 1916 Anti-Dumping Act in the EU. This Regulation does not affect any obligations of the EU and therefore did not require authorisation from the WTO.

Therefore, once a fully-fledged WTO member, Russia will be entitled to challenge the provisions of the EU Basic Anti-dumping Regulations, breaking Russia's lawful interests. This issue was already touched upon in the present work in regard to EU amendments of Basic Regulation of 2002.

V. Overview of the WTO dispute settlement procedure

The procedure is divided into two stages. The first stage, at the level of the WTO Members concerned, consists of a bilateral consultation. Upon failure of the consultation, the second stage can be opened by requesting the WTO Dispute Settlement Body to establish a panel. WTO Members, other than the complaining and defending party, with an interest in a given case, can intervene as "third parties" before the panel. The panel issues a report, which can be appealed before the Appellate Body (AB) (each appeal being heard by three members of a permanent seven-member body set up by the Dispute Settlement Understanding). Both the panel report and the report by the Appellate Body are adopted by the Dispute Settlement Body (DSB) unless the latter rejects the report by unanimity.

Anti-dumping, anti-subsidy and safeguards measures are among the most popular subject matters in WTO dispute settlement. Out of the 64 panel reports adopted between 1 January 1995 and 31 December 2002, 23 cases referred to these areas.[455]

Tables gives an overview of the procedural steps and the time involved in the WTO dispute resolution.

Table 27. Overview of procedural steps and time frames in WTO dispute settlement	
These approximate periods for each stage of a dispute settlement procedure are target figures — the agreement is flexible. In addition, the countries can settle their dispute themselves at any stage. Totals are also approximate.	
60 days	Consultations, mediation, etc
45 days	Panel set up and panellists appointed
6 months	Final panel report to parties
3 weeks	Final panel report to WTO members

---

[454] Council Regulation (EC) No 2238/2003 of 15 December 2003 protecting against the effects of the application of the United States Anti-Dumping Act of 1916, and actions based thereon or resulting therefrom, OJ L 333 , 20.12.2003 P. 0001 - 0002

[455] Commission of the European Communities, 21st Anti-dumping report, 2002, p. 71

60 days	Dispute Settlement Body adopts report (if no appeal)
Total = 1 year	**(without appeal)**
60-90 days	Appeals report
30 days	Dispute Settlement Body adopts appeals report
Total = 1year 3months	**(with appeal)**
Source: http://www.wto.org/english/thewto_e/whatis_e/tif_e/disp1_e.htm	

VI. Panel and Appellate Body Recommendations

The major part of anti-dumping complaints has been won, either completely or at least on some issues, by the complainants. The rare exception to this has been, e.g. Cotton yarns Panel Report, where the Panel rejected all Brazil's claims.[456]

The General provision of Art. 19 of the Dispute Settlement Understanding is also applicable to the anti-dumping cases. Thereunder, "where a panel or the Appellate Body concludes that a measure is inconsistent with a covered agreement, it shall recommend that the Member concerned bring the measure into conformity with that agreement. In addition to its recommendations, the panel or Appellate Body may suggest ways in which the Member concerned could implement the recommendations." The most far-reaching remedy that a panel could recommend would be revocation of a measure imposing anti-dumping duties, reimbursement of anti-dumping duties paid and compensation for losses suffered as a result of the anti-dumping measures. No panel have gone so far as to suggest that the importing country pay compensation for damages suffered. Panels thus far in general have been reluctant to make the abovementioned suggestions, rather limiting themselves to the standard Article 19 recommendations that the Member concerned bring the measure into conformity with the Agreement found to have been violated. In the case Steel Plate, e.g., the panel refused to suggest that the measure be revoked because it could not say that, had the Department of Commerce acted consistently with the Anti-dumping Agreement, it would not have found the existence of dumping.[457] By the way of exception, the Panels in cases Cement I and Cement II suggested that Guatemala revoke the measure.[458]

It should be noted that before the Uruguay Round a few GATT panels have recommended revocation of anti-dumping measures and reimbursement of anti-

---

[456] EC-Imposition of anti-dumping duties on imports of cotton yarns from Brazil, Report of the Panel, ADP-137, 4 July 1995

[457] Panel WT/DS179/R United States- Anti-dumping measures on stainless steel plate in coils and stainless steel sheet and strip from Korea, 22 December 2000

458 Panel WT/DS60/R Guatemala-Definitive anti-dumping investigation regarding Portland Cement from Mexico II,19 June 1998; Panel WT/DS156/R Guatemala-Definitive anti-dumping measures on grey Portland Cement from Mexico II, 24 October 2000

dumping duties paid.[459] Now in light of Article 19 of the Dispute Settlement Understanding such recommendations are no longer allowed, while suggestions to that effect are still possible.

VII. Special standard of review

The most relevant special procedures are set forth in Articles 17.5 (ii) and 17.6 of the WTO Anti-dumping Agreement.

Article 17.5 (ii) provides that a panel examining a matter in dispute under the WTO Anti-dumping Agreement shall do so based on the facts made available to the authorities of the importing Member in conformity with appropriate domestic producers. Effectively, this means that panels will limit their examination to the information that was actually before the investigating authorities at the time the challenged determinations were made and do not perform de novo review.[460]

Article 17.6 establishes a special standard of review to be applied by panels in examining disputes in anti-dumping cases with regard both to matters of fact and questions of interpretation of the WTO Anti-dumping Agreement.

Article 17.6 (i) provides with respect to review of the facts that the Panel shall determine whether the authorities' establishment of the facts was proper and whether their evaluation of those facts was unbiased and objective; if so, the evaluation shall not be overturned, even though the panel might have reached a different conclusion. The standard is designed to preclude de novo review by panels.

Article 17.6 (ii) offers rules on legal interpretation by providing that the Panel shall interpret the provisions of the Anti-dumping Agreement in accordance with customary rules of interpretation of public international law. Where the panel finds that a relevant provision of the Agreement admits of more than one permissible interpretation, the panel shall find the authorities' measure to be in conformity with the Agreement if it rests upon one of those permissible interpretations.

---

[459] See e.g. Panel L/5814- 32S/55 New Zealand- Electrical Transformers from Finnland, rec. 4.11, Report by the Panel adopted on 18 July 1985.

[460] See e.g. WT/DS156/R Guatemala-Definitive anti-dumping measures on grey Portland Cement from Mexico II, rec. 8.19: "We consider that it is not our role to perform a *de novo* review of the evidence which was before the investigating authority in this case. Rather, Article 17 makes it clear that our task is to review the determination of the investigating authorities. Specifically, we must determine whether its establishment of the facts was proper and the evaluation of those facts was unbiased and objective. In other words, we must determine whether an unbiased and objective investigating authority evaluating the evidence before it at the time of the investigation could properly have made the determinations made by Guatemala in this case. In our review of the investigating authorities' evaluation of the facts, we will first need to examine evidence considered by the investigating authority, and second, this examination is limited by Article 17.5(ii) to the facts before the investigating authority. That is, we are not to examine any new evidence that was not part of the record of the investigation."

From the perspective of the investigating authorities, the relevance of these provisions is to emphasise the need to fully document and explain all aspects of the determinations made, whether legal interpretations or factual conclusions.[461] Should it be a panel review of the determinations of an investigating authority, the panel is directed, by Article 17.6, not to make its own judgements, but to evaluate the judgements of the investigating authorities. This standard gives a degree of deference to the factual decisions and legal interpretations of national authorities, and is intended to prevent dispute settlement panels from making decisions based purely on their own views.

VIII. Non-appliance of exhaustion of local remedies rule

Very important is that the customary international law rule of exhaustion of local remedies does not apply to WTO dispute settlement proceedings. This means that the exporting country need not exhaust judicial remedies available in the importing country, i.e. in the case of the EU, appeal before the Court of First Instance and the European Court of Justice before resorting to the WTO dispute settlement. It should be noted that the application of the rule of exhaustion of local remedies in the area of anti-dumping disputes would be unbearable as a practical matter. Even in the EU, where the judicial institutions have had more than twenty years practice of arbitrating such disputes, experience shows, firstly, that it often takes a very long time, sometimes two to five years,[462] before judgements are reached and second, that the judiciary do not always double-check seriously the administrative determinations reached, limiting the review to the check of procedure.[463] Parties affected by administrative determinations, therefore, should not have to go through the expensive procedure of importing country unnecessary and it should be up to them to decide whether they have more faith in the dispute settlement provisions of the WTO or in those provided by importing country litigation. Furthermore, individual producers might have different interests to the exporting country government bringing the WTO case. It should be noted that, thus far, no panel has accepted this principle of exhaustion of local remedies.[464]

---

[461] Czako/Human/Miranda WTO handbook on Anti-dumping investigations, p. 87

[462] Judgment of the Court of First Instance of 29 September 2000, Case T-87/98, (International Potash Company v Council), ECR 2000 P. II-03179, Judgment of the Court of 14 March 1990, Case C-156/87,Gestetner Holdings plc v Council, ECR 1990 Page I-0078, Judgment of the Court of 10 March 1992, Case C-179/87, (Sharp v. Council),ECR 1992, P. I-01635. Although most of the issues raised in the appeals were hardly novel and all claims were eventually dismissed, it took the Court 2-5 years to reach the judgement.

[463] Vermulst/Komuro, Anti-Dumping Disputes in the GATT/WTO, p. 10

[464] Silvestre J. Martha, World Trade Disputes and the Exhaustion of Local Remedies Rule, argues that "Since, under general international law, the exhaustion of local remedies rule only applies to obligations of result of which private parties are the object, there is no way that the rule can be invoked in cases of anti-dumping duties".

IX. Conclusion

The WTO have established an impressive record of throughout review of anti-dumping measures taken by WTO Members. One of the major goals of the Russia's accession to the WTO is the access to the WTO dispute settlement procedure. From the moment of the accession Russia will have a choice of two judicial systems for challenging the EU anti-dumping measures – that of the EU and of the WTO. Once the Member of the WTO Russia will be a more respectable trade partner for the EU. Of course, anti-dumping measures against Russia will not be eliminated as such because they are allowed under international trade rules, but Russia will have better protection against arbitrary decisions and will be able to challenge EU anti-dumping laws as such.

(See Diagram 7 on page 187, Source - official web site of the WTO http://www.wto.org/english/thewto_e/whatis_e/tif_e/disp2_e.htm)

Joint Conclusion

The analysis made in the present paper finds that the EU has systematically been applying anti-dumping measures against Russia over the past two decades. It should be stressed, that the EU anti-dumping measures against Russian imports are characterised by very lengthy duration due to the active use of expiry review investigations by certain Community industries. The most suffering Russian industries are fertilizer, aluminium and metallurgy. The majority of the EU anti-dumping proceedings against Russian exporters lead to unfavourable results to Russia, the number of terminations without measures or accepted undertakings is very limited. The EU anti-dumping policy is especially acute on the eve of the two major events: unprecedented EU Enlargement, extending EU trade policy on ten new members, and accession of Russia to the WTO. The first issue might entail some negative consequences on EU anti-dumping treatment of Russia.

On the 8th November 2002 the EU granted Russia a market economy status. This event is of a paramount political importance as it was a big breakthrough on the Russia's way to the WTO. However, the advantages deriving from newly gained status were partly diminished by the amendments to the EU Anti-dumping Regulation.

Nevertheless, to end on a note of optimism, the author would like to touch upon the good that will come out of Russia's entry to the WTO.

After the accession to the WTO Russia will have at hand the WTO dispute settlement mechanisms, unprecedented in their powers, and discussion forum at its disposal, as well as the new-found respect of being within, rather than outside, the WTO club. Moreover, it will itself use the anti-dumping and other trade protection instruments against injurious imports into Russia. Just as observed in other countries, Russia can expect this to have chilling effect on the number of anti-dumping initiations by the large trade block. Nevertheless, it is unlikely that anti-dumping cases against it will diminish if they are WTO-conform.

In short, while Russia's future successes as an influential trading partner may lead, at times, to new obstacles placed in its path, it will always be possible to constructively make use of the armaments it will newly have, as a result of its membership to the WTO.

DIAGRAM 7 THE WTO DISPUTE SETTLEMENT PROCEDURE	
Consultations (Art. 4) 60 days	**During all stages** Good offices, conciliation, or mediation (Art. 5)
Panel established by Dispute Settlement Body (DSB) (Art. 6) by 2nd DSB meeting	**Note**: a panel can be composed (i.e. panellists chosen) up to about 30 days after its establishment (i.e. after DSB's decision to have a panel)
Terms of reference (Art. 7) Composition (Art.8) - 0-20 days	
Panel examination Normally 2 meetings with parties (Art. 12) 1 meeting with third parties (Art.10), 20 days (+10 if Director General asked to pick panel)	**Expert review group** (Art. 13, Appendix 4)
Interim review stage Descriptive part of report sent to parties for comment (Art. 15.1) Interim report sent to parties for comment (Art. 15.2)	**Review meeting with panel** upon request (Art. 15.2)
Panel report issued to parties (Art. 12.8; Appendix 3 par. 12 (j)) 6 months from panels composition, 3 months if urgent. 30 days for appellate report	**Total for report adoption:** up to 9 months (no appeal) or 12 months (with appeal) from establishment of panel to adoption of report (Art. 20)
Panel report issued to DSB (Art. 12.9; Appendix 3 par. 12 (k)) up to 9 months from panel's establishment	
DSB adopts panel/ appellate report (s) Including any changes to panel report made by appellate report (Art. 16.1, 16.4 and 17.4) 60 days for panel report unless appealed.	**Appellate review** (Art. 16.4 and 17) max. 90 days
Implementation Report by losing party of proposed implementation within "reasonable period of time"- approx. 15 months- (Art. 21.3)	**Dispute over implementation:** Proceedings possible, including referral to initial panel on implementation (Art. 21.5) - 90 days
In cases of non-implementation Parties negotiate compensation pending full implementation (Art. 22.2)	
Retaliation. (Art.22), **Cross-retaliation:** (Art. 22.3)30 days after "reasonable period expires"	**Possibility of arbitration** On level of suspension procedures and principles of retaliation (Art. 22.6 and 22.7)

Afterword

Between submitting of the present Dissertation at the Johann-Wolfgang Goethe-University in Frankfurt am Main in March 2004 and sending it for publishing in July 2004 two major events of high importance in the EU-Russia Relations took place. In the Afterword the Author will briefly describe and analyze the impact of these events on the topic of the Dissertation.

1. EU Enlargement and Russia

Just before the historical EU enlargement, on 27 April 2004 the Russian Federation and the European Union signed a Protocol to the Partnership and Cooperation Agreement between the EU and the Russian Federation, extending the Agreement to the ten new Member States of the enlarged EU on 1 May 2004.[465] The parties also adopted a Joint Statement on EU enlargement and EU-Russia relations, which contains inter alia, compromising clause regarding anti-dumping.[466] Therefore, in paragraph 5 of the Joint Statement parties agreed that special transitional measures concerning the most significant existing EU anti-dumping measures on Russian exports will be adopted. The purpose of such transitional special measures is to prevent a sudden sharp negative impact on traditional trade flows. The provision further provides, that the products subject to the anti-dumping measures concerned are potassium chloride, ammonium nitrate, grain oriented electrical sheets and products subject to measures incorporating quantitative thresholds, notably silicon carbide, aluminium foil. Reviews of other measures, such as steel wire ropes and cables, may also be initiated on the basis of justified requests by Russian interested parties. These reviews shall be treated by the EU as a priority. Furthermore, the provision confirmed, that as from 1 May 2004 all trade defence measures currently applied by the acceding countries on imports from third countries, including Russia, will cease to exist.

The paragraph 5 of the Joint Statement of 27th April 2004 is in accordance with Notice regarding the application of anti-dumping and anti-subsidy measures in force following the enlargement[467], published by the EU on 15th April 2004, where the Commission envisaged a two prolonged approach regarding potential

---

[465] http://europa.eu.int/comm/external_relations/russia/russia_docs/protocol_0404.htm

[466] http://europa.eu.int/comm/external_relations/russia/russia_docs/js_elarg_270404.htm

[467] Notice regarding the application of anti-dumping and anti-subsidy measures in force in the Community following enlargement to include the Czech Republic, the Republic of Estonia, the Republic of Cyprus, the Republic of Latvia, the Republic of Lithuania, the Republic of Hungary, the Republic of Malta, the Republic of Poland, the Republic of Slovenia and the Slovak Republic and the possibility of review (2004/C 91/02), OJ C91/2, 15.04.2004

reviews of measures in this context. Firstly, the automatic application of these measures in the twenty-five Member State Community may cause undue economic hardship for some operators, in particular in the new Member States. Therefore, the Commission considered whether interim arrangements were necessary during a temporary period to alleviate any such difficulties. Secondly, the Commission gave notice that it is prepared to carry out interim review pursuant to Article 11(3) of Regulation (EC) No 384/96, where any interested party so requests and submits evidence that the measures would have been significantly different if they were based on information including the new Member States. In this regard, it stressed on the separate note that enlargement per se, in the absence of such evidence, is not a sufficient basis for a review to be initiated.

Before enlargement the European Commission informed all known interested parties of the possibility of a partial interim review of any of the measures currently in force in order to identify the cases where unwanted and excessive negative impact could occur upon enlargement of the EU. As a result, meetings were held with several third country governments and/or their exporters, including Russian representatives.[468] Following the analysis, it was determined that the risk of an excessively negative impact was particularly high for eight products, five of which originated from Russia. The Commission decided by publishing the Notice of 20.03.2004[469] on its own initiative to initiate partial interim reviews for these few products in order to assess the possibilities for making interim arrangements to be applied for a temporary period.

Anti-dumping measures against inter alia Russian products chosen for the review fall into two categories:

1) two measures that are subject to undertakings with a quantitative and/or a price element (measures on imports of silicon carbide and aluminium foil originating in Russian Federation). The Commission will examine, whether these undertakings, which were drawn up on the basis of data for a Community of 15 Member States should be adapted to take account of the enlargement of the European Union to 25 Member States[470];

2) three measures that are characterized by high levels of duty and a significant level of imports into the new Member States, which indicates that interested parties including users, distributors and consumers could be subjected to excessively negative effects immediately after the EU enlargement (measures on imports of potassium chloride, ammonium nitrate and grain-oriented

---

[468] http://europa.eu.int/comm/trade/issues/respectrules/tdi_enlarg/faqs_ir.htm

[469] Notice of initiation of a partial interim review of the antidumping measures applicable to imports of certain products originating in the People's Republic of China, Russian Federation, Ukraine and the Republic of Belarus (OJ No C 70, 20.03.2004, p.15)

[470] Art. 2.1. of the Notice 2004/C 70/04

electrical steel sheets originating in the Russian Federation). Other factors taken into account when selecting measures for a review are the level of production and the level of prices in the acceding States. During the review, it will be examined whether, in the light of Community interest, there is a need to adapt these measures to avoid a sudden and excessively negative effect on interested parties including users, distributors and consumers.[471]

As a result of the interim review regarding potassium chloride the EU concluded that "it is in the Community interest to adapt the existing measures, provided that such adaptation does not significantly undermine the desired level of trade defense."[472] The Commission accepted Undertakings from Russian exporters and made their imports to the EU subject for registration. The outcome of the interim review have undoubtedly improved the situation of Russian exporter of potassium chloride and avoided sudden economic hardship, in spite of the fact that the measures were not abolished completely.

At the same time two Russian exporters of potassium chloride initiated interim reviews, based on the prima facia evidence, provided by the applicant, that the circumstances on the basis of which measures were established have changed and that these changes are of lasting nature. [473] The applicant alleged and provided evidence showing that a comparison of normal value based on its own cost/domestic prices and its export prices to the EU, would lead to a removal of dumping. Therefore, the continued imposition of measures at the existing levels, which were based on the level of dumping previously established, is no longer necessary to offset dumping.

It should be noted, however, that the although the EU-Russian Agreements concerning EU Enlargement represents the new level of compromise between the EU and Russia and is likely to reduce the anti-dumping burden of several Russian exports, it will not solve all problems regarding anti-dumping. Firstly, the European Commission stressed, that as in previous 1995 enlargement, the Commission will not automatically review all the existing EU trade defence measures due to enlargement. This means that except the cases listed in the examined above Notice 20/C70/04, the EU leaves it to interested parties to ask for reviews of individual measures. The interested party, requesting the interim review must submit evidence, that the measures would have been significantly dif-

---

[471] Art. 2.2. of the Notice 2004/C 70/04

[472] Commission Regulation (EC) No 1002/2004 of 18 May 2004 accepting undertakings offered in connection with the anti-dumping proceeding concerning imports of potassium chloride originating in the Republic of Belarus, the Russian Federation or Ukraine and making imports of potassium chloride originating in the Republic of Belarus and the Russian Federation subject to registration, OJ No. L182, 20.05.2004, p.16

[473] Notice of initiation of a partial interim review of the antidumping measures applicable to imports of potassium chloride originating in Russia, OJ C 093 , 17/04/2004 P. 0002 – 0003; Notice of initiation of a partial interim review of the anti-dumping measures applicable to imports of potassium chloride originating in Russia OJ C 093, 17/04/2004 P. 3 –4

ferent if they were based on information including the new Member States, whereas enlargement per se, in the absence of such evidence, is not a sufficient basis for a review to be initiated.[474] Secondly, the new anti-dumping cases are likely to be initiated in future and the measures will be applicable on the EU-25 level. Thus, in May 2004 two anti-dumping investigations were initiated: against Russian export of grain oriented flat-rolled products of silicon-electrical steel[475] and styrene-butadiene-styrene thermoplastic rubber[476]

2. EU-Russia WTO deal

21 May 2004 the Agreement concluding the bilateral market access negotiations for the accession of the Russian Federation to the WTO was signed. Taking into consideration, that the EU is Russia's largest trading partner, this Agreement is a major step in the process of Russia's WTO membership. Romano Prodi, President of the European Commission said: "Today the EU and Russia cement further their trade and economic relations. This deal brings Russia a step closer to the international trade family, the World Trade Organisation, where it belongs."[477] The deal covers the commitments that the Russian Federation will undertake in goods and services once it accedes to the WTO.

In addition, the Agreement has solved a range of trade related energy questions, in particular on the question of the domestic price for industrial users of gas. As it was mentioned in the Dissertation, the energetic issue have been a stumbling block of the EU-Russian relations for years. Russia committed that the price of gas for industrial users covers costs, profits and investment needed for exploitation of new fields. Russian gas prices to industrial users would be gradually increased, which is in line with Russia's own energy strategy. This deal was a compromise as Russia made some important concessions in other sectors.

It is hard to predict now which effect the gradual increase of gas prices in Russia will make on anti-dumping, as Russian gas prices will, at least for the next few years, still remain lower than European. However, in the following antidumping cases it might be possible to refer to the EU-Russian WTO deal regard-

---

[474] Notice of initiation of a partial interim review of the antidumping measures applicable to imports of certain products originating in the People's Republic of China, Russian Federation, Ukraine and the Republic of Belarus (OJ No C 70, 20.03.2004, p.15), paragraph. 5

[475] Notice of initiation of an anti-dumping proceeding concerning imports of grain oriented flat-rolled products of silicon-electrical steel originating in the United States of America and Russia and of the initiation of an interim review of the anti-dumping duty on imports of certain grain oriented electrical sheets originating in Russia (also known as grain oriented cold-rolled sheets and strips of silicon-electrical steel with a width of more than 500 mm) (OJ C 144, 28/05/04, P. 2)

[476] Notice of initiation of an anti-dumping proceeding concerning imports of styrene-butadienestyrene thermoplastic rubber originating in the Republic of Korea and Russia (OJ C 144, 28/05/04, P. 5)

[477] http://www.europa.eu.int/comm/trade/issues/bilateral/countries/russia/pr210504_en.htm

ing the energy compromise. The practice of the next years will show if the discretion of the European Commission will take into consideration this commitment of Russia. Moreover, as it was examined in the Dissertation, once in the WTO, Russia will have new legal instruments to challenge inter alia, anti-dumping cases.

WTO accession will anchor Russia into an international rules-based trading system. It will enhance openness, transparency and predictability, which provides a foundation for improved economic governance and will make Russia more reliable and respectable trading partner. This will in the long-term perspective have positive impact on access of Russian exports to the EU market.

Frankfurt am Main, July 2004

195

Literature

I. in Englisch

Aslund, Anders/ Warner, Andrew, EU Enlargement: consequences for the CIS countries, USA, 2002

Barysh, Katinka/ Cottrell, Robert/Frattini, Franko/Hare, Paul/ Lami, Paskal/ Medvedkov, Maxim/Yasin, Evgeny, Russia and the WTO, London: Centre for European Reform, 2002 (cited as: Barysh, Russia and the WTO)

Bordachov, Timofei, Russia and the European Union: the special department is needed? Library of Publications of Carnegi Moscow Centre, Issue 3, March 2002

Borovikov, Edward, Evtimov/ Bogdan, Law firm Hammonds, Brussels EC's Treatment of non-market economies in Anti-dumping law. Its history: an evolving disregard of international trade rules, its state of play: inconsistent with the GATT/WTO? (cited as: Borovikov/Evtimov, EC treatment of non-market economies in anti-dumping law.)

Broadman, Harry G., Global economic integration: prospects for WTO accession and continued Russian reforms, the Washington quarterly, Spring 2004, p. 79-98

Broude, Tomer, An anti-dumping "To be or not to be" in five acts: a new agenda for research and reform. Journal of World Trade , 37(2): 305-328, 2003

Czako, Judith/ Human, John/ Miranda, Jorge, A handbook on Anti-dumping investigations, Cambridge University Press, 2003 (cited as: Czako/Human/Miranda, WTO handbook on Anti-dumping investigations)

Didier, Pierre, The WTO Anti-dumping Code and EC Practice. Issues for review in trade negotiations. Journal of World Trade 35 (1): 33-54, 2001

Emerson, Michael, The elephant and the bear. The European Union, Russia and their near abroads, Centre for European Policy Studies Paper, Brussels, 2001 www.ceps.be

The painful EU-Russia summit in Rome, Commentary, Centre for European Policy Studies Paper, Brussels, November 2003

Institutionalising the Wider Europe, Centre for European Policy Studies Paper No. 42, October 2003 (cited as: Emerson, Institutionalising the Wider Europe)

Deepening the Wider Europe, Brussels, February, 2004, www.EuruJournal.org

Flemming, Splidsboel-Hansen, Russia's Relations with the European Union: a constructivist cut. International Politics, 39: 399-421, December 2002

Govan, David, How the EU can help Russia, London: Centre for European Reform, 2000 (cited as: Govan, How the EU can help Russia)

Hamilton, Carl B., Russia's European economic integration: escapism and realities, Centre for economic policy research, London, 2003 (cited as: Hamilton, Russia's European economic integration: escapism and realities)

Hanson, Peter, Russia-EU economic relations: dimensions and issues, Birmingham, 2002

Haukkala, Hiski, The Making of the European Union's Common Strategy on Russia, Helsinki, 2000

Haukkala, Hiski/ Medvedev, Sergei, The EU Common Strategy on Russia. Learning the Grammar of the CFSP, Helsinki, 2001

Havlik, Peter, Russia, European Union and EU Enlargement, Russian-European Centre for economic policy (RECEP), Moscow, 2002

Hillion, Christophe, Institutional aspects of the partnership between the European Union and the Newly Independent States of the former Soviet Union: Case studies of Russia and Ukraine. Common Market Law Review, 37: 1211-1235, 2000

Horowitz, Dan/Goddard, Theodore, EU Regulation on Russian Metals Trade, in: Metal Bulletin and Metal Supply and Demand, Materials of the second International Conference "Metallurgy of Russia in the context of the World Market", Moscow, 1998, (cited as Horowitz/Goddard, EU Regulation on Russian Metals trade)

Ivanov, Igor (former Russian Foreign Minister) Article "Association or dissociation? Will New Barriers Appear in a United Europe?", Newspaper Izvestia on January 11, 2003, www.mid.ru
Remarks by Minister of Foreign Affairs of the Russian Federation Igor Ivanov before Representatives of the Socio-political and Business Circles of the FRG on the Theme "Russia-European Union: The State of, and Prospects for Partnership," Munich, December 10, 2003, www.mid.ru

Kaveshnikov, Nikolay, Three stories about Strategic Partnership between Russia and the European Union, European Documentation Center, St. Petersburg, Russia and the European Union in a Wider Europe: New Openings and Old Barriers, International Academic Conference, St. Petersburg, 20–21 September 2002, http://www.edc.spb.ru/conf2002/kaveshnikov.html, (cited as: Kaveshnikov, Three stories about Strategic Partnership between Russia and the European Union)

EU-Russia Relations: How to overcome the deadlock of mutual misunderstanding?, Euro, January 2003
http://www.euro.ucl.ac.be

Kim, Jong Bum, Fair price comparison in the WTO anti-dumping agreement. Recent WTO Panel Decisions against the "Zeroing" method. Journal of World Trade, 36 (1): 39-56, 2002

Lanoszka, Anna, The World Trade Organization accession process. Negotiating participation in a globalizing economy. Journal of World Trade, 35 (4): 575-602, 2001

Lasagni, Andrea, Does country-targeted anti-dumping policy by the EU create trade diversion?, Journal of World Trade, 34 (4): 137-159, 2000

Lindsey, Brink, Daniel J. Ikenson, Antidumping exposed: the devilish details of unfair trade law, Cato Institute, Washington, S.C. 2001

Liu, Xiang / Vandenbussche, Hylke, European Union anti-dumping cases against China. An overview and future prospects with respect to China's World Trade Organisation Membership. Journal of World Trade, 36 (6): 1125-1144, 2002

Lynch, Dov, Russia's Strategic Partnership with Europe, in: The Washington quarterly, Spring 2004, p.99-118

Luff, Richard (Law firm Van Vael&Bellis), The Russian Steel Industry – Business as usual? To which extend will joining the WTO really help?, Eurasian Metals, Nr. 3, 2003 (cited as: Luff, The Russian Steel Industry – Business as usual? To which extend will joining the WTO really help?)

"Russia's proposed status as "market economy" country: a way forward or a status quo?" (cited as: Luff, Russia's proposed status as "market economy" country: a way forward or a status quo?). Speech at the Adam Smith Conference "Russia's accession to WTO", 16-17 October 2002, Moscow

Malfliet, Katlijn, The European Union and Russia: towards a Common Strategy? European Documentation Center, St. Petersburg, Russia and the European Union in a Wider Europe: New Openings and Old Barriers, International Academic ConferenceSt. Petersburg, 20–21 September 2002, (cited as: Malfliet, The European Union and Russia: towards a Common Strategy?)
http://www.edc.spb.ru/conf2002/malflietk.html

MacLean, Robert, Evaluating the impact of the EC's conditional market economy principle in Chinese and Russian anti-dumping cases, International trade law and regulation, vol.7, Issue 3, July 2001 (cited as: MacLean, The impact of the EC's conditional market economy principle in Chinese and Russian AD cases)

McGovern, Edmond, European Community Anti-dumping law and practice, Globefield Press, 2003, cited as: McGovern, EC Anti-dumping law and practice

Parenti, Antonio, Accession to the World Trade Organisation: a legal analysis. Legal Issues of Economic Integration, 27 (2): 141-157, 2000

Naray, Peter, Russia and the World Trade Organization, Great Britain, 2001

Pinder, John/ Shishkov, Juri The EU& Russia. The promise of partnership, London: Federal Trust for education and research, 2002 (cited as Pinder/ Shishkov. The EU& Russia. The promise of partnership)

Polouektov, Alexander, Non-market economy issues in the WTO. Anti-dumping law and accession negotiations. Revival of a two-tier membership?, Journal of World trade, 36 (1): 1-37, 2002, sited as: Polouektov, Non-market economy issues in the WTO. Anti-dumping law.

Qin, Julia Ya, "WTO-Plus" obligations and their implications for the World Trade organization legal system. An appraisal of the China Accession Protocol. Journal of World Trade, 37 (3): 483-522, 2003

Quereshi, Asif H., Drafting Anti-dumping legislation. Issues and tips. Journal of World Trade. 34 (6): 19-32, 2000

Rydelski, Michael Sanchez, Individual Treatment in EC. Antidumping Cases concerning State-Tarding countries, in: Europäische Zeitschrift für Wirtschaftsrecht (EuZW), 1997, S.138

The Community's New Anti-Dumping Practice towards China and Russia, in: Europäische Zeitschrift für Wirtschaftsrecht (EuZW), 1998, S.586 (cited as: Rydelski, The Community's New Anti-Dumping Practice towards China and Russia)

The WTO and EC on Safeguard Measures, in: Europäische Zeitschrift für Wirtschaftsrecht (EuZW), 1999, S.654 ff.

Silvestre J. Martha, World Trade Disputes and the Exhaustion of Local Remedies Rule, in: Journal of World trade, 30, 107-130, 1996

Sulamaa, Pekka/ Widgren, Mikka, EU-Enlargement and the opening of Russia: Lessons from the GTAP Reference Model, Helsinki: ETLA, The Research Institute of the Finnish Economy, Discussion Paper Nr. 825, 2002

Terenin, Dmitri, Russia within a "greater Europe", Library of publications of Carnegi Moscow Centre, Issue 10, October 2002

Timmermann, Heinz, European-Russian Partnership: What Future? European Foreign Affairs Review, 5: 165-174, 2000

Vahl, Marius, Just Good Friends? The EU-Russian "Strategic Partnership" and the Northern Dimension, The Centre for European Policy Studies Working Document, No. 166, March 2001

Van Bael, Ivo/Bellis, Jean-Francois, International Trade Law and Practice of the European Community: Anti-Dumping and other Trade Protection Laws of the EC, Third edition, CCH Europe, 1996 (cited as: Van Bael/Bellis, EC Anti-dumping Laws)

Van Bael, Ivo, EEC Anti-dumping enforcement: an overview of current problems, European Journal of International Law, Vol. 1, (1990), Nr.1/2, p.118-148

Vermulst, Edwin/ Waer, Paul, E.C. Anti-Dumping Law and Practice, London 1996, (cited as als: Vermulst/Waer, E.C. Anti-Dumping Law).

Vermulst, Edwin/ Komuro, Norio, Anti-Dumping Disputes in the GATT/WTO. Navigating Dire Straits, in: Journal of World trade, 31, 5-43, 1997(cited as: Vermulst/Komuro, Anti-Dumping Disputes in the GATT/WTO.)

Vermulst, Edwin/ Graafsma, Folkert, WTO Dispute Settlement with respect to Trade contingency measures. Selected issues. Journal of World Trade, 35 (2): 209-228, 2001

Wang, Lai/ Shengxing, Yu, China's new anti-dumping Regulations. Improvements to comply with the World Trade Organisation rules. Journal of World Trade, 36 (5): 903-920, 2000

Yudaeva, Ksenija, Joining the WTO: is a political decision an only hope?, Library of publications of the Carnegi Moscow Centre, Issue 6, 2003

II. in German

Bail, Theodor/ Schädel, Walter/ Hutter, Hans, Kommentar zum Zollrecht der Bundesrepublik Deutschland und den Europäischen Gemeinschaften, F III 1. Antidumping-VO; FIII 2 Antidumping-Entscheidung, 1984, (cited as: Bail/Schädel/Hutter, Antidumping VO)

Berrisch, Georg, M./ Kamann, Hans-Georg, Die neuesten Entwicklungen im Europäischen Außenhandelsrecht, in: Europäische Zeitschrift für Wirtschaftsrecht (EuZW), 1999, S. 714 ff.

Beseler, Johannes-Friedrich, Die Abwehr von Dumping und Subventionen durch die Europäischen Gemeinschaften, 1.Aufl. Baden-Baden 1980, (cited as: Beseler, Abwehr von Dumping)

Beseler, Johannes-Friedrich/Williams, Allan, Antidumping and Antisubsidy Law: The European Communities, London, 1986, (cited as Beseler/Williams, Antidumping and Antisubsidy Law)

Bierwagen, Rainer M., Entwicklungen im Verfahrensrecht bei der Anwendung außenhandelsrechtlicher Instrumente der EG, in:RabelsZ 58 (1994), S.667 ff.

Die neue Antidumpinggrundverordnung nach dem Abschluss der Uruguay-Runde, in: Europäische Zeitschrift für Wirtschaftsrecht (EuZW), 1995, S.231ff.

The Protectionist Bias in National Anti-Dumping Laws: An Appraisal of GATT Article VI and its implementation, and Proposals for Negotiation in the Uruguay-Round, Deventer/Boston 1990

Bogdandy, von/ Nettesheim, Martin, Strukturen des gemeinschaftlichen Außenhandelsrechts, in: Europäische Zeitschrift für Wirtschaftsrecht (EuZW) 1995, S. 465 ff.

Chu, Ching-Peng/Ludwig, Markus, Russland und die Osterweiterung der Europäischen Union.-geistesgeschichtliche und integrationstheoretische Überlegungen im Verfassungspolitischen und verfassungsrechtlichen Kontext zur potenziellen EU-Osterweiterung um Russland, Marburg, 1999

Dauses, Manfred. A., Handbuch des EU-Wirtschaftsrechts, Loseblattslg., Mai 2001, zitiert nach Verfassern

Egeln, Jurgen/Klann, Uwe, Die Antidumpingpolitik der Europäischen Gemeinschaft, 1. Aufl., Baden-Baden, 1997 (cited as: Egeln/Klann, Antidumpingpolitik der EG)

Fang, Xiaomin, Länder ohne Marktwirtschaft im Antidumpingrecht der EG unter besonderer Berücksichtigung der Praxis gegenüber China, Frankfurt am Main, Lang, 2002

Friedrichs, Rolf, Die Bindung der Gemeinschaft an die Wettbewerbsordnung des EGV bei der Anwendung des Antidumpingrechts, Trier, 1998 (cited as: Friedrichs, EGV/Antidumpingrecht)

Gabler, Thomas, Das Streitbeteiligungssystem der WTO und seine Auswirkungen auf das Antidumpingrecht der Europäischen Gemeinschaft, Frankfurt am Main, 1997

Gerner, Ivette, Die Europäische Union und Russland: Unterstützung der EU für die Transformationsprozesse in Russland am Beispiel des Technischen Hilfsprogramms Tacis, Frankfurt am Main, 1997

Grabitz, Eberhard/ Bogdandy, Armin, von/ Nettesheim, Martin, Europäisches Außenwirtschaftsrecht, München, 1994

Grabitz, Eberhard / Hilf, Meinhard, Kommentar zur Europäischen Union, Loseblattslg. Stand: Mai 2001

Hilf, Mainhard/ Göttsche, Götz, Chinas Beitritt zur WTO, Recht der Internationalen Wirtschaft, März 2003

Hilf, Mainhard/ Schlorkopf, Frank, WTO-Recht. Textsammlung Englisch/Deutsch, Mauke, Hamburg, 2001

Hilf, Mainhard, Allgemeine Prinyipien in der welthandelsrechtlichen Streitbeilegung. Die WTO auf dem Weg zu einer

Rechtsgemeinschaft? In: Europarecht (EuR) -Beiheft 1-2002, S. 173 ff.

Hummer, Waldemar, Die raumliche Erweiterung des Binnenmarktrechts, in: Europarecht (EuR) -Beiheft1-2002, S.75 ff.

Kinder, Hella, Die Außenindustriepolitik der Europäischen Gemeinschaft: dargestellt am Beispiel von Antidumpingmaßnahmen, Frankfurt am Main, 1996

Klann, Uwe, Das handelspolitische Instrument des Antidumping, Baden-Baden 1997

Landsittel, Ralph, Dumping im Außenhandels- und Wettbewerbsrecht, Baden-Baden 1987

Niedobitek, Matthias, Die Beziehungen der Europäischen Union zu Russland, Spreyer, 1996

Oppermann, Thomas, Europarecht: ein Studienbuch, 2. Aufl, München, 1999

Park, Sung-Kwan, Regelung und Paxis des Antidumpingrechts: eine vergleichende Analyse des Antidumpingrechts der Vereinigten Staaten, der Europäischen Gemeinschaft und Koreas nach der GATT Uruguay Runde, Frankfurt am Main, 1998

Peter, Manfred, Russlands Platz in Europa, Berlin, 2001

Prieß, Hans-Joachim/ Berrisch, Georg, WTO-Handbuch, Berlin/Brüssel, 2003

Reszel, Peter C., Die Feststellung der Schädigung im Antidumping und Antisubventionsrecht der Europäischen Gemeinschaften, Köln 1987,(cited as: Reszel, Feststellung der Schädigung)

Reuter, Alexander, Außenwirtschafts- und Exportkontrollrecht Deutschland/Europäische Union, Düsseldorf, 1995

Rolf, Reinhard, Die Rechtsstellung Betroffener bei der Anwendung außenhandelsrechtlicher Schutzinstrumente in den Vereinigten Staaten und der Europäischen Gemeinschaft. Eine vergleichende Untersuchung, Frankfurt/Bern/New York/Paris, 1991

Streinz, Rudolf, Europarecht, 5.Aufl., 2001

Schwarze, Jürgen/ Schmidt-Aßmann, Eberhard, Das Ausmaß der gerichtlichen Kontrolle im Wirtschaftsverwaltungs- und Umweltrecht, Baden-Baden, 1.Aufl. 1992, (cited as: Schwarze/Schmidt, Ausmaß gerichtlicher Kontrolle)

Schweitzer, Michael/Hummer, Waldemar, Europarecht, 4. Aufl., Berlin, 1993

Tarr, David/ Thomson, Peter, The Merits of Dual Pricing of Russian Natural Gas, The World Bank, 2003, www.wto.ru

Timmermann, Heinz, Die Beziehungen EU-Russland. Voraussetzungen und Perspektiven von Partnerschaft und Kooperation, Berichte des Bundesinstituts für ostwissenschaftliche und internationale Studium, Köln, 1994 (cited as: Timmermann, Die Beziehungen EU-Russland)

Wessely, Thomas W., Das Verhältnis von Antidumping- und Kartellrecht in der Europäischen Gemeinschaft: eine Untersuchung der wettbewerblichen Schranken des EG-Handelsschutzrechts, München: Beck, 1999 (cited as: Wessely, Antidumping- und Kartellrecht in der EG)

III. in Russian

Безбах В.В. / Капустин А.Я./ Пучинский В.К. (Bezbach VV./ Kapustin A.Y./ Puchinski V.K.), Право ЕС: Правовое регулирование торгового оборота, Москва, 1999 (EU law: Legal regulation of the external trade, Moscow, 1999)

Белов А.П. (Belov A.P), "Антидемпинговое регулирование в России и за рубежом", "Право и экономика", № 8, 2000 ("Anti-dumping regulation in Russia and abroad", "Law and economy", Nr. 8, 2000)

Борко Ю.А. (Yu.A. Borko), Документы, касающиеся взаимоотношений между Европейским Союзом и Россией, Москва, 1994
(Documents concerning relations between European Union and Russia, Moscow, 1994), cited as: Documents concerning relations between the EU and Russia, Moscow, 1994

Ван Дузер Э., Сутырин С.Ф., Капусткин В.И. (Van Duser E., Sutirin S.F., Kapustkin V.I.), Россия и международная торговая система, Санкт-Петербург, 2000 (Russia and International trade system, St. Petersburg, 2000)

Вилльемс. А/ Дудко А. (Villems.A/ Dudko A.), Антидемпинг: новые правовые возможности, Металлы Евразии, № 1, 2003 (Anti-dumping: new legal opportunities, Eurasian Metals, Nr. 1, 2003)

Герчикова И.Н. (Gertchikova I.N.), Международные экономические организации: регулирование мирохозяйственных связей и предпринимательской деятельности, Москва, 2002 (International economic organizations: regulating role in international economic relations and business activities, Moscow, 2002)

Зенкин И.В. (Zenkin I.V.), Право всемирной торговой организации, Москва, 2003 (Law of the World Trade Organization, Moscow, 2003)

Зименков Р.И. (Zimenkov, R.I.), Россия: интеграция в мировую экономику, Москва, 2002 (Russia: integration into the world economy, Moscow, 2002)

Ливенцов Н.Н./Лисоволик Я.Д. (Livenzov N.N., Lisovolik Ya.D.), Актуальные проблемы присоединения России к ВТО (Actual problems of Russia's accession to the WTO, Moscow, 2002)

Карро Д./ Жюйар П. (Carreau D./ Juillard P.), Международное экономическое право, Москва, 2002 (International economic law, Moscow, 2002)

Кашкин С.Ю. (Prof. Dr. Kashkin, S.Yu.), Россия и Европейский Союз, документы и материалы, Москва, 2003 (Russia and the EU, Documents and materials, Moscow, 2003)

Козырин, А.Н., Шепенко, Р.А. (Kozirin A.N./ Schepenko. R.A.), Конкуренция на международных рынках и антидемпинговое регулирование, Москва, 1999 (Competition and anti-dumping regulation on international markets, Moscow, 1999)

Сафонов И.А. (Safonov I.A.), Внешнеэкономические связи России со странами Европы в контексте расширения ЕС, Москва, 2003 (Foreign economical relations of Russia with European countries in view of EU Enlargement, Moscow, 2003)/ (cited as: Safonov, Foreign economical relations of Russia with European countries in view of EU Enlargement)

Сутела П. (Sutela P.), Россия и Европа: некоторые аспекты экономических взаимоотношений, Московский Центр Карнеги, 2003 (Russia and Europe: Some Economic Aspects, Carnegi Moscow Centre, 2003)

Медведков, М. (Medvedkov M) "Соглашение о партнерстве ЕС и России пока не оправдало возложенных надежд", Евро, № 12, 1999, 30-32 (The Partnership and Cooperation Agreement has not confirmed expectations yet, Euro, Nr. 12, 1999, p. 30-32)

Для России в расширении ЕС есть и достоинства, и недостатки, журнал Европейского Союза "Европа", Nr. 35, Январь 2004, http://www.eur.ru/em/39/eu35_04.htm (On advantages and disadvantages of the EU Enlargement for Russia, Journal of the delegation of the EU Commission in Russia, Nr. 35, January 2004, http://www.eur.ru/em/39/eu35_04.htm)

Топорнин Б.Н. (Topornin, B.N.), Европейское право, Учебник, Москва, 1998 (European law, Textbook, Moscow, 1998)

Шепенко Р.А. (Shepenko R.A.), Антидемпинговый процесс, Москва, 2002 (Anti-dumping procedure, Moscow, 2002)

Антидемпинговый процесс и применение антидемпинговых пошлин в ЕЭС, Внешняя торговля, 1997, № 4-7 (Anti-dumping procedure and imposition of anti-dumping duties in the EC, Foreign trade, 1997, Nr. 4-7)

Постатейный комментарий к федеральному закону "О мерах по защите экономических интересов Российской Федерации при осуществлении внешней торговли товарами", Москва, правовая система "Консультант", 2002 (Commentary to the

Federal Law "Measures on protection of economical interests of the Russian Federation in external trade of goods", Moscow, electronical law database "Consultant", 2002)

Энтин, Л.М. (Prof. Dr. Entin, L.M.), Европейское право, учебник для Вузов, Москва, 2000 (European law, Textbook, Moscow, 2000)

IV. Materials

Commission of the European Communities, the Directorate General for Trade http://www.europa.eu.int/comm/trade/issues/index_en.htm, 15th - 21st Anti-dumping report, Brussels, years 1996-2002; Anti-Dumping Statistics http://www.europa.eu.int/comm/trade/issues/respectrules/anti_du mping/legis/index_en.htm Weekly updated anti-dumping and anti-subsidy measures list of the EU, http://europa.eu.int/comm/trade/issues/respectrules/anti_dumping /stats.htm Communication from the Commission to the Council and the European Parliament. Wider Europe- Neighbourhood: a new framework for relations with our Eastern and Southern Neighbours, Brussels, 2003 Enlargement of the European Union, Good news for Russia, Brussels, 2003 Bilateral Trade Statistics. Russia Trade Statistics, 2003 http://europa.eu.int/comm/trade/issues/bilateral/countries/russia/i ndex_en.htm

Антидемпинговая служба Комиссии ЕС Постоянное представительство России при ЕС (Commission of the European Communities/ Russian Delegation at the EU in Brussels), Антидемпинговая политика Европейского Сообщества: Практическое пособие для российских экспортеров и производителей, 1999 служба ТАСИС ГД 1А, Европейская Коммиссия, Москва (The anti-dumping policy of the European Community: Practical Hand-book for Russian Exporters, 1999 TACIS services DG1A, European Commission, Moscow. (cited as: Anti-dumping Handbook for Russian Exporters)

Delegation of the European Commission in Russia (www.eur.ru), Frequently asked questions on Russia market economy status, Moscow, 2002, EU-Summit, Copenhagen, 12-13 December 2002;

Frequently asked questions on EU Enlargement and its impact on Russia; Russia and EU Enlargement: selected issues, Brussels, 2003;

The EU and Russia. Economic and Trade indicators, Moscow, 2003;

Communication from the Commission to the Council and the European Parliament on relations with Russia, COM (2004) 106, 09.02.04, (Commission calls for the strengthening of EU-Russia relations IP/04/187 - Brussels, 09 February 2004) http://europa.eu.int/comm/external_relations/russia/intro/ip04_18 7.htm

Conference Proceedings. St. Petersburg, 1999, Ten Years of Cooperation (1988 – 98): the European Union and Russia in Perspective, Center for integration research and projects, St. Petersburg, www.cirp.ru

Министерство экономического развития и торговли Российской Федерации (www.economy.gov.ru)/ (Ministry of economical development and trade of the Russian Federation) О торгово-экономическом сотрудничестве России и Европейского Сообщества (по итогам 2002 г.)/("On trade and economical co-operation between the EU and Russia", 2002)

Ограничительные меры, применяемые против российского экспорта (на 1 сентября 2003 г.)/(Trade defence measures applied against Russian exports as on 1 September 2003)

Памятка российским экспортерам по антидемпинговому процессу, 2002 (Instruction to Russian exporters on the anti-dumping procedure), 2002

Общие вопросы доступа российских экспортеров на внешние рынки, 2002(General issues on external markets access for Russian exporters, 2002)

House of Lords, United Kingdom, 3rd Report, EU-Russia relations, London, 2002

Financial Times, London, www.ft.com, Judy Dempsey "Europe& Asia-Pacific: Russia seeks to safeguard its interests after EU expands", By Tobias Buck and Judy Dempsey in Brussels, February 02, 2004

Russia rejects trade links with incoming EU members, By Judy Dempsey in Brussels, February 10, 2004

Comment: Europe must take a wider view of the future, By George Soros, March 30, 2004

Financial Times Deutschland, Europäer erhöhen Druck auf Russland, Von Nils Kreimeier, Berlin, aus der FTD vom 5.2.2004

Межд. конференция "Россия и Европейское право", Москва, 2000 (International conference "Russia and European Law", Moscow,

2000), Материалы конференции : Соглашение о партнерстве и сотрудничестве и комментарии к нему (Materials of the conference concerning Partnership and cooperation agreement and commentaries)

UCLA Eurasian, EU, US Conference, Los Angeles, 6 March 2003, Gough, Anthony, EU-Russia Relations& Russia's Accession to WTO.

Комитет "Россия в объединенной Европе", Москва (Committee "Russia in the United Europe", Moscow) Дискуссии "Расширение ЕС: угроза или шанс для России", Москва, 2002 (Discussion "EU Enlargement: a threat or a chance for Russia", Moscow, 2002)

Дискуссии "Общий рынок Россия-ЕС. Возможно ли это?", Москва, 2002 (Discussion "Common market Russia-EU. Is it possible?", Moscow, 2002)

Доклад "Как углубить сотрудничество России и Европейского Союза", Москва, 2003 (Report "How to deepen cooperation between Russia and the European Union", Moscow, 2003)

Российская академия наук, Национальный инвестиционный совет (Russian academy of science, National investment council) Народнохозяйственные последствия присоединения России к ВТО, Москва, 2000 (Economical consequences of Russia accession to the WTO, Moscow, 2000)

Müller, Wolfgang, Europäische Kommission, DG Handel, Brüssel Der rechtliche Rahmen des Antidumpings, in: Bundesministerium für Wirtschaft und Technologie- Handelspolitische Instrumente in der Unternehmenspraxis, Dokumentation 493, Bonn, 2001. www.bmwi.de/homepage/download/doku/doku493.pdf, abgerufen am 01.06.2002 (Zitiert als: Müller, Der AD-rechtliche Rahmen)

Россия на пути в ВТО. Информационный бюллетень, www.wto.ru (Russia on the way to the WTO. Informational bulletin.) Антидемпинговое законодательство ЕС и его применение против России, Май-июнь 2003 (EU anti-dumping law and its appliance against Russia, May-June 2003)

WTO-Welthandelsorganisation, Verlag C.H. Beck, 1.Auflage, München, 2000

Schriften zum Europa- und Völkerrecht
und zur Rechtsvergleichung

Herausgegeben von Prof. Dr. Manfred Zuleeg

Band 1 Mathias Mühlhans: Internationales Wassernutzungsrecht und Spieltheorie. Die Bedeutung der neueren völkerrechtlichen Vertragspraxis und der wirtschaftswissenschaftlichen Spieltheorie für das Prinzip der angemessenen Nutzung internationaler Binnengewässer. 1998.

Band 2 Michael Grüb: Europäische Niederlassungs- und Dienstleistungsfreiheit für Private mit hoheitlichen Befugnissen. 1999.

Band 3 Kathrin Bremer: Nationale Strafverfolgung internationaler Verbrechen gegen das humanitäre Völkerrecht. Am Beispiel einer Rechtsvergleichung Deutschlands, der Schweiz, Belgiens und Großbritanniens. 1999.

Band 4 Jon Marcus Meese: Das Petitionsrecht beim Europäischen Parlament und das Beschwerderecht beim Bürgerbeauftragten der Europäischen Union. 2000.

Band 5 Christoph Schalast: Umweltschutz und Wettbewerb als Wertwiderspruch im deregulierten deutschen und europäischen Elektrizitätsmarkt. 2001.

Band 6 Ralf Bauer: Das Recht auf eine gute Verwaltung im Europäischen Gemeinschaftsrecht. Inhalt, Anwendungsbereich und Einschränkungsvoraussetzungen des Grundrechts auf eine gute Verwaltung in Artikel 41 der Charta der Grundrechte der Europäischen Union. 2002.

Band 7 Kerstin Estler: Zur Effektivität des einstweiligen Rechtsschutzes im Gemeinschaftsrecht. 2003.

Band 8 Ali Hahin: Der Vertrag von Amsterdam: Vergemeinschaftetes Asylrecht. 2003.

Band 9 Amina Dammann: Die Beschwerdekammern der europäischen Agenturen. 2004.

Band 10 Nina Nolte: Deregulierung von Monopolen und Dienstleistungen von allgemeinem wirtschaftlichen Interesse. Zur Bedeutung des Art. 86. Abs. 2 EGV. Insbesondere in den Bereichen der Elektrizitätswirtschaft, der Bodendienstleistungen auf Flughäfen und der Abfallwirtschaft. 2004.

Band 11 Izumi Kazuhara: Einfluss der Marktintegration auf die Auslegung und Anwendung des europäischen Wettbewerbsrechts. 2004.

Band 12 Olesia Engelbutzeder: EU Anti-Dumping Measures Against Russian Exporters. In View of Russian Accession to the WTO and the EU Enlargement 2004. 2004.

www.peterlang.de

Gustav Dieckheuer / Boguslaw Fiedor (eds.)

Eastward Enlargement of the European Union

Economic Aspects

Frankfurt am Main, Berlin, Bern, Bruxelles, New York, Oxford, Wien, 2003.
VIII, 214 pp., num. fig., num. tab.
Internationale Marktwirtschaft.
Edited by Gustav Dieckheuer, Karl-Hans Hartwig and Theresia Theurl. Vol. 4
ISBN 3-631-51430-1 / US-ISBN 0-8204-6481-3 · pb. € 39.–*

After more than a decade of transformation and catching-up to the present members of the EU the applicant countries now comply with many of the political and economic requirements laid down at the Copenhagen summit in 1993. Because of such a clear direction it is necessary and advisable to take a close look at the chances and the risks of the enlargement for the old member countries as well as for the new ones. This is the background of a collection of articles published in this book. The papers cover a wide range of important aspects of the EU eastern enlargement, for instance trade effects, country-specific as well as EU politics, regional transborder co-operation and monetary issues concerning a country's currency regime.

Contents: Trade Creation and Trade Diversion by EU Enlargement · Globalization and Eastward Enlargement of the European Union · Poland's Accession to the EU from the Macroeconomic Perspective · Social Policy and Income Redistribution in an Enlarged European Union

Frankfurt am Main · Berlin · Bern · Bruxelles · New York · Oxford · Wien
Distribution: Verlag Peter Lang AG
Moosstr. 1, CH-2542 Pieterlen
Telefax 00 41 (0) 32 / 376 17 27

*The €-price includes German tax rate
Prices are subject to change without notice
Homepage http://www.peterlang.de

Peter Lang · Europäischer Verlag der Wissenschaften